Northern
NURSES II

More Nursing Adventures from Canada's North

Edited by J. Karen Scott and Joan E. Kieser

Published by Kokum Publications

Canadian Cataloguing in Publication Data

Scott, J. Karen; Kieser, Joan E.
Northern nurses II: more nursing adventures from Canada's North

ISBN 0-9730392-1-3

1. Nursing   2. Northern Nursing   3. Women's Studies   4. Nurse Practitioner   5. Northwest Territories
6. Nunavut   7. Outpost Nursing   8. Extended Practice   9. Yukon   10. RCMP   11. Northern Aviation
12. Autobiography, Nursing

Kokum Publications
199 Queen Mary Drive, Suite 1505
Oakville, Ontario
L6K 3K7

kokumpub@sympatico.ca

Also by Kokum Publications
Northern Nurses: True Nursing Adventures from Canada's North
Available in Braille

Printed and bound in Canada 2005
by Mothersill Printing (1988) Inc.

Photo design graphics by Kathleen Atkinson
Maps by Matt Pun
Front cover photo by Sue Pauhl

Proceeds from the sale of this book will be donated to a northern nursing scholarship fund.

Tribute to a Friend

Christine Egan
June 20, 1946 - September 11, 2001

Many tributes and accolades have been given to Christine Egan following her tragic death on September 11, 2001, at the World Trade Center in New York. Articles appeared in various newspapers and journals, on television, and during the very personal memorial service that was held in Winnipeg and attended by hundreds of friends, former patients, and colleagues.

These tributes recalled her northern nursing career that spanned over thirty years, her love of the North, and her dedication to nursing. They spoke of her academic achievements that ended with a PhD in Health Sciences in 1999. More importantly, all articles mentioned her generosity and her commitment to friends.

Chris had an ability that I have seen in very few people – she regarded everyone she met as her equal, from the highest-level government official to the homeless person on the street. And she treated each one with honesty and respect. I never heard her "speak down" to anyone. If she felt you needed advice, support, comfort or friendship, she gave of it freely.

She was a champion of many nursing causes and worked diligently to promote the nursing profession in the eyes of the public, the healthcare profession, and the government. She had no tolerance for any nurse in administration who did not respect or support her front-line workers. She did not suffer fools lightly. She worked diligently with her patients to optimize their health on an individual, community, and regional level.

Chris was selfless in both her friendships and acquaintances. When Chris was in the South, she would meet you at the airport and drive you to any destination. She knew precisely at which store you could purchase the items you were looking for, and without hesitation, she would take you there. She actively maintained her friendships with many people – through phone calls, emails, invitations to her home, or trips to visit others. Chris always kept in touch.

Chris was a great cook. I remember one time in the early 1980s when we worked together in Rankin Inlet. A public works crew was weathered in, and the hotel dining room and the grocery store were closed. I looked in the cupboards and freezer at the nursing station, and I could not imagine how we could make a meal to feed six hungry men, from the odds and ends of food that were there. Chris looked in the same cupboards and freezer and produced a banquet that not only fed everyone, but had food left over.

Chris had the most exotic foods in her cupboards, so people were always anxious for a dinner invitation. However, there were two downsides to these invitations. The first was doing the dishes after the meal. In preparing her exceptional meals, she used every pot and dish in the cupboard. The second downside was meeting Chris at the airport, when she arrived from a shopping trip down south. She always had the largest, heaviest, and most numerous pieces of luggage on the plane. There was very little complaining about helping her get the luggage home, because most of the luggage consisted of supplies for her dinner parties.

I have asked myself many times how a person who has spent most of her life in isolated Arctic communities could die at the hands of terrorists, in an international trading centre in one of the largest cities in the world. Ironically, the answer is simple. Chris was in New York visiting family and friends. *She was keeping in touch.* The last reports of Chris's whereabouts put her in the lobby of the South Tower. We will never know for sure, but these circumstances and her character tell us that she was most likely caring for people in her last minutes, just as she had done all of her life.

As we dedicate this book to Christine Egan, we give recognition, in a small way, to a special person who not only lived the life of a northern nurse, but who also set standards for professional and personal achievements that are attainable within each of us.

On September 11, 2001, the world lost a special nurse and a very good person. Many of us lost an exceptional friend.

Sue Pauhl RN(EC), OPN, PNC(C)

Introduction

Let us take you on a trip across the top of the world. Nurses and a few fellow adventurers who have lived and worked in Canada's North over the past 70 years will be your tour guides. Travel with them across five and half time zones, through many of Canada's isolated areas: from Vancouver Island to the Yukon, the Northwest Territories, Nunavut, Labrador, and Newfoundland, as well as remote northern communities in central Canada. We hope that in reading these stories you will have a sense of the vastness of our country and of the isolation in which nurses have chosen to work.

By entering into the experiences of these authors, you will appreciate that Canada's North is vast and varied. The terrain includes the rugged mountains of the Yukon, the permafrost and barren flats of the Central Arctic, and the fjords and glaciers of Baffin Island. Weather can be equally variable, with bitter High Arctic blizzards and 35° summer days on the surface, and the appearance and disappearance of the northern lights in the cosmos. All of these affect one's ability to move and communicate in the North, and so influence the way these stories unfold.

Distances and an unforgiving land make air travel indispensable. Northern pilots are expert flyers who are able to get a plane on or off the ground under hair-raising conditions. Northern nurses trust them. The heroism of nurses and pilots is evident in the risk to their own lives in their efforts to deliver patients safely to hospital. Uppermost in their minds is saving a life – it is all in a day's work. In the northern territories, a very limited road system is possible – which is better in the winter, when the rivers and lakes are used as roads. One main road leads north from Hay River to Yellowknife, with travel at the whim of the weather as you cross the Mackenzie at Fort Providence, either on the ice bridge or the ferry. During freeze-up or breakup, all traffic grinds to a halt, and fresh produce has to be flown in – charged by the pound. In the Yukon, the Alaska Highway provides more transportation options, but brings with it another set of health problems and emergencies. From the Alaska Highway, the Klondike leads to Dawson City, and the Dempster goes all the way to Inuvik in the NWT. Although these roads are useful, most travel is done by air. But the deciding factor of weather remains.

Many of these stories take place before the first Anik communications satellite was launched in 1972. Nursing stations had two-way radios that worked *most* of the time. Contact with the other stations and with the hospital in their zone depended on the northern lights, which could knock out the signals for days. Today, even with all the advanced communications technology, the experience and expert decision-making skills of the nurses are still essential.

With the added responsibilities of working in isolation, we had to meet the challenges of the extended role of nursing, before that role was recognized – before degrees and certificates were presented to confirm our added skills. And, we learned just how capable we all were! The northern experience cannot be duplicated here in the South. A sense of adventure, independence, and survival instincts set northern nurses apart from their southern sisters.

Most of the areas where northern nurses work are sparsely populated. Eighty percent of Canada's population lives within 160 kilometres of the Canada-US border – that leaves a lot of space for the remaining 20%. The Yukon, with 531,844 square kilometres, has a population of 31,227 (Stats. Canada, 2005) and eight language groups. The Northwest Territories covers 1,299,070 square kilometres, with a population of 42,944 and nine languages. In Yellowknife alone, 35 languages are actually spoken. Nunavut, with 1,900,000 square kilometres, has a population of 29,683 (2005), most of whom speak at least one of the six dialects of Inuktitut. In all three territories, French and English are official languages, along with Aboriginal languages.

Today in the North there are Inuit and First Nations nurses who speak the traditional languages. Many of us nurses, in earlier times and to this day, have relied heavily on our local clerk/interpreters. Work in the stations would have been impossible without them. They were constantly training nurses new to the North. Theirs was the hardest job of all, as they never were off duty, whether at the Bay, out in the community, or at home. I admire their work and the patience they showed all of us.

Most of the contributing authors were in the North before Nunavut came into being and know the communities by their former names. Therefore, we have provided maps with the old and new names. This was a challenge, as there are not consistent spellings for names of places. Each of the northern territories has a toponymist, someone who studies place names. One toponymist explained to me that the spelling of a community name may differ from village to village, depending on slight variances in local dialects.

Since work on this book began, three nurses who have contributed greatly to healthcare in the North have passed away: Vera Robert, a nursing legend in Baffin; Anne Pask Wilkinson, public health nurse extraordinaire in Yellowknife, and Margaret Campbell Jackson, pioneer in public health in north central British Columbia. Anne was pleased to give permission to use her story for this book. Margaret had started her piece, but was not able to complete it.

We nurses are lucky to have Joan Kieser as co-editor of this project. Her interest in our careers in the North and her long hours spent editing our stories have given us a voice and turned our stories into a very exciting book.

So sit back, read, and enjoy our stories in *Northern Nurses II*. Travel from coast to coast to coast with the authors, as they reveal their adventurous spirit, talent, and creativity in delivering health care to all of the citizens of Canada's North.

*J. Karen Scott **RN**, BScN*

Foreword

It was not until 2002 that the first collection of stories by nurses who have worked in Canada's North was published in book form. This unparalleled publication, entitled *Northern Nurses: True Nursing Adventures from Canada's North*, edited by J. Karen Scott and Joan E. Kieser, had scarcely come off the press, when a northern nurse sent a manuscript to Scott and encouraged her to produce another volume, reminding her that there were many other nurses who had stories to tell about their adventures. What you have before you is a second volume of fascinating and unique, true stories written by nurses and other people about their experiences, not only on the land, but also on the sea and in the air.

Most of the stories in this volume happened within the past 70 years. They range from giving health care to individuals, families, schoolchildren, and in many instances, to the community as a whole. Experiences in industrial and maritime nursing and in epidemics are also described. Many of the authors give their vivid first-person accounts of the expanded nursing roles, in what is now called Primary Health Care. Stories about the challenges and risks of using air transport in and out of remote areas in extreme weather conditions and the many maps and pictures help to give "outsiders" a beginning grasp of the vastness of Canada's North.

Historian Marc Bloch emphasizes that if we are to get meaningful grasps of "human history," it is essential that we have "accounts of eye-witnesses." These "eye-witness" narratives by nurses and others who have lived in the far North of Canada, collected by Scott and Kieser, constitute wonderful historical gems of the history of health care in Canada. To paraphrase nursing historian Arlee Hoyt McGee: Knowledge of the history of nursing in Canada's remote areas makes a difference in how nursing is understood. Both volumes of *Northern Nurses* are valuable sources for learning about many of the ways humans can help each other, even with limited resources and often amidst life-threatening circumstances.

Like the first volume, this book will be of primary interest to all those who live and work in the North. As it has significance far beyond nursing in remote areas, it is a "must" for all health science libraries, health educators, students in any of the health sciences and for health priority and policy-decision makers. It is also a "must" for all nurses, school teachers, clergy, Royal Canadian Mounted Police, diamond miners, oil drillers, and for anyone who may be thinking about living in remote areas of Canada's North.

Shirley Stinson OC, AOE, RN, EdD, LLD (Hon), DSc (Hon), DSL (Hon)
Dr. Stinson is Professor Emerita, Faculty of Nursing and Dept. of Public Health Sciences at the University of Alberta in Edmonton, Alberta.

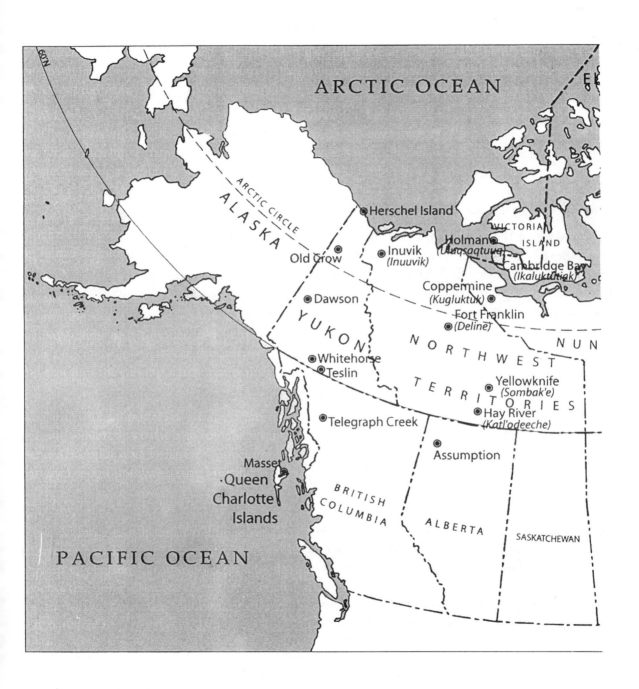

ARCTIC OCEAN

ALASKA

ARCTIC CIRCLE

60 N

Herschel Island

VICTORIA ISLAND

Holman
(Uluqsaqtuuq)

Cambridge Bay
(Ikaluktutiak)

Inuvik
(Inuuvik)

Old Crow

Coppermine
(Kugluktuk)

Fort Franklin
(Deline)

Dawson

YUKON

NORTHWEST

NUN

Whitehorse
Teslin

TERRITORIES

Yellowknife
(Sombak'e)

Telegraph Creek

Hay River
(Katl'odeeche)

Assumption

Masset
Queen
Charlotte
Islands

BRITISH
COLUMBIA

ALBERTA

SASKATCHEWAN

PACIFIC OCEAN

Acknowledgements

In addition to the many authors who contributed their stories to this book, a number of people have been extremely helpful in getting it into print.

Dr. Shirley Stinson, Professor Emerita at the University of Alberta in Edmonton, has supported this project with contacts, suggestions, and hours spent on the phone trying to get funding for the production of this work. We are indebted to her for her assistance and strategic advice.

Barbara Bromley of Yellowknife in the Northwest Territories has been a great backer of this project, getting permission for pictures and also attempting to find funding. She too has been a tremendous help and a cheerleader right from the beginning.

As she did for our first collection of stories, Gay Allison in Stratford, Ontario, read the draft and made many valuable recommendations. Mary Fitz-Gibbon also looked through the text and provided suggestions. Kathleen Atkinson of Mothersill Press, a graduate of Durham College in Oshawa, Ontario, took care of the picture graphics, and Matt Pun, a graduate of Sheridan College in Oakville, Ontario, produced the maps.

Joan's husband, Liam, was our computer/desktop publishing wizard. It was a change of pace from his day job as a physicist at the University of Toronto. Without his technical expertise and moral support, this and our earlier collection of stories would have taken much longer to complete.

Contents

A GLIMPSE OF NORTHERN LIFE

Karen Wood

Imagine endless prairie with skinny, stunted trees – a lot of birch – and bulrushes along lakes and swampy areas. Imagine a white blanket of snow reflecting pink and purple glowing sunsets. Imagine wild dogs barking in the distance, as you fall asleep in your small apartment, with the windows frozen open in winter, and swollen open in summer. Imagine skidoos roaring by on the main road which is right in front of your window, or a long stream of vehicles passing by in funeral processions, so common in town.

*

Imagine lengthy church services, no matter the denomination, with a congregation that bounces in merriment and speaks in accented English with Cree phrases. Imagine people with contagious giggles, character-lined faces, and kind hearts, singing off-key and off-beat.

*

Imagine the health clinic where nurses work, not only as nurses, but as doctors, x-ray technicians, pharmacists, counsellors, lab technicians, and occasionally, as veterinarians. In the nursing station vehicle, the ambulance driver picks up villagers whose homes are scattered about the community. (There are no addresses, but the driver knows where everyone lives.) He brings the people to the clinic where he lines them up, in order for them to be seen by the nurse.

*

Imagine it's your day off and you're called in to help deal with a suicide attempt, a car rollover, a dehydrated baby, and someone with an asthma attack. You pick up the infections you treat, as you struggle to stay awake while analyzing x-rays (that you have taken and developed yourself). Imagine peering into the sore throats of crying babies. Imagine taking, spinning, and packaging blood samples for the plane to take south. Imagine never having scheduled breaks, or suddenly being required to escort a sick patient on a plane to Winnipeg or Thompson. Imagine working with nurses who are replaced almost weekly due to burnout, and with doctors who vary from the best in the world, to the kind who will not answer the phone, because they are scared to come to the clinic after hours. Imagine trying to cope with 100 to 200 patients a day, some of whom complain to the chief about the three-hour wait to see the nurse. Consider a government that cannot afford to send nursing help or find other support staff, although a new jeep arrives – while layoffs down south leave hundreds of nurses jobless.

*

Imagine checking the weather daily for a two-month period to see if it's safe to take your baby outside. You venture out once for ten minutes and your baby almost gets frostbitten. Imagine garbage-bagging your laundry to the next building with your baby on your back, wondering how you can cut down on laundry, when you only brought one week's worth of clothing for each family member. Imagine never ironing – no one here ever does. How refreshing!

*

Imagine the phone rings and in a hard-to-understand drawl, the caller asks, "Monia's gas station?" You know the number well, as you redirect calls daily. Imagine eight more such calls after you set up the answering machine – kids phoning repeatedly to hear your new technology, leaving recorded giggles.

*

Imagine checking that the ice bridge is safe before leaving in your 1979 Suburban for a weekend break. Imagine being excited about a short holiday to the city of Winnipeg.

*

Imagine you've made good friends, but they leave two months after you arrive. You have enjoyed their company so much. Imagine the naked quietness after their departure.

*

Imagine all this – and you will have had a glimpse into northern life.

Karen Wood RN, BScN graduated from the University of Alberta Hospital School of Nursing in 1984 with her diploma in nursing and from the University of British Columbia in 1989 with her BScN. Before heading north, she worked in respiratory medicine, ICU, and general medicine, as well as home care and hospice. As a northern relief nurse in 1990, she worked in Tatla Lake, BC and Arviat which was then in the NWT, but is now in Nunavut. After she married, she followed her husband Chris when he worked in Cross Lake and South Indian Lake in Manitoba; in Sioux Lookout (where he did his Dalhousie Outpost internship) and in Fort Hope in Ontario. During their longest stint, which was in Iskut, BC, she joined him doing relief work. After years of cold, they decided on a warmer adventure in California. However, they still talk about working together in the North again, when their three children are in college.

THE CALL TO RETURN NORTH:
DIARY OF A NORTHERN NURSE

Dana Hawes

What keeps calling me back north of 60?

The winters in the North are bitterly long and dark and frigid. The summers are short, hot, and dry. To say bugs are plentiful is an understatement. I often try to dissect my choice of nursing as a profession, and I have spent countless hours trying to explain to people south of the 60th parallel what my life in the North is like – and why I do what I do. They wonder why I would I leave my comfortable life for the North, and my answers don't seem to satisfy them.

Having spent several years in Canada's Arctic, I thought it was time to leave. Long-time northerners cautioned me that after ten years there, you could not leave, because you would be unemployable south of 60. The level of independence you become accustomed to in your work in the North, they explained, would not be acceptable in the South. Northern nurses would find the transition extremely frustrating. However, I decided to say good-bye to the North, and I returned to where some think "real medicine" is practised. Emergency nursing had been my background, and I wanted to see what was happening on the cutting edge of medicine. I actually thought I may have been missing out on something in the fast-paced world of the ER.

As a new arrival in the emergency department of a northern Alberta hospital, I was actually reprimanded for applying a simple antibiotic cream without a physician's order. During orientation, I was told that a physician writes an acetaminophen order, but you have to call so that he can clarify whether the prescription is for regular or extra-strength. I gave two regular acetaminophens and was given a written reprimand for a medication error. What I came to realize was that I was unable to check my common sense at the door, before reporting for my shift. After wrestling with my conscience for a few years, I knew I had to go back to the North. It was the only way I could survive the Canadian healthcare system as a nurse.

I had my answer

For a northern nurse, priorities are common sense and a level head. No one cares how many letters you have after your name, how many courses you have taken, or how much nursing theory you have studied. At 0200 hours nursing theory is nice to have, but it does not mean you are competent. Nurses are still expected to rely on common sense, clinical expertise, and pure gut instincts. Although there are set clinic hours, if an emergency arises, a nurse must respond. It could be anything from a cardiac arrest to a dog needing sutures. There is no clock to punch and no support staff to perform x-rays or electrocardiograms, to do lab work or to fill in requisitions.

If the stretcher is dirty, you clean it; if there is restocking of supplies to be done, you do it; if the weather is bad and you require a medevac, you simply deal with it.

If only our politicians and professional associations would answer why it is that when I cross the 60th parallel northbound, I am able to perform child immunizations, well-child assessments, pap tests, well-woman checks, and pre-natal assessments? Why am I allowed to respond to emergencies of all kinds, to be the ambulance driver, the emergency dentist, the veterinarian? Why am I permitted to diagnose, treat, prescribe and dispense medication, perform x-rays, draw and spin blood, identify pathogens under the microscope, apply casts and splints, decide which lab tests are required and interpret the results? As soon as I cross the 60th parallel southbound, however, I am unable even to apply an over-the-counter antibiotic cream.

* * *

When I returned to northern nursing, I was just as apprehensive as I had been when I originally went north. The thought of the responsibility was overwhelming. Maybe the fear this time came from the known, as opposed the unknown. Ten years before, this world was totally unknown to me; now I was well aware of all the expectations. Perhaps some ignorance is bliss. Fortunately for me, I was welcomed back to the North with enthusiasm.

For several years, I had my "green dresser," my beloved green duffel bag that had travelled around the North with me and had become my only constant possession. This time, I had chosen to leave my old, sturdy, canvas friend at home in favour of a more modern companion: a black hard-sided case with wheels. (When one packs for a month or so, wheels are a fine luxury.) As usual, I packed my trunk full of goodies not available in northern communities. I felt a tremendous sense of freedom. Forget the politics of the South! I would be free to be "just a nurse."

Travelling to my first assignment took three days. There were no luxuries, just plain old propeller aircraft. When I arrived, a feeling of calm washed over me – it was all so comfortable and familiar. I knew I had made the right decision.

Once again, I was on a new adventure. This time, when I returned to nurse in the North, I kept a diary.

Day 1

I left home for the North today with my trunk of food and little pleasures, like books, and because of the season, I took my new bug jacket. Before I reached the airline counter, the ticket agent snarled at me and refused to lift my luggage onto the conveyor belt. I did not expect him to. I always insist on lifting my own bags. The luggage of a northern nurse is always heavy. After twelve-hours flying time, sustained only by airline peanuts and cookies, and followed by a four-hour ride on a dirt road that appeared to be the road to nowhere, I reached my destination – dead tired and hungry.

Day 2

Today was my first day of work in my new community. Funny, but it does not seem to matter how many times I have come north, I am still apprehensive and a bit frightened. The flow of patients in the clinic was steady. I saw children with impetigo, tonsillitis, and earaches. Mid-morning, a woman asked if I would remove stitches from her dog. The vet had put them in, but the trip to the vet is four hours back down the dirt road. I removed the stitches and moved on to the next medical problem. I chuckled to myself, thinking about how this request would have been perceived in the South, and how here it is as normal as bringing your child in for stitch removal.

Later in the day, I walked in the beauty of wild flowers and birch trees, and enjoyed the smell of wood stoves burning. Southerners ask me if I am afraid of bears. I respect bears. However, as I walk, I hum and sing. I doubt there is a bear brave enough to come within earshot of me.

Day 3

A gentle breeze brushing across my face and a chorus of bird songs provided a pleasant awakening this morning. The first patient in the clinic was an elderly gentleman. Because he spoke only Slavey, we communicated through our interpreter. He complained of sore toes. When he took his socks off, I was in no doubt that his toes were sore, for his nails were very thick. With daily soaking and filing, we should make headway, but it could take several visits. The rest of the day was routine, with the usual maladies of lice, scabies, earaches, and coughs.

After work, I walked to the local lake. I am amazed at the wild roses everywhere. Never have I seen so many shades of pink. I am originally from Alberta, which they call Wild Rose Country, but I must admit that Alberta has nothing on the Western Arctic when it comes to wild roses.

Day 4

It was a routine, fairly quiet day in the clinic. Many of the Dene are out at their camps. It is summertime, and it appears to be universal that we all feel better in the summer. The gentleman with the sore feet came for his daily foot care – we still have a long way to go. With school coming to an end, the students here, like children everywhere, are happy. This tends to keep business at the nursing station to a minimum. A young girl arrived for a pregnancy test. It is positive. I counsel her so she can make her own decisions. She has no idea about what it really means to be a mother, and I wonder how she will handle this. I will keep a close eye on her.

After work, I look forward to my walk. My bug jacket is now at the top of my list of prized possessions – a good investment. I take perverse pleasure in watching the annoying creatures trying, and failing, to attack me. What sweet revenge!

Day 5

I realize how lucky I am to simply walk downstairs to work. In these remote communities, most accommodations for the nurses are above the health centres or close by. This certainly beats having to supply your own vehicle, fight big city traffic for an hour, and pay dearly for parking and fuel – just to get to work.

The clinic was routine. My foot man arrived for his daily treatment. In the afternoon, there were home visits with the interpreter, because the elders do not speak English. It is a privilege to be welcomed into their homes. I feel inadequate doing home visits and always have. You go in with your little black bag, which really doesn't have much in it, certainly no miracles to cure old age. The elders have multiple age-related complaints. They must wonder why you always bring that black bag.

Later, as I headed away from the local lake on my evening walk, I spotted two bison in the ditch. I am very frightened of bison for they are unpredictable and do not frighten. I suppose, with their size, they have no reason to be afraid. Bison have poor eyesight, but they have an acute sense of smell. They may or may not attack. Tonight, I stayed back and waited to see if they were going to move from their spot. They did not move, and there was no other way to get around them. Fortunately, a truck pulled up and stopped. In it were a couple of fellows from another community who asked if I would like a ride past the bison. They hadn't taken me for a tourist. Tourists often have no fear and think that a close-up picture of a buffalo would be a perfect Kodak moment. I do have buffalo pictures, but none were taken up close.

Day 6

I awoke to the sound of rain on the tin roof. It will be a relief in more ways than one. The roads in town are unpaved, and there will be less dust today. For those with seasonal allergies, the rain cleanses the air. The rain is welcome.

In the clinic, I did many chest x-rays for tuberculosis surveillance. There has been TB in the North, but with our diligent follow-up programs, it has been kept under control. As I performed the x-rays, I knew I could not do this in the South.

After our regular hours, the RCMP brought a local man who had been bitten by a dog into the health centre. They had to shoot the dog. The only way for us to know if a dog is rabid, post-mortem, is to send the dog's head for analysis to a provincial lab in Alberta. I treated the man for the bite. Then the other nurse, the RCMP officer, and I went to work removing the head of the animal and preparing it to send via bus to Alberta. In the North, that is just the way it is. Because of this, I had to forego my daily walk.

Day 7

This morning, sunlight streaming through the crack in my curtains woke me. At this time of year in the North, the sun never really goes down. It becomes dusky around 1 a.m. as the sun partially sets, and it is bright again at 3 a.m. when the sun is high in the sky. I sleep well here and feel invigorated. All this daylight is energizing.

The janitor, who works in the health centre, is a grand gentleman. I am mesmerized when he shares his family history with me. His great-grandfather was a Scotsman who came here to work for the Hudson's Bay. He met his great-grandmother, who was a Dene, and married her. Their family has never left the community. He tells me that when he was walking beside the river two years ago, he found an old coin from the turn of the century. Engraved on it, were the initials of this same great-grandfather. He brought the coin in to show me. I find it amazing that for close to a hundred years the coin had been there and that he had discovered it.

Tonight, after talking to people in the community, I tried a different route for my walk. At the junction where two rivers meet, I sat and thought back to the days of the fur trade, and how the rivers were the highways. I imagined them busy with canoes piled high with pelts for trading. If only the rivers could talk. What stories they could tell!

Day 8

I bolted out of bed at 6 o'clock this morning to the incessant ringing of my apartment doorbell. (When a nurse is needed, people are expected to call. In a real emergency, they will just appear at your door. At times, however, *my* assessment of what is an emergency, and *theirs,* may be very different.) I wrestled to get my clothes on and flew down the stairs, my shirt on backwards.

There to greet me were several frantic adolescents who were under the influence of who knows what. They brought in a friend who had cut his wrist and was bleeding severely. I took the young man into the treatment room, and after reassuring his hysterical friends that he would be okay, I sent them outside to wait.

The boy told me that he and his friends had been partying last night. He had gotten very intoxicated, become depressed, and cut his wrist. He wanted to know if cocaine can make you depressed. I sewed his laceration, and then I had my drug and alcohol talk with him. I am sure it fell on deaf ears, as he was no different from any other adolescent. I called his parents and the RCMP. The kind officer came over to ensure they all got home safely. Twelve teens were sandwiched into a half-ton truck. No doubt they received a lecture from him as well.

Day 9

It is Sunday. Having most of the day to hike, explore, and visit, I headed down to the river where the landscape provided me with hours of entertainment. It was a feast for the eyes. The colourful explosion of wildflowers reminded me of an artist's palette. The diamond willow tree is plentiful in this area. It has very hard wood that does not rot and is popular for making willow furniture and walking sticks. However, it takes fifty years to grow a two-inch trunk. A lone buffalo grazed beside me, far enough away that I was not threatened. I felt lucky to be in this place. I ended my day losing myself with Captain Joshua Slocum in his tale about sailing alone around the world.

Day 10

Today I spent some time with a lovely Dene woman who works as our clerk at the nursing station. She is happy to share her tales of growing up in this area. As a child, she lived with her grandfather in a cabin which had old newspapers lining the walls for insulation. She could read well enough to understand some of the stories on the walls. She always wanted to go away and become a nurse; but in those days, that would have been next to impossible for her. For thirty years, she has worked at this nursing station, and I know that nursing would not be difficult for her. She told me how many of the nurses who come to work here for short periods want to change the local people. I apologized on behalf of my colleagues who, I know, are well-meaning, but naïve. I feel privileged to be a visitor in this community.

My patient with the toenail problem arrived for his pedicure. We are making headway with foot soaks and filing. At this time of year, many children have infected bug bites. These kids don't complain about their bites. They just scratch themselves raw. Some look as if they have chicken pox. Southern media has the public in a panic about illnesses that are carried by mosquitoes. No one here thinks about such things. These pests are just a fact of life.

Day 11

I lay in bed a bit this morning, just to listen to the birds. I'm glad I'm not in the South where I'd have to get up at 5:30 to be at work by 7:30. I don't have to be at the clinic until 8:30, so it's like sleeping in.

Many elders came in to get their medications refilled. The northern nurse takes care of that. If someone has a prescription for a medication not stocked at the health centre, the nurse orders several months' worth, and the individual comes in weekly for refills. It is the nurse who fills the prescription. The elders still like to go out into the bush for weeks at a time. I asked one of them what she remembered about her life, before the days of medications introduced by the white man. She recalled applying spruce gum to cuts, scrapes or burns, using eagle tears for eye infections and bear urine for certain maladies. Something must have worked, because there are people well into their 80s and 90s, living here independently.

Work was steady the rest of the day. We had the usual cuts and scrapes from falling off bikes onto gravel, more infected bug bites (which can be serious), earaches, and sore throats.

Day 12

When I awoke this morning, I was lulled by a steady soft rain on the tin roof. It has been hot and dry. I am sure the flora and fauna were relieved. I was, too, as I knew the clinic would be quiet. I don't know why, but people here don't come out in the rain. I asked the clerk/interpreter if her people disliked rain. She said, "They are made of sugar and they fear they would melt."

In the afternoon, we did home visits. I decided not to take the black bag, as there is not a thing in it that can help anyone. On our first stop, we looked in on a man who will turn 92 in a few days. He lives in a log shack about 12 feet by 12 feet, with no running water and with an outhouse. We found him lying on his single bed. There was lots of wood cut and split for his stove and a large rack of moose meat on his little table. Through the interpreter, he told me he was just fine. I am sure he is – as he is tougher than I. The interpreter informed me that the man's family ensures that he has wood and food, and that he is a fiercely independent man. I am amazed at him. I think he should be showing us how things are done, instead of us trying to meddle in his world. When I thanked him for the visit, he gave me a huge toothless grin. I handed the clerk ten dollars for a box of smokeless tobacco and asked her to give it to him on his birthday.

The next elder we visited was a woman well into her eighties. She was sitting on the edge of her bed, in a room not big enough to put a double bed and walk around it. In this tiny space, were all her worldly possessions. The interpreter told me that the woman's back was sore. I felt helpless, as I noticed that her mattress looked uncomfortably thin. She has all the bone disorders that accompany old age, and I know her pain is chronic. She told the clerk to ask the nurse to fix her pain, but I thought to myself, "Only God can do that and I am sure not her!" I gave her a back rub and tucked her into her old bed. I realized this was a very temporary fix.

Day 13

The rain has stopped and the sun is shining. Just as I do every morning, I put coffee on and take a moment to literally stop and smell the roses.

The clinic was the usual mix of injuries and illnesses – some obvious, some not. The RCMP brought in four adolescents who had rolled their vehicle on the gravel road around midnight, but were not found until this morning. They were all okay. However, one appeared to have a kidney contusion and perhaps a fractured collarbone. Because he required more diagnostics and treatment than we are capable of, my co-worker and I prepared him for a medevac. In the afternoon, we held the regular public health clinic, checking and immunizing babies.

After work, I strolled through the village. Children were out on their bikes, while older kids hung out at the recreation centre and at the local store. When it comes to the stages of development of children, there is no cultural divide. Such a big deal is made of the differences between cultures; but really, when it comes to human development, there are none. The adolescent boys here chase the girls and vice versa. They dress like teens anywhere else. The younger children ride bikes, skip rope, play catch, and enjoy candy and ice cream. These could be kids in any major city.

Day 14

During breakup, there is always the threat of flooding, because this is when the ice breaks into big pieces, and the river is partially thawed. The huge chunks of ice jam together and cause the river to dam. Now the river is totally thawed, and with the spring run off, it is very high and fast, and it sounds like a waterfall.

Since the clinic was quiet today, the clerk/interpreter and I decided to check on our woman with the sore back. She was sitting on the edge of her bed, dressed in her finery. I told her she looked pretty – because she did. Through the interpreter, she let me know that earlier today she had felt well enough to go to the store in her wheelchair. A family member had taken her. Although the store is only 100 feet away from her house, she had not been there for almost a year. I made a mental note that her wheelchair ramp was only a sheet of plywood which was not very strong. I made arrangements with the health board later to have a proper one installed.

In the afternoon, we made a quick visit to another strong-minded woman, a paraplegic confined to a wheelchair after an accident she suffered a few years ago. (Apparently, she had fallen from a balcony.) She took time from making birchbark baskets to give me a lesson. She showed me how she uses bark from birch trees, which has been peeled and sanded by hand until it is smooth. After she cuts the bark to create baskets of all shapes and sizes, she sews the pieces together with spruce root, which has been pulled from the ground and cleaned by hand until it is shiny. Then she reinforces the baskets with willow. Next, she dyes porcupine quills and sews them, one by one, onto the baskets, making beautiful flowers, birds or butterflies. These baskets are magnificent works of art, and I am lucky enough to own a few. Many local women make a living creating these masterpieces.

After work, I prepared and ate my dinner, which was rather boring, as I am running low on perishable foods. Once in a while, the store has some, but you can never compare the quality, choices or prices to what is available in the South. A stroll by the river with my cherished bug jacket – and the day is done.

Day 15

Usually, I am awake long before the alarm. Not this day. In the wee hours of the morning, there was a call. A young woman had been changing a light bulb. It had broken and small glass fragments were embedded in her eye. (I did not ask why she was changing a light bulb at 4:30 in the morning, as I did not really want to know the answer. However, the question did enter my mind.) I called for a medevac to take her to an eye specialist in Yellowknife.

The rest of the day was routine. The patient with the toenail problem no longer complains of pain, so we must be making headway. Through the interpreter, I explained that he should have the nails removed when the physician next makes his community visit.

After work, then my walk. It was very hot and dry. With the sun up 24 hours, it does not cool off much. Some think the North is always cold, but the opposite is true. It gets very hot, and stays hot, with the constant beaming of the sun. It is also very difficult to dress to keep cool, with the persistent mosquitoes that try to make a meal out of you. I have found bites on unmentionable places, and to this day, I wonder how they pulled that off.

Day 16

Because of the life and profession I have chosen, there are few constants. Today, I am grateful for old rivers, birds, and foliage. I have my lonely moments; but I overcome them with a good adventure story, long walks, and long distance telephone calls. Living here makes me appreciate the luxuries of life. When I head home over the 60th parallel, I realize how much we take for granted. I am not very patient with whining about prices in grocery stores, about the weather or about the lack of material possessions. I marvel at the people who are native to this area and at the nurses and teachers who choose to stay in remote communities, for years at a time.

* * *

Looking ahead

I know that the next two weeks of my contract will be steeped in routine: sick clinic in the morning and public health duties in the afternoon. I will spend my evenings, as usual, walking along the two rivers that hold so much Canadian history. I will pay attention to the geology and the secrets of another time. I will marvel at the flora and fauna. I will study the trees, the birds and the creatures both large and small, and I will try to imprint all this in my memory. I am grateful that I am able see places in Canada that most people can only dream of visiting. Perhaps most of all, I appreciate the warmth of the local people. I realize that they may live in such remote areas, but they have the same hopes and dreams as the rest of us. There isn't such a huge cultural divide as some might imagine – *we are all just Canadians.*

Dana Hawes RN graduated from Mount Royal College in Calgary. She began working in the North in 1994. She obtained her Occupational Health Certificate and her Critical Care Nursing Certificate, and she completed all the courses required by the Canadian Aeronautical Transport Systems for work as a flight nurse. Dana presently works at Foothills Hospital in Calgary, Alberta. Her story, "Adventures of a Northern Nurse" appears in *Northern Nurses: True Nursing Adventures from Canada's North* by J. Karen Scott and Joan E. Kieser.

SUNGLASSES AT MIDNIGHT

Bev Green

Nursing in the North is an unforgettable experience. I have many good memories of working at the nursing station in Cambridge Bay on the Arctic Ocean. It's on the southern shore of Victoria Island, in the northern territory now called Nunavut. When I was there in 1989, it was a town of about 1000 people. About 70% of the population were Inuit. The other 30% were "southerners" who came from all parts of Canada to work as healthcare personnel, teachers, Royal Canadian Mounted Police, as well as construction and public works staff.

* * *

Arctic nurses had to be adaptable and flexible. We soon became accustomed to the lack of supplies and equipment that we took for granted in the South. Many new tasks had to be learned quickly: suturing, doing lab tests and microscopic work, taking and developing x-rays and reading them (one of the more difficult skills), doing pelvic exams, and putting on casts. I soon realized that even more important than having these technical talents was the ability to do a good physical assessment, to take a thorough history, and to really listen. These steps were vital in working with patients. Northern nurses were given a lot of independence and at times, the responsibility was almost overwhelming. However, the responsibility, combined with learning about the people and their culture, made it a positive experience.

Weather was a big factor of life in the North. There were many things to get used to. I remember walking home from a call to the nursing station, shortly after midnight, and chuckling, as I realized I had just put on my sunglasses because the sunset was so bright. Later in the year, I watched the light disappear about 2 o'clock in the afternoon, after a very short and greyish daylight. Then there was the excitement of waiting for the sun to reappear, after the long days of midwinter darkness.

The one Christmas Day we spent in the Arctic was memorable. My husband and some of his co-workers poured hot water down the vents in our roof to de-ice them, and then they had the town water-truck bring water to our house and to several other homes. Earlier on that Christmas morning, we had to get the honey wagon to pump out the sewers. We had woken up to no water and to drainage from the kitchen sink coming up into the bathtub.

It was quickly apparent, not only at work but also in everyday life, how much we took for granted "down South." After a few months of living in a town without a hairdresser, I took the scissors to my own hair. There was no cosmetic improvement, but it felt better. Shortly after that, there was great excitement when we learned that an incoming RCMP officer would be accompanied by his wife who was a hairdresser. Needless to say, she did a booming business while she was in Cambridge Bay.

* * *

Life in the North was not all work. We enjoyed many social occasions. With frequent arrivals and departures of the various southerners who were in Cambridge Bay to work, it seemed we were always having a farewell party or a welcome event for someone. And there were the local celebrations. One of the biggest was the Omingmak Frolics, held in May to say goodbye to winter – although the weather still seemed very wintry to me. There was a parade with floats of all descriptions, pulled by the small number of vehicles we had in town. There was a float bearing an igloo, pulled by a grader. Even the nursing station Suburban was decorated and in the parade. In fact, there were not many spectators, since almost everyone participated. Following the parade, there were several games. The most unforgettable was the "Honey Bucket Race." The name tells it all. The nursing station entry in this race consisted of a pole-type stretcher bearing the lightest person on it. In this case, it was a visiting resident, perched on a honey bucket, with four of us carrying her. Sad to say, most of us, including me, ended up sprawled on the icy road. Not surprisingly, we lost the race.

In the evening, we enjoyed a talent show, listened to music, and watched the dancing, which included a jigging contest. While waiting for the judges' results, and with the music still playing, we were entertained by a little Inuit boy and girl about seven or eight years old doing a perfect two-step dance.

Christmas provided another opportunity to witness Inuit culture. On Inuit Games Night, we saw ankle pulls and musical chairs, with the men carrying the women on their backs, amid lots of laughter. For snacks, we sliced off chunks of raw frozen caribou.

* * *

Working in a northern nursing station was very different from nursing in the South. In the North, we dealt with *every* patient who came in, and we had to decide on a plan of action. History-taking was always an interesting exercise because some of the common Inuit expressions left me stumped. If I asked how long something had bothered the person, or when something had happened, the reply was, "Since before" or "Just before." My first reaction was to ask, "Just before what?" And the answer again was, "Just before" – as though it was a clear statement of fact. It took practice to ask the right questions to determine how long ago that was. If I asked how often a symptom occurred, the answer was, "Oh, once in a while" or "Once in a great long while." Again, it was not very informative, although I am sure the patient knew what it meant. I also had a hard time getting used to the response to a negative question. I would ask, "You don't have any allergies, do you?" and they would say "Yes" meaning, "Yes, I don't have any allergies." After a few such conversations, I learned to phrase the questions differently, and in a positive way such as, "Do you have any allergies?"

In addition, there was nonverbal communication with which we quickly became familiar. Raising of the eyebrows meant "Yes" and wrinkling of the nose meant "No." I noticed that it was most common among young adults and children. At first, I thought the kids were being rude and just refusing to answer. When I caught on, it was amazing how quickly it became a habit with me too. Once, when I was doing a developmental assessment on an infant, the young mother told me her four-month-old was already wrinkling her nose. One advantage of this particular form of communication was that it ensured that we looked at the patient, and not at the history form.

Most of the younger people in the town spoke English, but many of the elders did not. This was a problem if an interpreter was not available. On one occasion that I clearly remember, it landed me in a mess. I was driving an elderly woman home in the nursing station Suburban. It was dark and it had recently snowed, so it was difficult to see where the road was. After creeping along slowly and almost making several wrong turns, I took what I thought was the road. The elder said something to me. We were not communicating well, and I did not understand. The end result was that I got the Suburban hopelessly stuck. When the tow truck came to pull us out, the driver talked to the woman and then grinned. He told me that she had been trying to tell me, "That's not the road!"

* * *

The town of Cambridge Bay was one of the main centres in the Arctic. The nursing station served that town, as well as smaller satellite settlements. One was Bay Chimo, located about an hour's plane ride away, with a population of around 75. The other was Bathurst Inlet, a short plane ride further on, with a population of about 20. The nurse on call, besides having to see people after hours at the nursing station, was also available to talk to the lay dispenser in each of those satellite communities.

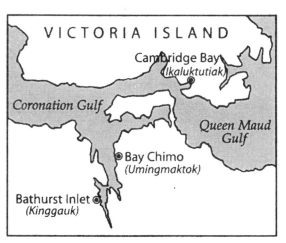

Lay dispensers were people native to the community who had some training. They were able to do basic treatments and they kept a small supply of medication to dispense. As those settlements had no phone service, they consulted with us by two-way radio. The only two-way radio in Cambridge Bay was located at the office of the Hunters and Trappers Association, which was a counter in Central Arctic Meats, a meat packing plant and meat store. The Association office would get a call from the lay dispenser in Bay Chimo or Bathurst Inlet, and then they would phone the nursing station. The nurse on call would have to go over to the meat store to discuss the case over the radio. Radio reception could be unreliable, especially when the weather was bad, so we had to have the volume as high as possible while getting information. One particular day, I found myself listening to a problem and to the description of the patient, and then shouting questions over the radio such as, "Does he have a fever? Is the urine foul-smelling and dark?" Meanwhile, people who were in the store buying fish and sausage heard the whole exchange. So much for patient confidentiality.

* * *

It was in Bay Chimo that I had one of my most unforgettable days in the North. About twice a year, the two settlements, Bay Chimo and Bathurst Inlet, received a routine visit from a doctor who travelled to communities in the Arctic, with a nurse from Cambridge Bay. The doctor saw people with chronic illnesses and those who were acutely ill. In a separate area, the nurse did preventive health care, such as vaccinations and well-woman checkups.

On the first of September, I had an opportunity to fly out on a day trip to Bay Chimo. It was common in the Arctic for planes to be delayed about an hour and a half due to fog. This day was no different. But then it turned beautiful. The scenery on the way to Bay Chimo (where there were real trees) was spectacular. We did not have trees in Cambridge Bay, so it seemed very green and lush. It was obviously a big day for the town, as half the population was there to greet us and to help me with my supplies

The lay dispenser showed me to the room at the back of the store, where I was to work. I was getting used to working without a lot of conveniences. However, I looked at this room in dismay. It contained twin beds – iron bedsteads with sagging mattresses. At the far end of the two feet of space between the beds, was a night table. On looking more closely, I was happy to see a new lamp, but I discovered that the generator was down, so the lamp could not be used. There was no electricity, no sink, no paper towels, or Kleenex.

There were about 15 people for me to see, the majority of cases being for well-woman checkups, including Pap smears. I had learned to do Paps about four months earlier. I always had a proper exam table, stirrups, a stool for me to sit on and a place to set slides. This was obviously going to be a bit more difficult.

The first woman who came in was about fifty years old and she spoke no English. With the lay dispenser acting as interpreter, I asked her how many pregnancies she had had. She beamed, and began counting on her fingers and naming her children. It hit me again how different the social norm was. In the South, I was more likely to hear "Two children." After taking the woman's history, it was time for the exam. I asked her to put on a gown and to lie down. I thought, surely it's not that hard to do a Pap on a bed without stirrups. I knew it could be done, but not by me, not that day. Between the sagging mattress, the lack of light, my inexperience, and the significant problem of the foot of the iron bedstead, it soon became obvious this was not going to work. Even if I had been able to insert a speculum, there was no way I could have seen anything. I had several other women to examine, and I was beginning to panic.

The lay dispenser looked expectantly at me and waited for me to solve the problem. And suddenly I did. I looked around frantically and saw a piece of plywood. Just how long it took, I cannot remember, but I finally came up with a perfectly workable – though quite unorthodox – plan. I placed all my equipment on one bed. Then I asked each woman to lie on her back, across the width of the two beds with the piece of plywood under her hips, thus solving the problem of the sagging mattresses. I had her prop her heels on the edge of the other bed. I got down on the floor, ducked under one leg and worked on my hands and knees. Once I had the speculum inserted, I used a flashlight to assist in the examination. My Pap slides were in readiness on the night table. The procedure was slower than usual, as I could barely see a thing. The women must have wondered what took so long and why they were in such a position. They were all most co-operative and cheerful, and grateful for the visit. By the end of our stop in Bay Chimo, I had perfected the system, and it worked quite well.

Another part of the well-woman examinations involved checking haemoglobins with a haemoglobinometer. Between patients, it was necessary to clean off the slide to remove blood. When I mentioned this to the lay dispenser, she brought me a small glass of cold water for the task. I began to long for the amenities of the nursing station in Cambridge Bay. However, I realized it is all relative.

Finally, I was finished. I emerged from the store to see the pilots, the doctor, and the schoolteachers patiently waiting for me, so we could continue on to Bathurst Inlet. It was an even smaller settlement, so there were fewer people to see. I cannot remember what kind of room I had for the examination, but it was not as challenging as the previous one. Both of the settlements we visited that day were a lot more traditional than Cambridge Bay. People in these smaller communities had much less influence from the South. In general, they probably led a healthier lifestyle. It was a great opportunity for me to see a more traditional way of life. The people were very friendly, and when several of them came to Cambridge Bay for a dental clinic a few months later, they greeted me like an old friend.

* * *

During my time up North, I had many memorable days and a variety of experiences. One thing became clear the longer I was there. Even though my background and upbringing was very different from that of the people I met in the North, we had many things in common. As patients and staff came to know me better and to confide in me, it was obvious that all of us shared many of the same struggles. The worries, sorrows, and stresses of our lives are very similar, as are life's joys. Treating people with respect and caring, and talking and listening to them, are an important part of nursing, no matter what the setting.

Bev Green RN, BScN graduated as a registered nurse in 1975 from the Misericordia Hospital in Edmonton, Alberta. Later, she took a post-basic BScN at the University of Alberta in Edmonton. She worked at both the Misericordia Hospital and the Hinton Hospital, and in public health in the Edson area in Alberta, before going north. Since then, she has been employed mostly in public health. Bev currently works in Sexual and Reproductive Health in the Calgary Health Region.

MY THREE YEARS IN ATTAWAPISKAT

Heather Thomson

Attawapiskat in Cree means "water between the rocks." It was my home for three years – from August 2000 to August 2003. I loved being a part of the small, but friendly, isolated community – even though it was often dusty and always windy. Working as a registered nurse was challenging, inspiring, and fulfilling. Life as a community member could be challenging; but I was welcomed, respected, and accepted. Throughout my three years in Attawapiskat, I kept a journal, and I sent stories through email messages, which I called "Dispatches from Attawapiskat," to friends and family. I've selected several of these stories and snippets from my journal that I hope will give a glimpse into my experiences of living in the North.

Sights, Sounds, Weather and Travel

The first snowfall covers the roadways, and the sound of winter begins with the roar of skidoos. All of a sudden, the population of the community seems to grow, as people come outdoors, eager for the cold weather. Cold weather? No, it's better to say freezing weather – because sometimes, with the wind chill factor, it is -50ºC. This means that the construction of the winter road will be started, so that community members can travel by truck or skidoo to points south. They may want to visit family or friends in other communities, get alcohol from Moosonee, attend a Monster Bingo, buy groceries in Moosonee at prices that are cheaper than in Attawapiskat, or it may be just to go on a road trip. My own experiences of travelling by different modes of transportation have definitely been expanded. I have been on a skidoo, on a sled pulled by a skidoo, in a kayak, in a large canoe powered by a motor, in a helicopter, aboard many sizes of Air Creebec planes, in an ambulance, and on cross-country skis.

At 6:30 each night, the church bells ring. Almost immediately, a chorus of dogs can be heard throughout the community. The dogs stop right where they are and begin to howl. One of the loudest and proudest howlers is Katie. I never tired of this daily, comical event.

The night sky here is immense. It is magnificent, with stars so bright and the northern lights, the *wawatay*, moving across the sky. Some say that, when the *wawatay* move, it is those who have already died, saying hello; others say it is someone in another community, saying hello by whistling. I experienced this one night – when all you could hear were whistles from different parts of Attawapiskat, and you could see the *wawatay* dancing amongst the stars.

Challenges and Opportunities

DeBeers, the international diamond corporation, began exploration in northern Ontario in the 1980s. They signed an agreement with the Attawapiskat First Nation in the fall of 1999. Today, the Victor Project is located in a wet muskeg area about 80 km to the northwest of Attawapiskat. A positive outcome (so far) has been employment opportunities for many community members, such as heavy machine operators, drilling assistants, kitchen staff, and administrative support staff. Projections from DeBeers – regarding the capacity of the diamond find – suggest that the mine could operate for ten to fifteen years. Negotiations are under way with DeBeers and the Attawapiskat First Nation Band concerning construction of the mine and its supporting infrastructure – as well as the economic and social impacts on the community of 1600 Cree people. The face of change appeared to me one day, after the Christmas community feast in 2002, when I saw dozens of children wearing new toques with the words "DeBeers ... a diamond is forever" printed on their foreheads.

*

The education system in this community is not very effective, despite the good intentions of many individuals, including teachers, teaching assistants, parents, and the education board. During my three years in Attawapiskat, the elementary school has had three different principals; most teachers leave after one school year. The lack of continuity is clearly seen in the poor behaviour and discipline challenges of many children, as well as in their lack of academic skills in the three Rs. The support structure of the school, as a place of learning and as a vital part of the community, is difficult to maintain if the players change each year. Another factor, debated by many, is the importance of children being taught initially in Cree, their first language, as they develop basic language and abstract thinking skills. At this time, English is still used in all grade levels.

*

The price of alcohol fluctuates with the seasons. Access to liquor stores, via the winter road, helps to bring down the price. In the summer, a mickey goes for about $150; in the winter, it's about $50. Remember that Attawapiskat is a "dry community," and I'm not referring to annual precipitation.

*

Attawapiskat has a very high unemployment rate, with many people living on social assistance. Overcrowded housing is also a significant problem, often with twelve to fifteen family members from different generations living together. Drinking water must be obtained in large jugs from the old water treatment plant, as the new plant's filtration system requires high amounts of chlorination, which makes the water impossible to drink.

One night at one o'clock, I was awakened suddenly by the sound of breaking glass. The cats scattered and my heart raced. I sat in my dark bedroom, disoriented. Was I being robbed? I ventured upstairs to find that the outer pane of my dining room window had a large hole in it, and a rock was lodged between the panes. I called the police. When they arrived, they asked if I had made anyone mad that day. "No, not that I'm aware of," I said. A report was written; they left and I went back down to bed.

At two o'clock, there was a louder bang. A bigger rock had broken a second pane, and glass was scattered all over the floor, on countertops, table and chairs – everywhere. The hospital maintenance worker was called to cover the broken window with plywood, until a new one could be ordered. I cleaned up the glass, and the police amended their earlier report. The incident was attributed to kids with a lot of time and nothing to do. Lexan, a glass-like material that will not break, was used as the outer pane of my window. Since then, it has withstood many rocks.

Health Care and Medical Emergencies

One snowy night, I talked to Medcom in Toronto regarding ground conditions at our airport. Medcom coordinates medical evacuations of patients from the North to hospitals in the South. My patient was destined for Moose Factory. They asked me to get a worker from the local Ministry of Transportation to go to the airport and measure the snow on the runway. After many phone calls, I got the snow condition report (less than one inch of snow on the runway). Then I relayed the information to the Medcom dispatcher, who would consult with the pilots and call me back. While I waited, I continued to prepare my patient (and the paperwork) for transfer. When the dispatcher called back, he told me that there were "conflicting reports of airport conditions," and that the plane would not be coming. Of course, there were conflicting weather reports – but ours was from here! Early the next morning, after the one inch of snow was cleared from the runway, the plane took off with the patient. Dagnabit!

*

The words "medical emergency" and "bad weather" conjure up memories of what can go wrong, when you are nursing in an isolated area. Thankfully, those patients who were held up due to bad weather during my time in Attawapiskat are all fine today. Their illnesses or injuries included: uterine hemorrhage with approximate blood loss of two to three litres, fractured femur (held up for five days), drug overdose of 250 plus pills, second-to-third-degree burns on 20% of a child's body, and acute appendicitis. As well, several babies were safely delivered. A solid nursing team was vital to these positive outcomes, and I was happy to be a part of the team.

*

Providing health care to a patient in Attawapiskat involves the extended family, especially in emergencies. Families can include half (or more) of the entire community. While

23

the nurses attempt to stabilize and care for the patient, it is not uncommon for the emergency room to be full of family members. Crowd control, and connecting with one or two family members, becomes a necessary skill that is learned quickly.

*

The lack of services for people with mental illness is by far one of the most challenging healthcare issues. If a person goes into a "crisis" and is suicidal, it means that he or she must go by plane to another hospital, often with police escort, to be assessed by a physician and then sent on another plane for admission to a psychiatric hospital. Once the "crisis" is over, the person is returned to Attawapiskat. There are no regular visits with a mental health worker, nor the structured activities needed to function at home and in the community. Thus, the cycle of medevacs for those in crisis becomes the norm for some patients.

*

As in many other First Nation communities, Type 2 diabetes, high blood pressure, and coronary artery disease are predominant chronic illnesses in the Attawapiskat population. A surprising point, however, is that these illnesses are seen in people in their mid-thirties. Therefore, it is not uncommon that a 38-year-old patient, brought in by ambulance for a minor household accident (such as slicing open his hand when gutting fish), might be taking three to five different prescription medications daily.

*

Gas sniffing remains a health problem for many families in Attawapiskat. Former gas-sniffers are often unable to maintain a job, or manage the basic life skills of cooking and personal hygiene. For those still involved, the daily battle to stop gas-sniffing often loses out to the feelings of hopelessness that can come from living in a poor, isolated Native community. When a gas-sniffer requires medical help, the nausea and shortness of breath that you get from the gas fumes on the person's clothing is overwhelming.

*

Once, an elderly man fell to his knees in the hospital hallway on his way to the dining room. Because he had fallen a few times before, it was decided that he needed a walker. After two days of "training," we let him go from his room to the dining room on his own. At lunch three days later, I saw him walking down the hallway *carrying* the walker. He was always eager to please, so he continued to take the walker with him into the dining room. I'm sure he must have wondered why we asked him to do this. (It became clear that the falls were related more to his rushing, than to a lack of balance.) We put the walker away and kept reminding him to *bay-ketch* (slow down) each time he headed to the dining room.

Social Activities

Attawapiskat is a small and isolated community. Compared to living in a city, there isn't much to do. However, social activities and events just seem to happen. At the arena, you can play volleyball, basketball, ball hockey, ice hockey, and broomball, and you can go skating. Each winter, annual tournaments for hockey and broomball are held with teams from other communities. Social get-togethers are held often with groups of nurses, teachers, paramedics, and a few community members. They usually include potluck dinners and games, games, games.

For exercise, I like to go on walks and hikes, and in the winter, I enjoy cross-country skiing. My transition from city girl to outdoor girl culminated in a fire-making award badge after a one-hour hike, deep into the woods. For this, I successfully prepared and maintained the fire for our snack of hot chocolate and hot dogs.

One fall day, I set out with a group of friends to pick cranberries, after learning where to find the best spot. When we arrived at the place, it became crystal clear to me that no one knew what a cranberry bush looked like. We searched the ground for loose cranberries, hoping they would show us the way, but we found none. The women from the community, who had been there the week before, had obviously picked the area clean. After we expanded our search area, a friend exclaimed that she had found a cranberry. We learned then that they grew close to the ground, in mossy areas. That day, we picked enough cranberries for our Thanksgiving turkey dinner. As we headed back to town, a friend noted that we definitely needed further training in cranberry picking, as it was easy to see where our group had been. The squished remains of cranberries littered the ground.

Embracing Cree Culture

Plucking a Canada goose for the first time was a challenging task for me. I had trouble keeping my hand in a cupped position and grabbing only small clumps of feathers. My hand got a cramp that needed to be massaged. While it took me about an hour and a half to pluck a large-sized goose, community women could do it in a half hour. It's a good thing I wasn't responsible for providing dinner for a family, because we might have starved.

*

Cree people have a very good sense of humour. A man with a prosthetic leg always got the new paramedic to check the pulse in his foot. And an elder, who lives at the hospital, wanted to throw her tissue into the garbage bin. She knew the bin was behind her, so tossed the tissue over her shoulder, in a textbook basketball manoeuvre. She's 94 years old.

*

I learned Cree words quickly, as I needed to communicate with the elders regarding their health. As with any new language, you tend to speak in a series of nouns in the hope of conveying your point and intersperse these with flailing hand gestures. I learned to say pain (*dak-a-sin*), good (*minn-ogin*), food (*meech-um*), breathe deeply (*esh-co-tam-o*), no (*mona*), yes (any affirmative sounding noise), tea (*tea*), stool (*mee-see*), urine (*wish-e-gin*), sit (*ap-pay*), stand (*nee-po-eh*), lie down (*mish-en-ey*) and many other important words. *Gee-miss-em* (boyfriend) always got a smile when I mentioned I was going to visit him on holidays.

It's All Part of Living in Attawapiskat

Presumably, many elders in this community were born on January 1. Coincidence? No. The church burned down many years ago, destroying the birth records, and most people only remembered the year they were born.

*

In Attawapiskat, time flies. Until September 2003, electrical power was supplied by diesel generators and the electrical frequency was not always consistent; thus electric clocks gained time, usually several minutes per day. It was always a funny joke to play on the new nurse who came to work too early.

*

One Christmas morning, as I was looking out my living room window and sipping coffee, I was startled by the sight of the police van pulling up into the hospital compound. The officers jumped out, drew their guns, and aimed them at some dogs they had been chasing. A rabid wolf had been in the community a few days before and had bitten a few dogs – thus necessitating a "dog shoot" for the safety of everyone. It was quite a sight.

*

New arrivals to Attawapiskat always experience incredible shock during their first visit to the Northern Store. The cost of groceries is directly related to the weight of the item – or the type of handling that is needed. A case of 24 cans of pop is $30, a two-litre container of Tropicana orange juice is over $9, broccoli averages $6, and laundry detergent can be $20 or more. After a short period, you adjust. When you are out on holidays, you begin to mail boxes of non-perishable items home and you stuff your carry-on luggage with cheeses, fresh fruits, and veggies. It is always fun for me to watch the expressions on the faces of people in the airport in Toronto, when a head of lettuce falls out as I get my plane ticket out of my knapsack.

* * *

I hope to go back to Attawapiskat some day. I miss the faces and the characters of the elders. I miss the extended job that nurses do, when physicians are only accessible by phone. I miss returning from a holiday and being welcomed back. I miss being stopped in the grocery store and asked for advice on a medical problem. I miss the craft people selling their handiwork at the hospital and door-to-door. I miss being involved with families, especially when new members are born, and watching them grow. I miss the crisp winter days – well, not all of them. I miss being part of the small, but friendly, isolated community of Attawapiskat – even though it was often dusty and always windy.

* * *

Postscript: August, 2004

Being a northern nurse in Attawapiskat, Ontario was the best preparation I could have had on my first mission with Médecins Sans Frontières (MSF)/Doctors Without Borders. From September 2003 to July 2004, I worked as a nurse in Baraka, in the Democratic Republic of Congo.

The Baraka project was a "start-up" project: the surrounding population had been without secondary health care for many years, and the first task was to get the hospital running. When I arrived, there were 20 in-patient beds for paediatric and internal medicine patients, and one emergency Cesarean section was performed per month. At the end of my mission, our hospital had grown to 98 beds for paediatric, internal medicine, maternity, surgical, and intensive care patients. Elective surgeries were scheduled four days per week, and the number of emergency surgeries had increased to 5-10 per month. A second task was to bring primary health care to an isolated population across Lake Tanganyika, through weekly mobile clinics. On these trips, which I made by boat, I was able to actually *touch* patients since I was the nurse practitioner. I developed special relationships with the pregnant women (*meembas* in Swahili), with the elders who suffered chronic pain, and with the little ones who boldly stared at the strange white woman (*muzungoo* in Swahili).

I was in charge of the nurses, and my role was to organize, coordinate, supervise, mentor, collaborate, teach, and learn. Since nursing is a central element in the provision of health care, my role extended to the coordination of all hospital services. When I worked in the North, I learned how to navigate the healthcare system, to advocate for patients, to stabilize and prepare a patient for evacuation, to problem-solve first and then consult with the physician, and to manage the numerous competing priorities. Having these skills was vital to the success of my mission

My northern experiences of isolation, and of living and working with a diverse group of people, were similar to the "culture shocks" that I encountered in Baraka. However, what was new was living and working in an insecure region, where our movements were restricted, and where we were in constant contact by radio. It was an interesting coincidence that the radios we had in Baraka were identical to those that I used when I was on call in Attawapiskat. Except when we went to Bujumbura, the capital city of Burundi where our mission headquarters was, there was limited access to email and no Internet access. Food was low on variety, but sometimes high on flavour. The mangoes and fish tasted great; but the main staple, *foo-foo*, a pasty glob of flour and water, was not too tasty. As for the temperature, it was as hot in Baraka as it was cold in Attawapiskat – usually 30 to 40 °C.

During my time in Baraka, I encountered MSF nurses from Europe, as well as other Canadian nurses. By far, those nurses who had worked in isolated northern communities adapted and integrated easily into their role. In Baraka, as I did in the North, I aimed to become part of the strong, courageous Congolese community, and I was welcomed by generous, humourous, and resourceful people. I will never forget them.

Heather Thomson RN, BScN graduated from the University of Ottawa in 1992 with a BSc (Honours) in Computer Science. Before becoming a nurse, she spent over 10 years in computer consulting as a programmer, systems analyst, and team leader. She completed her final nursing practicum at the Nellie Fiddler Health Centre in Muskrat Dam, Ontario and received her Baccalaureate of Nursing at the University of Ottawa in 2000. She then moved to Attawapiskat, Ontario, where she worked until 2003 as a registered nurse at the James Bay General Hospital. From October 2003 to July 2004, Heather was on mission as a registered nurse with Médecins Sans Frontières/Doctors Without Borders in Baraka, in the Democratic Republic of Congo. Heather's stories: "Go North for an Experience like no Other," "Attawapiskat: One Nurse's Experiences," and "What the Survey Says" appear in *Northern Nurses: True Nursing Adventures from Canada's North*.

IN A HEARTBEAT

Susan Pauhl

Why, you might ask, would I choose to leave a nursing position that I loved, medical and nursing staff who were great to work with, and a place to live that was close to family, friends, fine dining, entertainment, and great shopping? The only answer I can give is, "To add a little adventure to my life." I felt that, if I did not leave all of these comforts, I would probably stay in the same place for the rest of my life. I knew there was a whole new world out there – waiting to be explored. So from 1971 until 1991, I explored Canada's Arctic.

How does one begin a story that spans twenty years? I could start with the sheer beauty of Canada's North. The amazing geography of mountains, tundra, rivers, oceans, and barrens is far more breathtaking in real life than in any picture you have ever seen. Northern lights, in vivid blues, greens, pinks, and white, zinging and crackling across the clear, black northern sky are a common, yet always spectacular, occurrence. They make you stop and watch their dance. I could tell about weather extremes: from summers in Inuvik under the twenty-four hour sun that were so hot that my air conditioner could not keep my apartment cool, to winter storms in Rankin Inlet with whiteout conditions and wind-chill factors of -80°F that kept you housebound for days. Never in my dreams, could I have imagined the wildlife that I would encounter. I have sat on a skidoo in the middle of a caribou herd near Chesterfield Inlet, observed a group of walrus off the shore of Hall Beach, helped care for an abandoned polar bear cub in Rankin Inlet, and watched ravens, as big as turkeys, steal groceries from the back of pickup trucks.

* * *

Moving from large cities, such as Hamilton and Toronto, to small communities with populations from 300 to 3,500 people, was relatively smooth. Leaving traffic, noise, crowds, and the everyday rush of life was a plus. In no time, a short walk to the Northern Store took much longer than expected, as you stopped to talk to everyone you knew along the way. Weekend shopping sprees to the mall were replaced by catalogue shopping. You soon realized that you could purchase everything from a catalogue, or by making a phone call to the customer service department of any store. A trip south, no matter how brief, brought new meaning to the phrase "excess baggage."

Shopping for groceries definitely improved over the twenty years that I spent in the North. In the beginning, fresh fruit and vegetables were only seen when you carried them in your hand luggage on a return flight from holidays or a medevac. By 1991, fresh produce was readily available in most communities. The prices, however, did not make it accessible for most families, especially in smaller places.

Making out a barge order for the first time was quite an experience. A barge order, which was placed once a year, was to include all of the dry goods, non-perishable and heavy items that would be needed by the nursing station during the next year. The order would be filled in the South and shipped north by barge when the ice was out of the straits and inlets, usually in late fall. How do you figure out how many rolls of toilet paper you would need for the whole nursing station? I don't think I ever got that one right. Errors frequently occurred, such as when someone thought they were ordering 12 bottles of HP Sauce, and 12 cases of HP Sauce arrived. Since there were no returns, trading the surplus items between nursing stations was a common practice.

* * *

Housing varied greatly, depending on the year and the community in which you were living. When I first went north, most nurses were single, so housing accommodation consisted of individual bedrooms or bed-sitting rooms. You shared the kitchen, living and dining room, and washrooms with the rest of the nursing staff. These accommodations were usually part of the nursing station building. The advantage of this arrangement was that you didn't have to leave the building to see clients after hours. The disadvantage was that you heard the on-call doorbell ring every night. This made it difficult to distance yourself from work, even on your time off. As married nurses were hired, individual apartments were built for the staff. Some of the apartments were attached to the clinic, while others were located in the community. This was a great improvement for everyone as it offered more individual privacy, distance from work when you were not on call, and the ability to hire married nurses and nurses with families.

A frequently-asked question of a northern nurse would be, "What do you do in your spare time?" I wished I'd had more spare time. Work kept me so busy that I never had hours of time with nothing to do. More than one person in my life has mentioned that I am a bit obsessive-compulsive so, needless to say, I was usually able to find something that needed to be reorganized, filed, followed up, or rechecked. A significant amount of time was spent with on-call duties, and in the larger communities, this always meant being busy with patient care.

* * *

The most amazing and rewarding part of working up north was the scope of nursing practice. As a nurse, you don't realize how much you have been taught in your basic nurses' training, until you are actually expected to assess and treat your patients on your own. We were never taught to put all of the patient's signs and symptoms together, and come up with a diagnosis – much less a treatment plan. The transition from thinking as a hospital nurse to thinking as a nursing station nurse takes courage, confidence, independence, and a huge willingness to learn and to seek answers.

* * *

Learning on the job is good, but it cannot always be done fast enough to carry your own client load and still be able to help the other staff, by working independently and on call. I am eternally grateful to all of the nurses who shared their knowledge and skills, and who guided me through my orientation. Acquiring new technical skills was the easy part of the job. Starting an intravenous, suturing, taking and wet-developing x-rays, putting on casts, doing venepuncture and electrocardiograms were some of the new skills to be mastered while working in the North. I still get a headache whenever I think of all the manual white blood cell counts I had to do.

Working and living in a different cultural setting posed minimal difficulties. Treating people with respect and dignity crosses all cultural borders. The hardest part for me was the inability to learn another language – I think I have the worst aptitude for languages of anyone I know. Except for a few words, I relied entirely on my clerk/interpreters when I treated patients. I cannot say that everyone spoke highly of the "white" people in the North. But, on a one-to-one level, I never had any problems.

* * *

In 1979, I was selected to attend the eighteen-month Outpost Nursing Program at Dalhousie University. I gained a great deal from instructors like Ruth May, Dorothy Myhal, and the many physicians who worked with me during my internship. Not only did my patients benefit tremendously from the skills I acquired during the program, but also I was less worried about diagnosing and treating patients incorrectly.

I loved obstetrics and delivered many babies when I worked in the North. A trip to Coral Harbour to medevac a woman in premature labour, who was expecting twins, proved quite the challenge. By the time the doctor and I arrived at the nursing station and assessed the patient, it was evident that we would not make it to Churchill before the babies arrived. The first baby was born uneventfully, and then we waited for the second. This one, however, had no plans to leave the comforts of home. The uterus stopped contracting, and we waited and waited and waited.

After two and a half hours of no contractions, it was obvious the mother's labour needed to be augmented. I called the Inuvik Hospital for their protocol. Administering the suggested drug without an infusion pump or a fetal monitor is not recommended. However, if you don't have either of these pieces of equipment, you make do with what you have. What we had was a handheld fetal Doppler, with which we had been monitoring the fetal heart, and a paediatric intravenous infusion set. Within thirty minutes of starting the procedure, and a full three hours after her sister, Baby Number Two decided to make an appearance. Each baby weighed about four pounds, and both were in good condition upon arrival in Winnipeg.

* * *

In another community, an Inuit man presented himself at the health centre with lower intestinal bleeding. Although he had lost a significant amount of blood, he was stable. We started intravenous lines, arranged for an emergency medical evacuation, did the paper work, and waited for the plane to arrive. We were less then two hours from Frobisher Bay Hospital, so it was not long before we heard the plane overhead. As we were getting the patient ready for transport to the airport, we received a call from the airport saying that the plane had begun to ice up at 5,000 feet and that it was returning to base until the weather cleared.

"When will the weather be clearing?" we asked.

"Maybe tomorrow," was their response.

To make a long story very short, the plane returned to base at three o'clock in the afternoon and was not able to land in our community until eleven o'clock the next morning. During those twenty hours, the patient became quite unstable, his bleeding increased, and his blood pressure plummeted. It was obvious that he needed blood transfusions. Fortunately for this patient, the nursing stations used to stock blood donor kits. During the night, we gave him three units of uncross-matched O negative blood from "walking donors" in town, and his condition stabilized. Most Inuit men have haemoglobin levels of 15 to 18 gm/100cc. When he arrived at the hospital in Frobisher Bay, after receiving the three units of blood, his haemoglobin was only 4 gm. Had it not been for those donor kits, he certainly would have died.

* * *

Not long after getting into bed one cold winter night, I received a call from someone who said his brother had cut his hand. Not being thrilled about getting dressed and going into work, I questioned him as to just how big the cut was. "Oh it's really big. His hand is nearly cut off." Realizing there was more than a little room for exaggeration in that last statement, I asked the fellow how badly the cut was bleeding. "It isn't bleeding at all," he said. A nearly cut-off hand and no bleeding simply did not add up. I had no choice but to get out of my warm bed, dress for -40° weather, try to start my skidoo (that I could only get started if it was kept in a heated garage, which I did not have) and meet the boys at the health centre.

When I arrived, I found the older brother pacing nervously back and forth. His fourteen-year-old brother sat quietly on a chair in the foyer, with a scarf wrapped around his right hand. Although the patient looked pale, there was no blood on the scarf. While getting him to the emergency room, taking off his coat, and putting him on a stretcher, I learned that he had cut his hand on a Zamboni at the ice rink. If I had known what a Zamboni was, I might have been a little more concerned. I took the scarf off his hand. Except for a small band of skin on the top, it was completely severed just below the wrist. He had also lost the tips of his fingers. The injury had occurred while he was riding on top of the Zamboni, when the ice rink was being cleaned and he was scooping ice out of the auger, as it was turning. Since the blade was ice-cold, it promptly sent the arteries into spasm, which was the cause of so little blood loss. He was immediately medevac'd to Winnipeg, where surgeons spent eight hours reattaching his right hand. As luck would have it, he was one of very few left-hand dominant Inuit. When I saw this patient ten years later, he had excellent function in his right hand.

* * *

After attending the Emergency Preparedness course in Ottawa, I returned to my community and with the help of the staff, reorganized our medical response equipment at the health centre. The plan was that if an emergency occurred, the equipment could be taken to the scene where treatment could be initiated. All the planning in the world does not make for a smooth-running, emergency situation. One day at noon, a helicopter crashed into the fuel tanks at our airport. Immediately, we sent all of the staff, except one clerk/interpreter and me, to the airport with our emergency equipment. The plan was for the staff to assess the number of injured, triage them at the site, and send the injured back to the health centre for treatment, along with some of the staff.

What we did not count on was that during the time we were collecting our supplies and getting to the airport, personnel at the airport would bring the injured people to the clinic in private vehicles. So what actually ended up happening was that while my staff and equipment were en route to the airport, the injured arrived at the clinic with only Theresa Aklunark, the clerk/interpreter, and me there to treat them. It took about fifteen minutes before the clinic staff at the airport were told that the survivors were already at the health centre. Needless to say, that half-hour spent with the three injured patients was about the longest thirty minutes of my life.

* * *

Perhaps even more important than dealing with individual cases is the nurse's ability to effect change within a family, and also within a community. Family counselling pertaining to alcohol, smoking, diabetes, and care of a sick or an elderly person was a daily practice. Health instruction, in order to have people less dependent on the health centre and more able to make good lifestyle choices, was a huge part of our role. The nurse would do health instruction at the schools, hold community awareness programs on such issues as smoking, hepatitis, HIV, and botulism, as well as include some form of health teaching with each clinic visit.

One example of the results of an individual, family, and community program that produced good results was the smoking cessation program. When I first went north, nearly everyone smoked. No one considered the ramifications of cigarette smoking and pregnancy, of second-hand smoke on children and on those with asthma or other lung or heart problems. Through individual counselling, community awareness programs, television, radio and magazine advertisements, there is far less smoking in the North. Many homes have "No Smoking" signs on their doors. Only a few years ago, these signs would have been unheard of.

* * *

Career opportunities abound in the North. I arrived as a new graduate, straight out of a two-year diploma program. I had, however, worked for eleven years as a registered nursing assistant in Ontario. Those years were spent in the operating, emergency, and delivery rooms of busy city hospitals. I started as a community health nurse; then after completion of the Outpost Nursing Program, I became the charge nurse in Rankin Inlet. Feeling pleased with my new title, I called my mother. Her comment to me was, "Well, you are finally getting paid for what you do best – being bossy." Who knows you better than your mother?

Other positions I held while working in the North included nursing supervisor, assistant director of nursing, head nurse of a combined labour/delivery/nursery and surgery ward at the Inuvik General Hospital (my favourite position), senior nursing officer for the Inuvik Regional Health Board, and acting regional nursing officer for both Baffin and Kitikmeot Regional Health Boards. I was also a coroner in the Northwest Territories.

Such career opportunities don't just happen. They come about through mentoring by respected supervisors. These people approved time off and training programs to allow me to grow in my role as a nurse and to take on new challenges. In the Keewatin Zone, Esmond Smith and Rosemary Brown were wonderful, caring administrators. When I was in Inuvik, Norman Hatlevik and Ed Norwich, both hospital administrators, taught me the meaning of "management by walking around" and always listening to, and supporting, your staff. They also showed that you could be a manager and a friend, and do both well.

Making friends in the North is mandatory. Most nurses who go north are single, and when they first arrive, they are very unlikely to meet anyone they know in the community. The pool of people you get together with is small and there is no social hierarchy. I have learned that people you would never have socialized with in the South, you were now forced to interact with out of sheer necessity. You could even become close friends. Friends made in the North are yours forever. Even if it's only a card at Christmas, or a phone call every few years, when you next get together, it is just as if you had seen each other last week. Friends such as Meg McDonagh, Mary and Marion MacInnis, Frank Smith, John and Gail Borkovick, Lesley and Gary Singer, Ev and Juliene Summerfield, Bette and Don Palfrey, Karen Archbell, and Bridget Ellwood-Love became my family. These friends, plus many others in the community, gave me the support I needed to spend twenty years in a position that was both emotionally and physically demanding – but was one that I loved.

* * *

Assimilating back into the South is easy, as far as climate, shopping, housing, friends, and entertainment go. But what is lacking is career satisfaction. Independent thinking is certainly not encouraged. There are too many rules. It is difficult to return to hospital nursing, especially in large city hospitals, where a nurse's role has strict limitations. The extended class nurse practitioner's role in Ontario offers the closest match to northern nursing. When I returned to

Ontario, I was able to challenge the nurse practitioner program and go straight to writing the licensing examination.

Working in the nurse's extended class role, having my family around me, and keeping in touch with northern friends has made the transition to southern life relatively smooth. Northern nursing has remained close to my heart. Since my return south, I have given many talks, career-day presentations, and slide shows on nursing in the North. Many have asked me why I don't return to the North, because I speak about it with such passion. Time does take its toll, and with the role of the northern nurse as physically and emotionally demanding as it is, I feel my time has passed and that younger blood is needed. I have been asked several times, if I had a choice to do my career over again, would I spend twenty years in the cold, Canadian Arctic. My answer is always the same, "I would spend another twenty years as a nurse in the incredible and unforgettable Canadian Arctic. *In a heartbeat.*"

Susan Pauhl RN(EC), OPN, PNC(C) graduated in 1964 as a registered nursing assistant and in 1967 as an operating room technician. She worked for 11 years in Hamilton, Ontario, in labour and delivery, OR and ER. From 1971 to 1974, she worked for Medical Services at Moose Factory Hospital in northern Ontario. After earning her RN from Humber College in Toronto in 1976, she headed straight for the Yukon. From 1978 to 1979, she worked in several communities in the NWT before entering Dalhousie University Outpost Nursing program in Halifax, NS. Following her graduation in 1981, she was nurse in charge in Rankin Inlet. From 1981 until 1991, she moved between the Rankin and Inuvik hospitals, holding several positions including nursing supervisor, head nurse, director of nursing/senior nursing officer and acting regional nursing officer. In 1991, she returned to Ontario and worked as a nurse practitioner in several community health centres. Currently, Sue works in obstetrics at the Stevenson Memorial Hospital in Alliston, Ontario.

PREPARE TO BE TRANSFERRED

Karen Stauffer

Being married to an RCMP officer means that you have to be prepared to pack up and move periodically – which in the North is generally every two years. In 1983, after my husband Scott and I had spent two years in Snowdrift in the Mackenzie Zone, we were informed that we were being transferred to Rankin Inlet in the Keewatin Zone. The RCMP and Northern Health collaborated to bring in another RCMP and nurse couple to replace us. The couple they had in mind came from Fort Smith. They were flown in for one day in June to size up the community. We gave them a tour of the nursing station and the RCMP office, introduced them around, and then we set up a barbecue in the RCMP compound and invited various local people.

One of the problems in Snowdrift was stray dogs. These dogs had a tendency to run in packs, and as there had been an attack two years previously, the RCMP were often required to shoot homeless dogs that wandered around. Because Scott was always on call, he wore his RCMP shirt and gun belt all the time. We were sitting there, enjoying a steak barbecue and talking about what a wonderful community this was, when a stray dog came into the compound. It was a dog that the RCMP members had been trying to locate, because it had a big fishhook caught in its leg, and it was quite vicious. Scott stood up, pulled his revolver, and started to shoot the dog from the table. Those of us from Snowdrift, who were used to this, calmly kept eating. Scott fired away and then ran off into the bush, to make sure the dog was dead. However, the new couple was completely disgusted. Ultimately, they still agreed to come to Snowdrift, and in time, I'm sure they also got used to other unsavory jobs.

* * *

We left Snowdrift in early August, on a day of record heat (30°C). I knew it would be cooler in the Central Arctic, so I had taken a light jacket on the police plane. But I was unprepared for the minus 10°C, when we landed late that night in Rankin Inlet. On top of this, a prisoner had kicked out the side windows of the RCMP truck, so we were completely frozen by the time we got to our new house.

Because the nursing station in Rankin Inlet was fully staffed, there wasn't a job opening for me when we arrived. I was happy to take it easy, and I even worked at a few casual office jobs in the community. This was very short-lived, however, as a call soon came from the zone nursing officer. I was needed, immediately, to fill in at a one-nurse station in a tiny community within the zone. The circumstances were very sad. The interpreter at the nursing station had committed suicide. He had been discovered when he had not shown up for work and the nurse had gone to his house to look for him. Naturally, the nurse was very distraught and was given a two-week leave. My husband accompanied me into the community, as the situation required that the RCMP attend as well.

Although it was a stormy fall day, we needed to get there as soon as possible. We had to go by helicopter, flying very close to the ground, due to the limited visibility. I barely caught a glimpse of the community as we landed close to the RCMP office. Together we attended to the sad, but necessary, tasks before Scott and the community nurse stepped on the helicopter and flew off, leaving me on my own for two weeks.

* * *

There I was, by myself, in a strange community, and in a new zone. Inuktitut was a new language to me, and I didn't have an interpreter (because he had committed suicide). There had been no orientation to the nursing station, there were no other employees, and I didn't even know which direction the store was in. Besides, it was the start of a long weekend, so everything was closed.

I had been told that the nursing station was fully-stocked with everything I would need, but I had brought a few groceries with me. The nurse who had made the grocery order must have been a health food nut. There was only a very coarse type of whole wheat flour, lots of dried fruits, granola, and nut-type things, and unrecognizable cuts of wild meat in the freezer. There was very little of what I called real food. I had brought chocolate chips with me, knowing they were an essential requirement. However, the cookies I made with the coarse flour were not very satisfactory. Thank goodness there was popcorn.

I spent that first weekend checking everything in the nursing station, to become familiar with its stock and procedures, before I started seeing patients. I also went for walks in the community, trying to find my way around. This usually took no more than ten or fifteen minutes, as it was very small place. The entire community was also in mourning and everything was extremely quiet, since most people stayed inside. I discovered that I had two TV channels. Although both were CBC (one from British Columbia, the other from Newfoundland), it seemed as if I was getting two different channels. I was happy when Tuesday morning came and I could at least try to talk to some patients.

One of the first people to arrive was an elderly man in an agitated state. He was gesturing and trying to show me something outside. He was a very tiny man, and outside was a very tiny three-wheeled ATV. He pointed to it, and then beyond, which I took to mean he needed me to go somewhere with him. I got on, even though it was like two clowns on a circus bike, and we rode off for about a block. Then he stopped, and made a gesture that clearly meant "Get off!" I got off the ATV, and he continued on without even saying goodbye. I never did find out what he wanted.

The clinic was very quiet for that first week – no more than two or three patients a day. Without an interpreter, I didn't even try to call in patients from the chronic disease list or well-baby list. I'm sure the patients who came to the nursing station were amazed at how happy the nurse was to see them.

Things picked up, after a while. One person came in with a fractured arm. Although the x-ray machine was even more ancient than the one I had left behind in Snowdrift, I eventually figured out how to operate it. I had to arrange only one medevac from the community: a baby with pneumonia. I called the zone nursing office, and got them to talk me through the travel procedure in the zone, including how to get the patient to the airport. I also needed to know in what direction the airport was. It was all handled very efficiently, with help from the local taxi service.

By the end of the second week, I knew a few people well enough to visit them in their homes and I made daily visits to the store. Finally, a new relief nurse came to take over and I returned by plane to Rankin Inlet where a position had opened up at the nursing station.

Karen Stauffer RN, CHN, BSc was born and raised in Biggar, Saskatchewan. She received her nursing education at Kelsey Institute in Saskatoon and Wascana Institute in Regina. (CNA in 1974, OR Tech in 1976, RN in 1979, plus CHN upgrading in Ottawa, in 1983) In June, 1998, Karen graduated from Athabasca University with a BSc in Computing and Information Systems. She is working towards a MSc in Information Systems. She also works for Athabasca University as a programmer analyst. Her husband, now a Staff Sergeant, is still in the RCMP. Since leaving the NWT in 1994, they have made Fort McMurray, Alberta, their home. Karen's story "My Life as a Northern Underfill" appears in *Northern Nurses: True Nursing Adventures from Canada's North*.

NURSING ON THE FIRE LINES

Ildiko Luxemburger

My experience with northern nursing is somewhat limited, but greatly treasured. During the 1998 forest fires north of Thunder Bay, I worked as an occupational health nurse. My job was to look after the firefighters in their working environment. I didn't take any special courses before I went to the fires. To be hired, I needed to have recent emergency room and medical/surgical experience, and a thorough orientation. This was considered a "hardship assignment"– but to be truthful, a person can tolerate just about anything for a month. We (the crew, the nurse, and the fire chiefs) were dropped in by helicopter into an area about 50 km north of Armstrong, where camp was set up.

Accommodations for the firefighters depended on the location (the camp usually moved, following the fire) and on the group. When close to a town, a school gym might be used. Tents were issued by the Ministry of Natural Resources. Other standard issue arrangements were either cots or rubber mattresses. Native firefighters preferred sleeping on inflatable mattresses on the ground. I was given preferential treatment – I slept on a mattress on a door, which was placed on four milk crates, in an abandoned cabin. Except for some shelves, there was absolutely nothing else in the cabin, not even a door to close, since I was sleeping on it. The crews usually stayed in the forest for two or three days, then came back to camp for a night's rest, while another group fought the fires in their place.

A person might wonder what a nurse did in a camp full of healthy, young people. To begin with, there was the usual foot inspection every day. Almost all of the men had blisters and fungal infection on their feet from being in wet boots, day and night. Then, there was the issue of food safety. I fired a cook at one of the locations for seriously ignoring every rule in the book about meat preparation. Latrine hygiene was also my department. And there were always cuts to suture, respiratory illnesses to look after, chainsaw accidents to treat, infected insect bites to clean out. Whenever I could, I visited the men close to the fire line and made sure they had enough fluids to drink. Some work groups were better at safety than others. I made my health inspections with the permission of the fire chief. The health inspectors and the fire chief respected my (and the other nurses') assessments and recommendations regarding safety, hygiene, and food preparation. This is not to say that their setup was lacking, because they had good safety officers; it is simply different when a nurse does the assessing – another point of view.

The "nursing station" was the back of a tent. I was on call 24 hours a day, the usual hours in northern nursing. Many firefighters came in just to talk, for the isolation sometimes wore them down. One night, while one of the rookie firemen was trying to light a kerosene lantern, it blew up in his face. All I heard was screaming and cursing. You can imagine how difficult it was to see a burn and examine an eye with a flashlight. Because the kitchen had a generator, we "camped out" there while it was dark, so I could monitor his facial burns and his sight. With continuous cold compresses, we were able to keep the swelling and blisters down to a minimum. At the crack of dawn, he was flown out. His sight was saved, but for a while he would be called "ruggedly handsome."

These men and women were tough. There was a female firefighter who miscarried in the bush and had to be flown to Thunder Bay for treatment. She had been unaware that she was pregnant. A couple of days later, I diagnosed a young man with *epiglottitis*. Just before sunset, we were able to fly him out (the helicopters don't fly after dark). He was taken straight to the intensive care unit and it wasn't until I finished my tour of duty that I saw him again. He thanked me profusely. Apparently, he spent two full weeks in the ICU unit, and they told him several times that without immediate medical treatment, he wouldn't have made it. There was a case of a man with appendicitis. Since it was dark, this poor fellow had to be driven out. That meant a four-to-six-hour drive on unmaintained logging roads in an old truck that lurched. He had his surgery and recovered quickly. I never once had to treat a burn due to a fire. Most burns were on the forearms, and they were caused by the mufflers of the chainsaws.

Ordinarily, Emergency Medical Service personnel and safety officers tended to the health needs of these workers. I was part of a two-year trial by the Ministry of Natural Resources. With nurses on staff, health care needs of the fire crews were met superbly and comprehensively. A study concluded that, when they were using EMS, there were many more trips out for medical help, since EMS personnel had less training than nurses. With us, almost everything was handled in camp, which meant that the firefighters spent fewer hours away from work. During that summer, I flew only four people out; whereas, in other years, close to 15 people were removed for consultation during the same period of time. The safety officers were well-trained in first aid and they cost less; but even though more holistic care was provided by RNs, we were considered too expensive. For that reason, provision of emergency health services was returned to the EMS the following year.

During that summer, I worked at three different locations, and there was not a boring day. One week, due to bad weather (and miscommunication), our food supply had not been delivered, so for three days we ate Kraft dinner with fried potatoes for breakfast, lunch, and dinner. The fire chief had to order the trapping and removal of two black bears that had developed a taste for spaghetti and had been hanging around the camp day after day. Considering the wildlife, the rough terrain, the heat of the summer, the number of men, and the roaring fires that just wouldn't let themselves be put out, I was surprised how safe the whole operation was. The fire chiefs and the staff knew what they were doing. I am very thankful for this experience.

DAWSON CITY

Ildiko Luxemburger

My most recent northern experience was in the Yukon during the summer of 2003, when I spent two months in Dawson City as a community health nurse.

The flight from Toronto to Vancouver was pleasant. The Canada Jazz plane that was to take us to Whitehorse was late leaving, due to mechanical problems. It stood right in front of us, just outside of the glass wall, in plain sight. About fifteen of us waited and watched as a mechanic on a stepladder tried to fix something under one wing. He was looking for the correct size of screw, but he couldn't find what he needed. We were close enough that we could clearly see into his toolbox. After about ten minutes, he left and came back with a roll of duct tape. Some of us stopped watching and started praying. Once the baggage handlers started to haul in our suitcases, we all cheered up. We tried to ignore a coffin, the first item loaded in the luggage compartment. Other than that, we had a comfortable flight.

After a well-organized orientation in Whitehorse, I was on my way to historic Dawson City. During the seven-hour drive, I enjoyed the breathtaking scenery along the Klondike Highway. I saw moose, elk, and several foxes along the road. On arrival at Dawson, one of the resident nurses, Michelle, showed me around and took on the role of mentor.

There were times when I wondered what I was doing up there. What made me think I could perform well enough to meet all the challenges? Even though I had had over 25 years of nursing experience, the learning curve was steep. What helped me through was the trust the nurses and physicians had in me, their friendly reminders, the relaxed workshops, and how everyone was approachable and willing to mentor a newcomer. My confidence grew quickly and I was able to relax and get back to nursing mode. I needed to learn how to take x-rays (and do the basic interpretation of them), how to use the slit-lamp to examine eye-injuries, how to do basic lab work, and how to fill out the dozens of different forms. The staff of the clinic was fantastic.

Our clients were not only local people, but also tourists, temporary workers, and visitors for special events, like the Dawson City Music Festival. I truly enjoyed the variety and excitement of this position. The camaraderie of everyone (Michelle and Steve Caws, Rosemary Graham, Tatum Arts, Lisa Joinson, Linda, Dr. Katrina White, Adam, Sean, Dr. Jo Devenish, Chris, Jennifer – I hope I haven't forgotten anyone) helped me through sleepless nights on call and weekends without my family. They made those two months unforgettable.

Many colourful characters lived in and around Dawson. There was the "caveman," a fortyish gentleman, who actually lived in a cave on the bank of the Yukon River, and whose broken finger I had the opportunity to treat. Then there was the local coroner: a jovial, rotund man, who came on duty wearing a T-shirt that said, "Jesus is coming! Look busy!" I met several gold miners who lived out on the dredge all summer without electricity or running water. They showed great respect for us by coming to town early and taking a shower in one of the motels, before meeting us at the clinic. There were many artists, First Nations characters, I will never forget.

Those who live and work in the Yukon are made of something stronger than the rest of us. You need to be tough, tenacious, intelligent, and creative to live there. You have to know yourself and you have to have a great sense of humour. Yukon nurses obviously love their role in the community. They take the long hours, unpredictable difficulties, harsh weather, and lack of frivolities in stride. They enjoy the land they live on, the friends they have, and the memories they make together. Everyone I met and worked with inspired me. I thank everyone at the Dawson City Nursing Station for their hospitality, kindness, and friendship.

Ildiko Luxemburger RN, Dipl.Ed became a certified midwife in 1975 in her native Hungary. She immigrated to Canada and graduated as a registered nurse from Humber College. She worked in numerous hospitals in southern Ontario, mostly in ER, cardiac care, and medical/surgical. With the Canadian Red Cross, she has been involved in assignments such as the Kosavar refugees, the Quebec Ice Storm, and the aftermath of Hurricane Georges in Puerto Rico. She has been an interpreter and first aid provider at Canadian Special Olympic Games. After receiving her teaching certificate from Queen's University in Kingston in 2000, Ildiko joined the teaching team for the Registered Practical Nurse Program of Huron Heights Secondary School in Newmarket, Ontario. She is also a member of the Emergency Response Team of York Region. In 1999, she won the Staff Achievement Award at the York County Hospital. In 2000, she was honoured as the Woman of the Year in Newmarket and given an Outstanding Achievement Award for the same municipality. She has two children, Tom and Julia, and lives with her husband, Robert, in Newmarket, Ontario. Poetry written by Ildiko appears in *Healing Words, Poems Inspired by the Healing Professions,* published in 2004 by the Nursing Department of Huron Heights Secondary School.

TOUR OF NURSING IN CANADA'S NORTH, 1969

Verna Huffman Splane

The Principal Nursing Officer (PNO) position was established in 1967 to advise the Deputy Minister of Health on all matters related to nursing in the Department of National Health and Welfare (NHW) within Canada and abroad. This was to ensure that national health policies were based on knowledge of current nursing needs, trends, and developments. To fulfill that function, the PNO maintained constant contact with nursing leaders in Canada and around the world, with specialist nursing consultants in NHW, and through visits to educational institutions, nursing and health organizations, as well as provincial and territorial governments.

It was as Principal Nursing Officer that I undertook a tour of Canada's northern health facilities from the east coast, through the Central and High Arctic, to the most westerly nursing stations in 1969. Plans for the trip were made in collaboration with Alice Smith, nursing adviser to the Director General of Medical Services who was responsible for Indian and Northern Health Services, and with Catherine Keith, a former supervisor of nursing for the Western Arctic and, in 1969, nursing adviser to the Deputy Director General. Catherine was assigned as my tour guide and mentor. As the Principal Nursing Officer, I was particularly interested in the chain of isolated nursing stations, the care that nurses were able to provide, and the conditions under which they lived and worked.

* * *

I have three recollections of Baffin Island, beginning with a dental clinic where we saw advanced dental caries among the Aboriginal children – attributed, we heard, to dietary habits, especially the substitution of candy for the traditional piece of walrus meat. A second memorable experience was a church service where clergy and congregation defied the subzero temperature as they worshipped in their fur-lined parkas, moccasins, and mitts. By far, my clearest memory was a flight to Clyde Inlet on the northern coast of the island, where our plane used the frozen inlet for a runway. It seemed as if the whole population came down to meet us and escort us, along with yelping huskies, through the village to the nursing station – my first nursing station. The three-room building provided a treatment room, a two-bed room for patients, and the nurse's quarters. The day was full of excitement, lively nursing discussion, exchange of views, and messages to take back to headquarters. As our plane prepared for departure to Frobisher Bay (now called Iqaluit), we were accompanied by much the same crowd as had greeted our arrival.

Leaving Baffin, the next port of call was on the main coast of Canada's Arctic. As our flight involved crossing the Distant Early Warning (DEW) line, we were required to have permission from the United States government to cross into our own country. A first of many surprises on this trip. Notes I kept at the time record some of the problems we faced:

- January 30: Charter flight to settlements cancelled due to weather conditions.
- January 31: Charter flight to settlements cancelled due to security clearance at DEW Line.
- February 5: Appointment for VH in Frobisher cancelled due to whiteout. Miss Keith stranded 4½ hours in vehicle between Apex and Frobisher. With aid of DIAND and a snowplough, she was taken back to Apex where she remained until February 7.
- February 6: Immobilized in residence due to whiteout.

From the DEW line, we flew into the High Arctic calling at hospitals and nursing stations at Inuvik, Tuktoyaktuk and Aklavik, on to the Yukon where we stopped at Old Crow, Dawson and Whitehorse, completing the trip on the west coast at Lower Post, the most northerly point in British Columbia.

In the course of three full weeks of flying across the far reaches of Canada's North and visiting health facilities in remote regions, we saw public health in operation, in the fullest sense of the word. We listened to nurses, doctors, and other health workers describe their work and their lives; we talked with people and patients in each community, as well as the RCMP and mission personnel, who were clearly in strong support. We also saw the means of transport available for home visits: foot, dogsled, automobile, skidoo, plane, and in summer, canoe.

* * *

What had I learned in this cross-country northern tour? In the chain of nursing stations, I saw differences and similarities. The differences related largely to the degree of isolation of location; to the size and construction of the building; to staffing patterns and, to a degree, to the personality of the nurses themselves. The similarities in how nurses functioned were striking. Nurses, in general, had developed a high degree of professional independence, often due to circumstances that forced them to draw on the utmost limits of their nursing knowledge and skills, and on their capacity to innovate – features seldom encouraged in southern parts of the country. And, of course, they were on call 24 hours a day. Especially in more isolated regions, nurses were vulnerable to the vagaries of weather that could prevent evacuation of an emergency patient to more appropriate treatment centres. We heard of cases where nurses had to take on an extended role, even that of surgery, working under the telephone guidance of a physician miles away. Not all activity took place within the stations. Home visiting, whether on a regular or an emergency basis, was part of nurses' traditional public health responsibility for the wellbeing of the community at large. Another similarity we observed was the mutual support and respect among nurses, the RCMP, and mission personnel. It clearly exceeded the bounds of traditional linkages. Whatever the differences and similarities, nursing stations in 1969 were the centre of the community, forming the backbone of health services for the country's scattered northern population.

The multicultural makeup of the nursing staff was noteworthy. We met nurses from the Caribbean, Pakistan, the United Kingdom, and Scandinavia. What had attracted them? For some, it was adventure and travel. For others, it was the unique central nursing aspect of an outpost service that focused on "primary health care," a principle later enunciated as the key to "Health for All" in the 1978 UNICEF/WHO accord. Many of these nurses were trained in midwifery, a particularly valuable qualification in under-doctored regions, and a qualification that in 1969 was still denied to Canadian nurses in their own country through medically imposed restriction.

* * *

The stories of the nurses themselves intrigued me the most. They were stories of hardship, challenge, courage, innovation, and fun! I remember an unusual story I heard from a public health nurse who used the Canada/Alaska Highway to cover her district of thousands of miles. In her area, she had some trappers with whom she had developed a way of communicating if they needed her help. The presence of a certain formation of boughs, in a strategic spot along the roadside, was a signal for assistance. Sighting one such signal, the nurse went in to the trapper's hut and found him injured. She was able to deal with that situation. However, the trapper had a bigger problem. He had fur pelts that were due for auction in Edmonton, and he was unable to travel. Would the nurse act on his behalf? He coached her on prices and negotiation, and using her own free weekend, the nurse agreed to assume an extended role as proxy at the fur auction. She did it well. What a story!

Nurses who worked outside the stations and drove cars, too light for safe travel on highways and gravel trails, faced dangerous seasonal road conditions. We heard of cars in the ditch on the Canada/Alaska Highway and nurses without means to communicate for help. They were largely dependent on helpful truckers working in that region.

* * *

What came about from that trip? On returning to Ottawa, my report to the Deputy Minister was well received. It included recommendations for safer cars and systems of communications, federal support for changes in Canadian nursing education to include midwifery for nurses working in the North, and increased opportunity and financial support for educational leave. Alice Smith and I had worked closely together for some years, and many of my recommendations had been made previously by Alice to her Director General – without success.

Over time, many voices brought about change and reinforcement for nurses working in the North – the dedicated leadership of Alice Smith and her staff, the influence of the PNO in the Deputy Minister's office, and modern technology: each played a part.

My cross-country tour of Canada's North was enriched in many ways by the light-hearted mentoring of the now-deceased Catherine Keith. Cay showed me how to dress for the Arctic, how to keep going in 50° below zero weather, how to appreciate the splendour of the Arctic and the beauty of our Aboriginal people, and how to enjoy the nurses, wherever they worked.

At the end of the strenuous journey, I stepped out of a pair of long johns that had kept me warm for three weeks. They had become sufficiently worn and fashioned to my form that when I removed them, they remained standing, with buckled knees.

My life experience in national and international health has taken me on projects in many parts of the world. As I reflect on the Tour of Nursing in Canada's North, 1969, I count it among the most privileged and memorable journeys of my 65 year professional career.

Verna Huffman Splane OC, RN, BSc, MPH, LL.D graduated in 1937 from Nichols Hospital in Peterborough, Ontario. She earned her Diploma in Public Health Nursing at the University of Toronto in 1939, her Bachelor of Nursing at Columbia in 1957, and her Master of Public Health from the University of Michigan in 1964. She worked for the Victorian Order of Nurses and for the Government of Canada as the Principal Nursing Officer. She has worked for the WHO in the Caribbean, South America, North Africa, and Geneva. She was Vice President of the International Council of Nurses and Vice President of International Social Service. Verna co-authored a study of CNO Positions in 50 countries and has been a lecturer at the School of Nursing at the University of British Columbia. She has been on the Canadian Red Cross Executive and the President of ISS Canada. Among honours she has received are Canadian Red Cross, Distinguished Service Award; International Council of Nurses, Citation; Canadian Nurses Association, Jeanne Mance Award; YWCA, First Women of Distinction; Officer, Order of Canada; Emory University, Lillian Carter Centre for International Nursing Award (shared with husband Richard Splane); Honorary Professor, School of Nursing, UBC and the Queen's Golden Jubilee Medal. Verna has received Honorary Doctorates from the following universities: Queen's, St. Francis Xavier, and British Columbia.

ZIPLOC BABY

Beryl Belbin

In September of 1981, as a young bride and a new graduate, only a year out of nursing school, I began working in Nain, Labrador. I planned to stay for only one year and ended up staying for 23 years. My life there was very interesting, and I had many stories to tell: some of them sad and tragic and others full of hope and perseverance.

One story that I remember well started on a Saturday while I was at work. The morning was very quiet. Around lunch time, I received a call from a distressed mother who told me that her daughter was having pains and that she refused to come to the clinic. Being acquainted with the young woman and her family, I asked to speak to her. She wouldn't talk to me, but I could hear her screaming at her mother to get off the phone. Her mother said, "You know what she's like. You better come and get her. I think she is going to have her baby." I knew this woman had had several babies of her own, so I respected her judgment regarding labour pains. So much for a quiet day at the clinic.

A short time later, I walked into their home. The daughter was crying on her knees in the living room. She told me she was having awful pains. Without saying a word, I managed to get her into her coat. Before she could refuse, I proceeded to drag her out of the house and get her on the skidoo with me. Halfway over to the clinic, she attempted to get off. Fortunately, she was sitting in front of me, and I held on to her with my legs. It must have been quite a sight!

When we reached the clinic about ten minutes later, I took her to the Emergency Room, where I quickly removed her clothes. Just as I pulled off her pants, "a little black head" greeted me. Within seconds, the rest of the baby came into the world. The personal care attendant and I had to scramble. This little angel was the most beautiful creature I had ever seen. She jerked her arms and legs, and she mewed like a kitten. I wrapped her in warm towels, dried her off, and put her in the not-so-warm incubator. The young mother was not impressed and wanted to know what was happening.

I helped the little baby to breathe, and she began to pink up. I knew that if she were to survive, this three-pound newborn could not stay in Nain, as she needed more help than we could give her. I called for a plane. A problem with living in this community was that there was little daylight during the midwinter months, and to make matters worse, there were no lights on the runway. The airline informed me that they didn't think they had enough daylight to fly to Nain, pick up the baby, and then fly across to St. Anthony in Newfoundland, where there was a hospital. They could only make it if they had a quick turnaround. I said, "No problem. Just get here."

My next challenge was getting the baby from the clinic to the plane. Our incubator wasn't transportable, and the medevac team had no time to come up to the clinic to get her. The temperature was minus 25°, not counting the wind chill. While we waited for the plane, we warmed up the baby. She held her own: there was no grunting, and no cyanosis, and she was very bright. We put a knitted cap on her, placed her in a Ziploc bag (which acted as a sauna), and lay her between my bare breasts. (Unfortunately, they were not that big, but she would be warm.) I covered her with a blanket and then put on my shirt and my big down-filled coat. Before leaving the clinic, I took one last look at her, with her little head sticking out of the Ziploc bag. I zipped up my coat and prayed.

When we reached the airstrip, the plane was just landing. As I walked towards it, the door opened and the stairway came down. All I could hear over the noise of the engine was, "The incubator won't heat up. It's just too cold." There was no way this baby was not going to survive – not after all she had been through in her short life. I climbed aboard the plane with my mewing infant. Who should greet me, besides a flat-chested doctor, but a wonderfully well-endowed nurse! She must have thought I was crazy when all I could say was, "What wonderful breasts you have. Open your top. I have something for you." She began to laugh as she read my mind. After we settled our baby in between her breasts and put the oxygen tubing near her face, the nurse strapped herself into her seat. They flew to St. Anthony, where a paediatrician was waiting for her.

The newborn impressed everyone, not only with her tenacity to live, but with her beauty as well. My Ziploc baby is now thirteen years old, and in grade seven. To this day, I don't know how she survived. And yes, she is still beautiful.

* * *

My husband, Wilson, was the principal of the all-grade school in Nain. One morning in 2003 we woke up and realized that it was time to move on. We had been in the community for 23 years, and our children, whom we had raised there, had grown up and moved away. After selling our home with all the furniture, we left Nain in July of that year. There was a very emotional sendoff with about 150 people turning up to say goodbye. The Moravian choir came to the airstrip and sang hymns to us in Inuktitut. To be sure, we left a part of ourselves in Nain, Labrador. But we also took a part of Nain with us.

Beryl Belbin RN, BN graduated in 1980 with her degree in nursing from Memorial University of Newfoundland in St. John's. She worked in St. John's for a year. In 1981, having recently married, she and her husband moved to Nain, Labrador, where they stayed for 23 years.

NURSING THE ICE DANCER

Hazel Booth

Christmas was going to be different this year. For the first time ever, I was not working on Christmas Day, nor was I going back to be with my family in Ottawa, which for many years had been "home" for me. Now, home was in the Yukon. This was also to be my first Christmas with my friend Matt. Intrigued by my stories of Canada's Yukon, my brother Grant had recently moved up here to check it out for himself. We had made arrangements to stay for a few nights at a cabin in the Haines Pass, a gorgeous area along the edge of Kluane National Park with mountains and lakes galore – a winter wonderland. Matt's friend Sean was to join us for the cabin adventures as well. I was looking forward to experiencing a true Yukon Christmas.

We jammed our gear into every little nook in the back of Sean's small truck and secured the snowboard and skis on top. The four of us crammed inside and left Whitehorse late Christmas afternoon, just as it was starting to get dark. Our plan was to get gas in Haines Junction, but it was Christmas Day and every station in town was closed. It is never a good idea to run out of gas on the Haines Road in minus 30 degree weather. At Matt's suggestion, we headed to Kathleen Lake, where there is a day-use cabin with a woodstove. We would spend the night there and double back to Haines Junction for gas in the morning.

With the woodstove roaring, we settled in and made Christmas dinner. No turkey for us – instead a yummy fondue of caribou, sheep and buffalo; a chocolate fondue for dessert, and our favourite winter camping beverage, Fireball. After dinner, feeling overstuffed with food, we walked around the lake. The night was cold, very cold. The lake seemed unsettled – it gurgled and groaned, sounding exactly like a stomach digesting food. I've never heard anything like it.

On Boxing Day, Sean drove back to Haines Junction to fill the truck with gas, while Matt, Grant, and I prepared breakfast. Matt and Sean had heard of some ice climbing at the far end of Kathleen Lake and were interested in trying to find it, so we thought we'd spend the day at Kathleen Lake and head out to the Haines Pass cabin in the early evening. I put on my new *mukluks* and snowshoes, handmade for me by community members from Teslin. Grant wore his modern snowshoes. Matt and Sean, both on skis, pulled the ice climbing gear on toboggans. Off we went on the frozen lake. It was around minus 22 degrees.

About an hour out across the lake, my brother Grant called to me, "Hey, Hazel, are moose supposed to be in the water this time of year?" I wasn't sure what the answer was. He pointed to what he thought was a moose. It looked like a rock to me. Then, the rock moved. As we got closer, we realized it *was* a moose and she had fallen through lake ice weakened by an avalanche. Not sure if she was going to stand up and charge at us, we approached cautiously, but soon realized that we were in no danger at all. The moose was stuck in the ice and shivering uncontrollably. She was exhausted. There was a horseshoe-shaped path through the ice where she had struggled to paw her way out. Clearly, this moose wasn't much of an ice dancer. Covered in ice, she sounded like a Christmas tree when she moved. She was helpless. Powerless as we felt, we knew we needed to help or she was going to die.

First we yelled at the moose (by now, we had given her the name Morris), trying to scare her out of the water. It didn't work. We chipped away with ski poles at the ice around her. That didn't work. Thinking she just needed a little energy, I ran over to the sled and grabbed my curried tuna wrap. Matt tried to feed it to her, but she wouldn't eat it. Perhaps she just wasn't big on curried tuna. She wouldn't eat a bagel or trail mix either. Then we ran back again to the toboggans to get the rope that Matt and Sean had brought for ice climbing. We tied it loosely around her neck and we pulled. That didn't work. The moose lost her leverage and sank deeper into the water. We had made matters worse. To keep her head afloat, we kept constant tension on the rope. Matt and Sean had the idea of setting up a crevasse pulley system that would give us a four to one mechanical advantage. The closest ice that would hold the ice screws was about 50 metres away. Sean hurried to set up the pulley system, while Matt and I kept constant tension on the rope around the moose's head to keep it from sinking under the ice. We also worked to position the rope in a safer place around her. To get the rope through the ice cold water and under her shoulders was a bit of a challenge.

Next, Grant took over at the moose's side and put her in a headlock. As Grant would say, he was "cheek to cheek and eye to eye with the moose." Morris pushed against Grant, and they both used the side of the mountain as leverage as Matt, Sean, and I pulled on the rope. Morris didn't resist; neither did she help. Slowly we pulled her up out of the water and over about a metre from where she had fallen through the ice. We had done it.

Now what were we to do with a moose lying on the ice shivering? It just seemed to come together. We put Matt's very expensive tarp over her and built a shelter from the wind out of snow. We gathered wood to build a fire in the shelter. Prying open her mouth, we dumped warm water from our Nalgene bottles down her throat. For hours we tried to warm her, massaging the muscles in her hind legs and pulling the ice off her fur.

Careful as we were, Matt fell up to his waist through the ice in Morris's hole. He quickly used his arms to pull himself out. Later, as I was carrying a big boulder over for the snow fort, my right leg slipped through the ice up to my knee. Sean was next to break through the ice. We teased Grant that his turn was coming. After all, four out of the five of us (including Morris) had gone through already. Meanwhile, Morris just lay there, turning her head every once in a while to get a better look at us, much like a pet dog lazing around the fire. At times we almost forgot she was there, until all of a sudden one of us would giggle and say, "Um, is that a moose right there?"

About 6 or 7 in the evening, Morris started to perk up, paying more attention to her surroundings and even starting to drool. At one point, she tried to stand up, but fell down again. It was kind of funny, as she fell in such a way that her butt was almost in the fire. We aren't sure if this was coincidental, or if Morris moved purposefully in order to warm her behind. We ourselves were starting to get cold and hungry. Not knowing what else we could do for Morris, we put on our snowshoes and skis and returned to the cabin in the dark. By the time we got back, we were all too tired to set out for the other cabin, so decided just to stay where we were another night. Besides, we wanted to check on Morris in the morning.

* * *

The following day, we went out to look for Morris and also to see if we could find the ice climbing location. We were all very quiet, without words, and anxious about what we would find. Would Morris be there? Would she have fallen through the ice again, and would we have to pull her out again? Would she be dead? Peering over the wall of the snow shelter, we discovered that she was gone and one wall of the snow fort was broken. The remnants of the fire and the two untouched bagels were left behind. We were ecstatic.

Grant and Matt immediately began following Morris's tracks. Grant spotted her a couple of hundred metres away in the first bush where she could find shelter. She was standing initially and then fell down. We were pleased to see that she had been eating some of the willows and that there was moose poop and pee in the snow. Morris was looking much stronger, which was great to see. Although it did not bother her when we approached her, we decided to leave her be and check on her on our way back.

We continued across the lake in search of the ice climb – which we never did find. On our return in the late afternoon, we stopped to check on Morris. This time she was standing and a bit more cautious about our being there. Interestingly, Morris would not let Matt, Sean or me go closer than a few metres. However, Grant, the one who had been "cheek to cheek and eye to eye" with Morris, put his hand out and she slowly brought her nose down, briefly touching Grant's hand, as if to say, "Hey, man, thanks." I think we half expected Morris to follow us back to camp. I know I caught myself looking behind me every once in a while. We noticed that the lake was quiet, no gurgles – the indigestion seemed to have cleared.

With only one night of our holidays left, we headed out to try to find the cabin we had originally set out for. The road was pure ice, the wind was blowing, and it was a whiteout. We ended up staying at a tiny old cabin at the side of the road. When we awoke in the morning, we discovered two feet of snow had come through the crack of the door. Driving back to Whitehorse, we experienced huge snowdrifts, poor visibility, giant winds, and icy roads; yet I loved it. We never did reach the Haines Pass cabin, but what a great adventure we had. We could not have had a more truly Yukon Christmas.

EMERGENCY ON THE ALASKA HIGHWAY

Hazel Booth

My heart fluttered with excitement at what I saw as the plane approached Whitehorse: mountains everywhere, wildflowers galore, and Caribbean blue waters. I was working towards my Master's Degree as a nurse practitioner and had come to the Yukon to work between semesters. Completely naïve, I had fully expected to arrive at a vast and barren land. Instead, I found not only the land of the midnight sun, but also an outdoor enthusiast's playground.

* * *

The main difference between nursing in the Yukon and other northern nursing assignments is that there is a major highway that joins all of the communities – except Old Crow, which can be reached only by plane. Other northern villages where I had worked were accessible only by air. The Alaska Highway attracts thousands of visitors every summer. A common sighting is "Northbound to Alaska," etched in the dust on the back of the RVs, cars, and VW hippie vans that flow north. The highway brings people from all walks of life – from outdoor enthusiasts, fishermen, and cruise line tourists, to retirees undertaking their trip of a lifetime. The reality of working beside the highway, with the extra volume of vehicles, is the number of car crashes you have to deal with. Vehicular accidents are often the result of drivers falling asleep at the wheel or losing control from driving too fast.

As a nurse practitioner, one of my roles was to respond to motor vehicle accidents, along with the local volunteer ambulance attendants. This role is one of the most challenging aspects of community nursing, because of the amount of time involved, the unpredictability, and the emotional turmoil of dealing with death and mangled human bodies. On the other hand, responding to car crashes can be a very rewarding experience. How could that possibly be rewarding? Here is a glimpse into my role as a community nurse practitioner working along the highway in the Yukon.

* * *

I recall the first time I was called out to one of these car crashes on the Alaska Highway. The clinic hours were finished for the day. As I was walking home from work, the new RCMP Corporal in town, Mark Groves, pulled up beside me in his car to say hello. He grinned from ear to ear, excited to be in the community. I assured him that it was a great place, and that after-hours on call had been quiet for several weeks. His happy disposition was refreshing, and I continued my short walk home, with a smile on my face. Not half an hour later, the health centre phone rang: "There's been a terrible accident. Two adults and a child are hurt – really, really badly." In order to save time, I asked the caller to inform the RCMP, while I notified the ambulance volunteers. I grabbed my portable radio and keyed in the mdmrs channel, the one specifically for the ambulance volunteers, and I reported the crash. Within seconds, two community ambulance volunteers replied that they were on their way to the health centre. I changed from my shorts into jeans. I pulled on my low-cut hiking boots and was out the door, running to the health centre garage, where the ambulance was parked. The ambulance attendants are community members who volunteer to be on call 24 hours a day, seven days a week. When a call comes in, they immediately drop whatever they are doing to help, no matter if they are working, eating dinner with their family, or taking a shower. They are amazing people who deserve heaps of gratitude.

While I ran to the health centre, I managed to dial the handheld radio to contact Whitehorse ambulance. I knew that if I had three critically injured patients, I was beyond the limits of my resources – and I was going to need help, fast. I wanted to give Whitehorse ambulance and the medevac team standby notice. As I rounded the corner, I noticed the RCMP car screaming out of town. RCMP dispatch in Whitehorse called me to let me know they were en route to the scene. It was reassuring to hear that the caller had followed through, and that the RCMP were on their way. I waved to the RCMP vehicle, to let them know I saw them, and I continued my run to the health centre.

I had just enough time to grab my bag of emergency first aid supplies, medications, and the automated external defibrillator. The ambulance attendants had already arrived, and we quickly threw in an extra spine board and straps to ensure we had enough equipment for all three injured. We left immediately. As we drove to the scene, we all put on medical gloves and doused ourselves in bug spray. Having responded to car crashes in the summertime in the North, I learned that an early application of bug dope saves a lot of grief at the scene. I also carry bug spray for accident victims in my first-aid bag, because mosquitoes are often one of the worst enemies.

Meanwhile, I received a call from one of the fire department volunteers. Word travels fast in small town. "Hazel, I heard there was a car crash. Do you need the Jaws?"

"Copy that. We haven't arrived at the scene yet. I don't know."

"All right. We'll head out there – just in case."

* * *

As we crested a hill, it was evident that we had arrived at the location of the car crash. Right away, we noticed the lights from the RCMP vehicles. A sport utility vehicle was at the side of the road, upright, but with extensive damage. It had obviously rolled a number of times. Personal belongings were scattered for at least a 100 metres along the road. I had never seen so much debris from one vehicle. The RCMP had already closed the highway. I jumped out the back of the ambulance for a quick briefing from them. "There is an unconscious woman trapped in the driver's side of the vehicle. She is being attended to by a paramedic, a passerby from British Columbia. There is a little girl who goes in and out of consciousness. She was thrown from the vehicle and is on the side of the road over there, attended to by a passerby with first aid training. The dad is over there under the blanket – deceased."

Calmly and quickly, the two ambulance attendants split up, one going to each victim. I decided to do a rapid assessment of each person – to get an idea of how serious the situation really was. I ran first to the woman trapped in the vehicle, assessed her quickly, and then ran over to the little girl. After a brief look at her, I ran over to the "dad" under the blanket. I thought it was best that I confirm he was deceased – just in case. I knew I needed to be brave, yet I was afraid of what I would find. I lifted one corner of the blanket and even today, I still remember feeling as if the blood had drained to my toes. What I saw wasn't a man, but a beautiful girl who I guessed was probably around 15 years old. Clearly, she was not alive. Still hopeful, I listened for a heart rate and breathing, and I checked her pupils. There was nothing I could do but cover her again. Everyone else directed their attention to the woman and the little girl. It wouldn't help anyone now to know that it wasn't the dad, but a young teenager. I didn't say anything to anyone. I pushed the image out of my mind and hurried back to the little girl. I had two lives to focus on and hopefully, maintain.

Normal protocol for medical evacuation is to go out to the scene, bring the accident victims by ambulance back to the health centre to be stabilized, consult with the physician on call in the Whitehorse hospital emergency, and finally, coordinate with their medical evacuation team. In this case, I was aware that normal protocol was not sufficient. I was the only medical person there. And both the child and the mother needed to get to a hospital immediately. It was clear to me that the girl had internal injuries and needed surgery. Taking her to the health centre first was not an option for me, because that would have wasted valuable time.

I remember saying to myself, "Think Hazel, think. How can we do this?" Just then, one of the passersby said that he had seen two helicopters sitting by the side of the road, about an hour south of our location. They were there because of the forest fires burning in the area. Several options whirled through my mind. I could secure the little girl to a spine board, start the intravenous therapy, and quickly have her ready for transport. However, I couldn't transport her, because her mother was still trapped in the car and needed medical attention. I couldn't be in both places at once. There were people milling around, anxious to help out, so I took charge, gave encouragement and support, and directed them on how to give first aid.

* * *

In a normal situation, the ambulance attendants would communicate with Whitehorse ambulance to update them, but in this case, the attendants were too busy to go to the radio. I asked the new RCMP Corporal, who was eager to help, to use his radio to give Whitehorse an update on the situation and to get the medical evacuation team here – as soon as possible. I also asked him to notify Whitehorse ambulance that there were two choppers just one hour away, and also to let them know I was beyond the limits of my resources and required assistance. This communication was vital to ensure a fast transport to the hospital. Very shortly, he returned to my side, to tell me that Whitehorse ambulance was aware and that they were working on mobilizing their crew. I was grateful.

The ambulance attendant started oxygen on the little girl, while a passerby soothed her and held her head to protect her spinal cord. I recruited someone to hold her arm, so that I could start intravenous therapy, and I asked someone else to be an IV pole for me. A number of people from the village helped strap her to a spinal board, with the ambulance attendant guiding them on how to proceed. Another person was given the task of wrapping gauze around a deep wound on her arm. Seeing that she was in good hands, and nearly ready for transport, I ran back to her mother. The people attending to her were doing a fabulous job. The other ambulance attendant had done his best to protect her spinal cord by supporting her head. He was in an awkward position though, because the roof of the vehicle was crushed, and there wasn't much room to reach her easily.

I felt overwhelmed, but I took a deep breath and started some positive self-talk. The woman was trapped in the vehicle in such a way that I couldn't reach her to give her medical care. I could see that her airway had great potential to be compromised, so I inserted a nasal airway that worked – until she removed it. This was a good sign because it meant she was conscious enough to do this. Still, I knew that her level of consciousness could change at any second, and I was worried. Her arm was mangled, but because it was the only part of her body I could reach, I started an intravenous there. I enlisted another passerby to be my second IV pole for the mother. At least she was getting fluids that would delay her shock.

At some point in time, I ran to the police vehicle to speak with the team in Whitehorse to discuss how to get the casualties to the hospital. I emphasized their critical status. With the mother still trapped in the vehicle, it was impossible for me to go to the health centre with the girl. I had a decision to make – the girl was in the ambulance, and ready for transport, and I didn't want to delay.

The Corporal "patched" me via RCMP dispatch radio in Whitehorse through to the ambulance dispatch in Whitehorse, and together, we figured out a solution. Within 15 minutes, a fixed-wing plane would land at the community airport, with a medevac nurse on board. I would send the little girl via land ambulance, with the local community volunteers, to meet this plane. Once the local attendants dropped the girl off at the airport, they would return here, to continue helping with the mother. Meanwhile, we would work on extricating her from the vehicle. The Whitehorse ambulance dispatcher managed to get in touch with the forest fire crew down the road and they promised to send a helicopter.

Since it was fifteen minutes to the airport, the ambulance crew left immediately with the little girl. I knew I had made an important judgment call when I sent her with the volunteer ambulance attendants and without me. I saw the panicked look on the ambulance volunteers' faces, but it was our best chance at getting her to the hospital as quickly as possible. They had been doing a tremendous job of caring for her, and I was appreciative of their assistance. They were a great crew and they would be just fine. Because of them, this child had a chance.

* * *

The fire department volunteers prepared the Jaws of Life so they could cut away the metal, to enable extrication of the mother. The rear door was cut away first – to allow me to reach her. Once the door was removed, I climbed into the back seat of the mangled vehicle. Workers placed blankets over both of us, and I closed my eyes when fire department volunteers began to bend and cut metal, and remove the shards of glass. It was a weird sensation, being under the blanket. I could hear them cutting and bending the metal, and I felt someone place a hand on my back, to keep the blanket tight against me for protection. I didn't know exactly what was unfolding outside, but I trusted these volunteers to keep us both safe. Moments later, the roof was free, and we were able to remove the woman to the side of the road, where I was able to stabilize her.

With the highway closed, tourists gathered in the distance and watched the scene unfold. I could hear the swirling, rhythmic beat of a helicopter. As in a scene from M*A*S*H, two helicopters appeared on the horizon. They had sent both of them. It's difficult to describe the sense of gratitude and relief I felt, at the sight of those helicopters.

The helicopters landed directly on the highway, on either side of the crash site. With so much debris and so many personal belongings strewn along the road, the wind created by the propeller blades resulted in what looked like a war zone. Things flew everywhere. People protected themselves by kneeling on the ground with their heads tucked between their knees. It was a heart-wrenching moment when the wind lifted the blanket off the deceased girl at the side of the road. Only then, did people realize the sad and shocking truth – that this was a young girl, and not the father.

Each helicopter arrived complete with forest fire crews who were trained in first aid. Finally, more help had arrived. We transferred the mother to one of the helicopters, and the pilots prepared to leave for the hospital in Whitehorse. Just as the doors closed, I heard the sound of sirens in the distance. *Something told me to wait.* Over the brow of the hill, the ambulance came into view; it drove directly to a helicopter and stopped. A medevac nurse jumped out the side door. Whitehorse had sent two medevac nurses on the fixed wing plane: one had returned to Whitehorse with the little girl, and the other nurse had come back with the ambulance to assist with the stabilization and transferring of the second patient by helicopter to Whitehorse. It was such a relief to see him. He promptly took over the patient's care, and they were off the ground within minutes.

As the tick-tick-tick of the helicopter blades faded in the distance, an enormous sense of relief and grief overwhelmed me. Something special had happened this evening. I had watched and helped a whole community come together to assist this family whom we knew nothing about – not even their names. So many people and resources had worked together. This was the community I lived in, and I felt extremely lucky. I looked at the debris all around me, the grey flat faces of my fellow community members, and the blanket at the side of the road. I felt a lump in my throat, my vision blurred, and I took in another deep breath. Moments later, a community member approached me, with two kittens in a small travel cage that had been found near the crash site. He offered to care for them for as long as we needed. I made a mental note to be sure to let the family know the kittens were safe – once we knew who this family was.

I went over to the vehicle and sorted through some papers I found, trying to put a name or some sort of identity to these people. Strewn over the back seat, was a tax return with the names of two children listed as dependents. There also was a photo of the two girls together, smiling broadly, and a birthday card. Inside the card, was the name of the older sister, the one who had died, and a note that said something like, "*I hear you have your first boyfriend and that he is really nice. I can't wait to see you soon. Love, Dad.*" Suddenly, these people became real. I could not even begin to imagine their loss. I sensed the significance of these items, and I gave them to the coroner, who said she would pass them on to the family.

With the help of the ambulance attendants, we removed the girl's body from the side of the road, to await transfer to a funeral home. People from the community continued to comb through the ditches and helped to gather the family's belongings. The RCMP piloted a long line of vehicles with passengers who had been waiting patiently and watching. They drove by slowly. A few people were operating video cameras; others were taking photos; some just looked sad.

* * *

We returned to the health centre. It took me a long time to document in the charts what had unfolded that evening, and to restock the supplies I had used – in case there was another call. My eyes pained with fatigue; nevertheless, I pushed myself to finish up. In the midst of this, the phone rang. Then a client appeared at the front door, a local man well-known to me for his alcoholism, who said he was throwing up blood. I couldn't believe it. He was vomiting blood in a way I had never seen before, and his blood pressure was "in his boots." Immediately, I flew back into emergency work mode. I checked his vital signs, did some bloodwork, started an IV to get some fluids into him, and prepared him for transport to the Whitehorse hospital. The medevac team met us halfway there. At 6:30 in the morning, I went to bed, knowing I needed to be at the health centre for the walk-in clinic in two hours. I was 15 minutes late for work, but I chuckled when I realized, "Hey, I'm on Yukon Time."

I spent the day organizing a critical incident debriefing for the front-line workers, along with looking after the regular functioning of the clinic. I came to appreciate having a sense of humour. When you sleep for only two hours in two days, funny things happen. I was still thinking about the helicopters landing on either side of me, the debris flying around, and everyone protecting themselves. In each helicopter, there had been four forest firefighters. As the doors opened, eight healthy, muscular, young men with tanned, sooty faces had come running towards me – ready to do whatever I said. I couldn't help but chuckle and think, "Wow! Every woman's dream come true!"

* * *

Later that day, we learned that, among other injuries, the little girl had a ruptured spleen. The time from the crash to the operating table in Whitehorse was less than four hours. During the night, both she and her mom were transferred to a trauma centre in the United States, where they were from. I had made some difficult judgment calls and decisions that night, as I had chosen not to follow the usual protocol for transporting clients. Things went so well there is already talk of using this night as a model for future emergency scenarios.

So what was so rewarding about going to the scene of a car crash? I didn't get these people into this situation; but with the help of many others, I got them out of it. Had we not made the choices we made, I honestly believe that the mother and her daughter might not have lived. (I say this as I think of the scar on my tummy, thankful to the people who saved my life, when I was in a car crash with a ruptured spleen at the age of 13.) I knew we would get them to the hospital in time. A week later, the kittens were returned to the family. *Life is precious.* I see that every day.

Now, where are those firefighters?

Hazel Booth RN(EC), MScN, PHCNP graduated in 1997 from the University of Ottawa School of Nursing. In 2002, she obtained her combined Master of Science in Nursing and Primary Health Care Nurse Practitioner degree from the University of Ottawa. She worked in neonatal intensive care at the Children's Hospital of Eastern Ontario in Ottawa. She also worked as a relief nurse practitioner in a number of Yukon Communities and as community nurse practitioner for Shibogama Health Authority in the Sioux Lookout Zone of Northwestern Ontario. She was an executive member of the Nurse Practitioner Association of Ontario, as the 2001-2002 student representative for the Primary Health Care Nurse Practitioner program. Hazel is presently the community nurse practitioner for the health centre in Teslin, in the Yukon, and is vice-president of the Yukon Registered Nurses Association.

THAT SINKING FEELING

Anne Pask Wilkinson

A four-day stay in a bush camp with bona fide Native trappers is not such a difficult experience. There is much to be learned and enjoyed. This is what our experience after a near tragedy revealed, when the Aboriginal family in question acted quickly and resourcefully. Native people have numerous ways of living figured out in detail, each with a lesson for us. In fact, I think all of us involved found the brief, intimate association valuable.

* * *

On November 28, 1962, Ken Kerr (our Indian Superintendent), a convalescent Indian mother with her infant, and I were flying on a routine charter to Snowdrift, some 115 miles east of Yellowknife. It was the first time I had been in that strange aircraft, a heliocourier, with its door on the left for the front seat only, and its door on the right for the back seat. Our departure had been much delayed because of the late freeze-up. It was made more urgent – after five days of bad weather – by the report of an injured boy in Snowdrift.

The weather had not been ideal for flying, but acceptable, until a blinding snow squall struck us abruptly from behind, from over the open water of Great Slave Lake. Our pilot, Mike Thomas, inspected and landed promptly near the shoreline on what appeared to be a narrow lake. We thought we had landed in uninhabited wilderness; however, unknown to us, human eyes had seen our aircraft, and the events which followed were heard. We were very fortunate, because soon we would need their help – urgently.

On reconnoitering the ice after landing, we were surprised to find a trail of fresh human tracks in a place where we had thought there was no one for at least 35 miles. Since this was not a dogteam trail, it appeared likely that a camp was close. As the eight-month-old baby was just over chickenpox (on top of more serious illnesses) and since the weather was not improving, we agreed that we should seek out the camp.

We had taxied along only a short distance beyond the stretch we had investigated, when the ice suddenly gave way and the nose of the aircraft quickly sank. The pilot called, "Bail out" and in a flash, he and Ken were out of the front seat, although Ken's foot was caught briefly when the door closed with the pressure of the water. I had been putting away the records I was

This story was originally published in the *Medical Services Newsletter, Summer, 1963*. It appears here, with minor changes, with permission of the author, who passed away during the preparation of this book.

working on, not watching. Now, my patients and I were trapped in the sinking aircraft. The wings settled on the ice – but not before we were nearly up to our necks in frigid water.

This was frightening for a woman with a small child, especially when she could not understand the reassurances, or the instructions and the efforts of the men outside the plane. She spoke only Chipewyan, which I could not speak. Nevertheless, she seemed to comprehend my repeated instructions. I pushed her as far up as I could in the available air space among the sleeping bags and mail sacks, just to keep the baby's head above water. The child's loud protests about the cold did not help the mother's composure. Nor could I hear the instructions from the men working desperately to rescue us. Mike opened my door below water, and they were able to get a window out, only to find it hopelessly plugged with mail sacks. My hands rapidly lost sensation. I could no longer follow directions or co-operate with him, and we had no space in which to move.

While the water was slowing coming up to my face, the baby quieted and the mother sang softly. About the time the men had exhausted their resources outside, a Native man appeared. He told Mike and Ken that his partner was coming with the dogs and an axe. They had seen us fly over and had heard us land. His eight-year-old son, George, heard us taxi and break through the ice, and he had run to tell them. We later found out that this was the one day they had not gone out on the traplines.

As soon as the second man arrived, and they realized that there were three people in the slowly sinking aircraft, they chopped frantically to open a hole in the roof of the plane. When we were pulled out through the opening, very numb and half-conscious, I remember thinking, "There goes the last of my hairdo," and "This must be what a Caesarian baby feels like!" Moments later, when I was being taken by dog team to the trappers' cabin, I thought, "Santa's reindeer never had the hard time these poor dogs are having."

During the first hour, I was unaware of the warmth of the cabin, being the last to respond. I was told that the infant, who had been rigid and cold, was warm and smiling in less than half an hour, even before her mother. I vaguely recall my own disbelief of this as I came to, and I remember the comfort it felt to be allowed to hold and rock the lively little baby. I remember the sun coming in the window, and the pleasure of recognizing that our hosts in that warm, steamy cabin were among my favourite people of the community of Snowdrift.

It was something of a shock to find myself bereft of clothing (except for someone's wool plaid shirt, later seen on the back of the man of the house), and confined to some bedding on a large sleeping bench. Our efficient hostess first rubbed my back and extremities – it was like a thousand demons needling my body. Then she wrung out all my clothing and hung it to dry on lines near the stove. Earlier, in a moment of consciousness, I had apparently recognized her and said, "Oh, Antoinette, it is you," and stopped struggling.

I remember, too, having concern for her, and ordering her to sit down and rest in her advanced state of pregnancy. However, after patiently sitting for a while, until it appeared I had finished asking everyone questions regarding the situation, Antoinette asked her own familiar, but at that time, startling question, "How is my baby?" It was a very distressing question, for her tiny daughter, whom I had flown out months ago and who had known ups and downs in an Edmonton hospital, had died two weeks earlier from a congenital defect. It had been impossible for Ken Kerr to inform the family, because their whereabouts were unknown. It so happened that when we were out on the escort trip (to bring the baby that was with us on the plane back from hospital), I had had a talk with the paediatrician who had attended Antoinette's baby. I was able to give her much more comforting information than ordinarily possible. Nevertheless, her sobs were heartbreaking, and it was hard to have to sit by helplessly, still without clothing, in circumstances where it was customary to offer comforting arms. Antoinette was a devoted mother who had previously lost two children to illness and accident, and her sorrow was not brief. She referred to the baby several times throughout our stay.

* * *

Antoinette was a good housekeeper, even with only a black-birch twig broom, and she tried to make us comfortable in her cabin. She had expected to be home in Snowdrift two weeks earlier, across safe ice not yet formed, and her family was almost out of food and staples. I think they were a little surprised that we shared what we had, and they enjoyed the variety, such as it was. There were eleven of us altogether, and we had some jolly times, with the aircraft emergency kit rations and the family's fresh moose meat. It was accepted that I was chief cook and bottle washer, though a very unskilled one, with only Ken's mess tins to cook in, his sponge from his personal emergency kit to wash and dry the dishes, and my stupid fingers not functioning very well because of the frostbite. I think everyone appreciated my efforts to practise what I constantly preached to them about washing and cleaning things, even with limited facilities. I allowed no one to drink out of a cup after someone else had used it, until it had been washed. At bedtime, we all enjoyed drinking hot chocolate from an assortment of tins and bowls.

The little cabin was tidy and well-organized, with the wash basin on the shelf over the wood box and the "slop pail" at hand. In fact, a funny incident happened one morning when a single edible fish that had been caught in a net was placed in a pan on the shelf. I went to get some wood for the fire and as I was returning, I remarked, "You know, that fish doesn't look dead." At that moment, behind my back, the fish flung itself down into the unpalatable contents of the "slop pail." Everyone laughed at my reaction – and at the poor fish's evident distaste for its location. So out went our lunch to the dogs. At least the fourth dog (which until then had gone without, because only three fish had been available) had a meal.

The first night was pretty miserable and chilly for some of us without sleeping bags and with our coats still damp – and considering the nightmares that came when you did doze off. Ken and Mike had both gotten wet climbing out of the plane, and Mike had dislocated his toe while trying to kick in a window. He had been putting his weight on it without thinking, so that even with what treatment I could give (my medical bags deep in the plane), it was painful. We kept the fires going, and a candle burned all night, as the family slept soundly. Mink skins hung over my head where I was lying on a blanket on the floor; lynx and other skins hung over Ken's and Mike's heads near the door. Later in our stay, I watched Big Joe, our host, scrape and stretch a skin. It was amusing to see his three-year-old son, Gilbert, work away similarly with his bit of squirrel hide nailed to a stick and watch his concern when he thought Mike was going to swipe it from him.

* * *

The accident occurred around midday. That afternoon, Little Joe, Antoinette's grown brother, headed out with his dogs for Yellowknife, 80 miles away. Long after dark, which came early, he returned, having found it impossible to travel in the deep snow and over the rough overflows. He suggested taking gasoline from the plane, and trying to get to Snowdrift over the open water with the canoe and outboard motor (they call it a "kicker") the next day. Someone suggested that they siphon out the gas with my enema equipment. However, the next morning, after fishing in the submerged aircraft with a gaff, all the mail, sleeping bags, and many other important things were retrieved; but none of my expensive medical equipment could be located. The front part of the wings (where the gas cap was) was underwater, so a hole had to be cut in the wing for gas. It was not very cold – around zero – and it was a sunny day. Even to approach the aircraft in that thin spot, over what we later found was a current in a channel 150 feet deep, would be dangerous.

Under Mike's direction, the men worked hard preparing signs on the ice to guide rescue craft, and they marked out a runway near the cabin where the ice was 12 inches thick. They also prepared for the canoe trip to Snowdrift. After a delicious moose steak lunch, the four men carefully pushed the big canoe over more than two miles of treacherous ice, in places only one and a half inches thick, until finally, the two Native men went on alone toward the edge, climbing in as they broke through, and disappearing around the island.

In the meantime, near the cabin, six-year-old Dorothy and I were hauling pails of water up the steep slope from the water hole in the ice for her mother, who was doing some laundry in a tub, and for Mary Louise Nitah, the mother of the baby, who kept her own supply of diapers washed. She was very content to be among friends and appeared to have had no residual effects at all from her icy experience. Little Mary Annie bounced happily if we fed her enough of the dehydrated cream, which was the only milk preparation we had.

At eight years old, George was a skilled trapper, with his own preserves near home. He showed me a number of interesting things. We sawed wood together, while his little sister sat on the log and laughed, as I sang to the rhythm of the saw, "*Land of the silver birch, home of the beaver, where still the mighty moose wanders at will.*" Then we split the wood, filled the wood-box, talking about safety measures with tools like axes and saws. Dorothy came along with an ice birthday cake in two layers, with little sticks for candles and dusted with sawdust, and presented it to me – remarkably, on the eve of a birthday I almost didn't get to celebrate. The big clumsy pup who added to our fun, the youngsters snow-sliding, and the other play things – all were reminiscent of my own country childhood. I really enjoyed that day.

* * *

We were tired and discouraged, when our male hosts returned after dark, unable to make the boat motor function on aviation gasoline, but delighted to have brought back a beautiful otter which they had shot – a rare find. We spent that evening drying out family allowance cheques and other important pieces of mail, and all my medical records which had miraculously floated up. The diapers scarcely had any room on the lines, and I believe we got one less-wet sleeping bag dry. Because their radio batteries were weak, we could not get any news of the search – if it had started.

The women and I discussed a number of things we rarely have time to talk about. Antoinette had many questions. Ken found it a good chance to talk with the men about better ways of marketing their furs and fish, something that he had long been trying to make them comprehend, effectively enough this time for them to give him the present catch to take out.

The following day was dull and snowy, not very good for search planes. I tried fishing through the ice, without a bite, and watched the men set out a fish net under the ice. We built a large pile of evergreen boughs to make a smoke-signal fire, if we heard a plane. Antoinette used up the last of her lard and flour for her delicious bannock. As the daylight faded, we saw a plane approach in the snowing clouds, but he turned just before he might have seen our fire. That evening, we had a fine time trying to beat Joe, the head of the house, at checkers, but we couldn't do it. The family had its own homemade set and board, and Joe was really good at the game. I was quickly eliminated, so I gathered up a couple of pens and wrinkled paper, to work with the youngsters. George had some difficulty with my arithmetic questions, yet he enjoyed doing them; so he made up his own, while Dorothy and I were printing. They obviously loved learning, and one wondered how their hunting season losses and gains stacked up.

The next morning we had very little to eat, just coffee and the remains of the biscuit mix (what would we have done without that oven?). Saturday was a better day. Soon after 9:00 a.m., we heard the drone of motors – the Air Force on its grid searching. We became excited as Mike recognized the procedures of the craft we heard. Even Antoinette came running down to pile boughs on the fire, as the plane was coming very close. Both the Joes and the children ran out on the ice, waving their arms. Mike stood ready with his flare gun (the cartridge had dried out in the oven), and at his shout, we piled on the green boughs. Over the treetops came a Cessna, dipping its wings and landing down the runway they had marked with boughs. We had been found!

Never was there a more excited, delighted group of people. As Ken and I, replacing two spotters in the plane, took our departure, little Dorothy hung onto my hand and said, "You my friend, yes?" while George waved cautiously. I wanted to bring him in for examination of a resolving abscess on his jaw; however, he would not enter the aircraft under any pretext. Neither would Mrs. Nitah. She preferred to stay where she was, until she could go the rest of the way home with her baby, by dogsled.

An hour or two later, I was at home making a phone call to my kin, while anxious friends invaded the apartment. Freed of smelly clothing, I luxuriated in a fragrant tub. Meanwhile, in the cabin in the woods, joy also reigned. The eyes of the family filled with tears at the sight of the unheard-of supply of food and candles (for we had used their last) that Ken and I had ordered to go back out on the returning plane – enough for a safety margin of another three weeks. In farewell, Antoinette picked up the fine wolverine skin (that Joe had proudly described her tanning) and deftly sliced out the choice centre back, put it into Mike's hands, and said, "For your new parka."

Anne Pask Wilkinson RN, PHN graduated in 1944 with her RN from Wellesley Hospital in Toronto, Ontario. In 1951, she attained her PHN. For several years, she worked with the Victorian Order of Nurses in Ontario, Nova Scotia, and Saskatchewan. In 1955, she went to Edinburgh, Scotland, for her midwifery qualifications and on her return, joined Medical Services. She was the nurse at Baker Lake Nursing Station where she did research with Inuit women on child-bearing and the raising of children. In the early 1960s, in Yellowknife, she conducted a survey with white and Dene women on breastfeeding of infants. She later moved to the Yukon where she was zone supervisor with Medical Services for five years. Anne did volunteer nursing work in Victoria, British Columbia. She was a member of "The Raging Grannies" and was concerned about women's rights and the ecology of our world. In June 2004, Anne passed away at her home at Wildwood Forest, near Nanaimo, BC.

A MOUNTIE TRIES HIS HAND AT NURSING

Dennis Minion

I was a member of the Royal Canadian Mounted Police from 1955 to 1975. For thirteen years, from 1957 to 1970, I worked in isolated areas of the Northwest Territories. Because of the nature of my work during that time, I had a lot to do with nurses. I also had the privilege of working with two female doctors, who made life a lot easier in our isolated conditions.

From 1963 to 1967, I was stationed at Eskimo Point, now called Arviat, in the new territory of Nunavut. We lived next door to the nursing station, which was run by a lovely Czechoslovakian nurse named Tania. (For the life of me, I can't recall her last name.) When I got up one morning, I discovered that our three-year-old twin daughters, Dianne and Debbie, had somehow climbed up onto the sink. From there, they had been able to open the medicine cabinet and had consumed two boxes of Ex-Lax. As soon as my wife, who was also a nurse, realized this, she got very upset. She said we had to pump their stomachs or else they would go into shock – and maybe die. I ran to the nursing station and got Tania, who hurried over with a narrow rubber hose.

We first tried to induce vomiting, but to no effect. I almost "lost it" trying to make the twins throw up. Finally, Tania said we had to try to pump their stomachs. Because Dianne was the better climber and had eaten the most Ex-Lax (Debbie only got what Dianne passed down to her), we worked on her first. My job was to hold Dianne down on the table, and keep a wooden spoon in her mouth, to prevent her from biting the tube. Meanwhile, Tania and my wife tried to ram a tube down the throat of a fighting kid. These two nurses did a great job. Much to my amazement, within moments, the Ex-Lax started to come up. It all came gushing out, as if there was a little pump in her stomach.

It wasn't long before Dianne was finished. Next came Debbie, who had watched the procedure used on Dianne and, I suspect, had decided she wasn't having anything to do with it. I was able to subdue her and get the wooden spoon into her mouth. But just as the pump started to do its work, Debbie somehow got the spoon out of her mouth, so the only thing that kept her teeth from severing the tube was my thumb. I didn't dare take out my thumb. We couldn't get the wooden spoon back in, so I tried to ignore the pain, and my bleeding thumb, until no more Ex-Lax came through the tube. During the whole time, Tania was amazing, calm, and controlled. She even praised my bravery.

These stories are part of a collection which Dennis Minion wrote for his children, who were too young at the time to remember their family life in the North.

Tania saved my life on another occasion. It was during an epidemic of rabies in the dog population of the community. Since every family had a dog team, there were lots of dogs. Whenever we found a rabid dog, the procedure which we were to follow was to kill the animal, cut off its head, and ship the head to the Federal Agriculture Laboratory in Hull, Quebec.

One day, while I was packing up a potentially rabid dog's head for shipment, I accidentally came into contact with some blood, which I thought might have gotten into a cut on my hand. I had watched a movie about a fellow who had rabies, and I knew that if the disease incubated, you were dead. When I sheepishly told Tania about it, she said I had to be treated. The treatment involved injecting a huge needle into the stomach muscle *every* day, for fourteen days.

I vividly recall making the torturous trip to the nursing station each morning at nine. In those days, I was lean and hard, and try as I might, I could not relax my stomach muscles. That meant that Tania really had to lean on the needle, all the while saying, "Sorry, sorry." Believe it or not, she actually broke a needle on me. I think Nurse Tania was more grateful than I was when the fourteen days were up.

* * *

In addition to the rabies epidemic, Eskimo Point was hit with a meningitis epidemic. By that time, there were two nurses at Eskimo Point: Tania and Mary Voisey. I recall how these women struggled to save the lives of the Eskimo children who got the disease. They were ill-equipped to treat patients who were that sick, and they could only contact the doctor in Churchill by radio. On several occasions, because the weather prevented evacuation of patients, these nurses had to manage with what they had in the station. In spite of their efforts, they watched at least three little children die. All white children were evacuated from the community; the Eskimos were left to do the best they could. The epidemic lasted for several months, and the nurses were right in the middle of it. It was a terrible time for them.

Dennis Minion served with the Royal Canadian Mounted Police from 1955 to 1975, in various northern communities such as Fort Smith, Fort Simpson, Eskimo Point (Arviat), and Yellowknife.

DELIVERY IN URANIUM CITY

Cecilia Rockel

While we hear stories of how important the Royal Canadian Mounted Police are to nurses in the North, my husband – and any RCMP members who have worked in isolated locations – have always admired the professionalism and dedication of northern nurses. In many instances, doctors fly in only once a week, and the rest of the time, nurses run the clinics on their own. In our case, the nurses were our lifeline.

Dale and I were married; he graduated from Depot (the RCMP training academy in Regina, Saskatchewan), and we were posted to Maple Creek, Saskatchewan, in May of 1999 – all in one week. Sixteen months later, we were blessed with our first child, a baby girl named Peyton. In February of 2000, when Peyton was five months old, we were transferred to the Black Lake Reserve in the far north of Saskatchewan, a remote fly-in posting, 22 km southeast of Stony Rapids and 80 km south of the Northwest Territories. When I was a young girl, my grandparents, who are lovers of the North, instilled in me a love of camping, fishing, and hiking. The places we frequented, however, were not nearly as far north as Black Lake.

* * *

The Christmas after we arrived in Black Lake, we were pleasantly surprised to find out we were expecting another baby. I had a difficult pregnancy and worried constantly about the fate of our unborn child. Consequently, I spent a lot of my time at the clinic, which was located directly across the road from the RCMP compound. I got to know all of the nurses and doctors, even though many of them worked on a rotating basis throughout the North. During our stay, both Dale and I developed friendships with many of the northern nurses, often sharing special occasions like Thanksgiving and Christmas with them.

* * *

The story I would like to share begins during the night of Saturday, July 14, 2001, when I was in my 36th week of pregnancy. Since we were scheduled to fly to Regina on the RCMP plane the following Tuesday morning, I had spent the night busily packing, baking, and cleaning the house. In fact, I was so involved in my cleaning regimen, that I was shocked when Dale arrived home from his shift at 2 a.m. and insisted we go to sleep. In retrospect, I'm glad that I hadn't had time to contemplate any of the old wives' tales about how to encourage the onset of labour, because they obviously have merit.

After two hours of sleep, I awoke suddenly. Since our bedding was soaking wet, I assumed that my water had broken. Dale outright refused to entertain this possibility. After all, we were scheduled to deliver in Regina, and it was three days before we were supposed to leave. Nevertheless, we called the nurse at the clinic, my mother in Regina, and our next door neighbour, Constable Craig Matatall. Each of the three people we spoke to gave us the much needed reality check: I *was* in labour.

Craig ran over to our place in his housecoat to watch our sleeping toddler, Peyton. Dale and I headed for the clinic, where the nurses quickly confirmed that I was in active labour. When reality finally sank in, my nervous husband returned home to pack a hospital bag for me. In the meantime, the nurses monitored me and made arrangements to have a bush plane in Stony Rapids ready to take me to Uranium City. The Black Lake clinic is small, with only basic equipment, and it is not equipped for emergency procedures. The plan was that we would pick up Dr. Botha in Uranium City and continue flying to Prince Albert, the largest northern hospital, where the baby could safely be delivered.

At 5 a.m., I was loaded onto a stretcher and put into the back of a makeshift ambulance, an old van commonly used as the taxicab in Black Lake. While the "ambulance" sped away, Dale, Craig, and Peyton all packed into the RCMP Suburban and raced down the road to meet us in Stony Rapids so Dale could come with me. Once we arrived, I was transferred onto the waiting bush plane, at which point I caught a glimpse of the young-looking pilot. Already in a state of panic, I asked Nurse Su-Ann Crawford whether he was old enough to hold a pilot's license. She assured me that the flight would be fine.

Since I was 3 cm dilated in Black Lake, and my contractions were getting closer together, Nurse Su-Ann took every precaution to ensure that I would not deliver on the plane. For example, they positioned the stretcher so that my head was towards the back of the plane – the force of take-off can speed up labour. Also, the plane flew at a very low elevation, because we were in an unpressurized airplane, and as much oxygen as possible was needed. Finally, the doctor in Uranium City was notified that we were on our way, and he was ready with suction and other medical devices, should they be needed. Once we landed in Uranium City, Dr. Botha examined me and determined that I was 5 cm dilated. He insisted that we should not continue to Prince Albert, and that I would have to deliver in Uranium City.

* * *

Once again, I felt a twinge of panic. At one time, the hospital in Uranium City had been a thriving place, serving about 5,000 people. When the uranium mine closed in 1983, the population declined severely, and the hospital now provided medical care to only about 120 people. I knew that they were not fully-equipped to deliver babies, and I had heard that only seven babies had been born in the hospital in the last four years – and then only out of absolute necessity. Furthermore, I knew that the closest neonatal unit was in Saskatoon, a flight of at least two and a half hours away. Dr. Botha and Dr. Martens (who came in on his day off) tried to reassure me, while Nurses Linda Crawford and Alida Silverthorn used humour to calm my nerves. Dale announced that he was feeling tired. Granted, he had just worked the night shift; but, apparently, he had momentarily forgotten that *I* was the one in labour. Nurse Linda, whom we knew from her time at the Black Lake clinic, graciously offered Dale her room in the hospital so that he could take a nap.

Thankfully, my labour was extremely easy, and a short while later, Dale was awakened from his slumber, just in time to see the delivery of our son. Caleb John Kenneth Rockel was born at 10:04 a.m. To my relief, I heard his cry, and I was told everything was all right. Dale watched as our baby boy was weighed: 7 lb 8 oz, surprisingly big for a preemie.

After our baby was thoroughly checked and deemed healthy, the nurses soon took on the role of kitchen staff and made us a wonderful lunch of soup and sandwiches. They enjoyed holding Caleb and talking to him; in fact, he turned out to be "the talk of the town." We were embraced by the community with love. Complete strangers showed up at the hospital to pass along their best wishes and to bring presents for our baby. Dr. Botha took a digital picture of us, which he emailed to our families, and his wife brought a singing teddy. A conservation officer who visited hinted that Caleb may have inherent trapping and fishing rights because of his northern birthplace. (Could he have been serious?) The funniest moment for the nurses and me, however, was looking into the hospital bag my husband had packed. The contents included three pairs of shoes, four pairs of pants, two shirts and a variety of toiletries – all for Dale. In his early morning excitement, he hadn't even packed me a toothbrush.

We were grateful to the women in the community, who provided many of the essentials that Dale had forgotten to bring. The local church ladies' group gave us hand-knit baby blankets, and the nurses were kind enough to find a take-me-home outfit for our baby: a light blue sleeper with "Property of Uranium City Hospital" stamped on the back.

The hospital staff were professional and knowledgeable; but just as important, they were very caring and friendly. The nurses were always available to answer our questions. They even took family photos of us in front of the hospital. When we left Uranium City the next morning to return to Black Lake, I remember looking back and seeing a picture I will never forget. Standing in the doorway waving goodbye, with huge smiles on their faces, were all the staff of the hospital.

* * *

When our small plane touched down on the landing strip at Black Lake, Craig and our daughter Peyton were there to greet us. Since RCMP members usually do not have their own private vehicles in the North, Caleb's first ride home was in the back of the RCMP Suburban, complete with bullet-proof glass between him and his dad. In the evening, Nurse Su-Ann came by to visit the child she had almost delivered. She and the other Black Lake nurses were thrilled that everything had gone well.

That night, Caleb slept in a laundry basket, and the next morning, he and I boarded the RCMP plane to fly south to Prince Albert. We were driven to the hospital to have Caleb's bilirubin checked. To our astonishment, when the nurses weighed him, he was only 5 lb 11 oz – not 7 lb 8 oz. We were soon put at ease when we realized that he could not have lost almost two pounds in two days. We assumed that the seldom-used Uranium City baby scale must have been incorrect.

* * *

From conversations with his nurses, we have learned that Caleb was one of the last babies to be born in the hospital in Uranium City. He is now an extremely active child whose scrapbook is full of memories of his birth day. Photos of the hospital include not only the building that now stands empty and faces demolition, but also the special doctors and nurses who helped to make Caleb's birth such a wonderful and special experience.

Cecilia Rockel, her husband, Dale, and their children, Peyton and Caleb, moved south in 2002, from Black Lake to Regina, Saskatchewan, where Cecilia is employed part-time at a therapeutic group home for teenage girls. Now that Dale does not have to concern himself with delivery situations, he can fully concentrate on his work in the RCMP General Investigation Section.

AN ARCTIC JOURNEY

Audrey Steenbeek

The Arctic regions of Canada evoke images of a hostile and an inhospitable environment. It is a land in which extreme seasonal variations in temperature, sunlight, and ice conditions are normal. Despite these challenging conditions, Inuit people have successfully inhabited these regions for thousands of years and have learned to adapt successfully to the barrenness and the isolation of the Arctic.

Contemporary Inuit communities stand in significant contrast to the populations first encountered by explorers, whalers, and missionaries in the 18th and 19th centuries, when the Arctic regions were first exposed to southern explorers. For instance, the traditional snow house has now been replaced by housing, complete with central heating and electricity. The traditional nomadic existence has been replaced by permanent residence in centralized communities. Inuit reliance upon resident and migratory wildlife has been overtaken by a partial dependence upon southern food, various forms of paid employment, and government assistance. Nevertheless, Arctic life remains unique, and many Inuit people today pride themselves on maintaining close ties with the land, their heritage, and their ancient traditions. Perhaps it is these elements of Inuit life that have attracted many adventure-minded travellers to the desolate beauty of the Arctic. It is certainly what lured me to the fascinating world of outpost nursing in the eastern Canadian Arctic.

The Journey Begins

As my husband, my two-year-old son and I flew on the First Air flight from Ottawa to Iqaluit, on the first leg of our trip to Qikiqtarjuaq, I felt like an explorer setting forth on the biggest adventure of a lifetime. At the same time, I felt some trepidation and I wondered if I had been foolhardy to accept such an employment offer. I noticed the in-flight magazine *Above and Beyond* carefully placed behind each seat. Glancing through it, I found an assortment of advertisements, including skidoos for sale, Inuit art galleries, and sealift companies. The plane was filled with people who were engaged in cheerful discussion. The flight attendants appeared to recognize many of the passengers on board and readily exchanged stories of their vacations in "the South" – a term, I later found out, which refers to anything south of Iqaluit.

We flew for a few hours over barren land and icy water, and finally reached Iqaluit (Frobisher Bay), the capital of Nunavut. Iqaluit, which is home to approximately 5,000 people, is the "metropolis" of the Baffin Region. To the inexperienced explorer such as myself, Iqaluit did not look like much more than a desolate, little community with a bright yellow airport terminal, distinctly resembling something built with a child's Lego set. In fact, Iqaluit is the pride of

Nunavut. It boasts its own hospital, fire department, elementary and secondary schools, a college, a string of restaurants and bars, various banks, several grocery and convenience stores, and even a movie theatre. In reality, it is far more than just a little community with an airport terminal built out of Lego blocks.

When we landed in Iqaluit, we were escorted by a First Air representative to the terminal where we waited for our connecting flight to Qikiqtarjuaq (which was formerly known as Broughton Island). Inside the terminal, excitement and noise filled the air. Inuit and southerners (or *kabloona*) eagerly awaited their loved ones. Tourists, dressed in very expensive Gortex and fleece, waited patiently for their flights or luggage, while children ran around happily, sucking candy, munching chips, or sipping pop. When we finally managed to check in with First Air, we were advised that our flight to Qikiqtarjuaq was delayed due to weather. This is the dreaded announcement that every traveller hopes never to hear – especially after travelling for nearly eight hours with a two-year-old boy and a weary husband.

What could possibly be wrong with the weather, I thought. It was July. The sky was blue in Iqaluit and it was 28 degrees in Ottawa. However, this is the Arctic, where weather is unpredictable, and a simple case of fog or strong winds will ground even the most seasoned pilot. On the other hand, seeing how young some of the pilots looked (they seemed to me too young to have a driver's license), I was thankful that they were not in a kamikaze mood. Besides, my son was not at all bothered by the delay. There were people to watch; there was plenty of noise and excitement to attract his attention, and more importantly, lots of space to run around in. In this airport, if you are not preoccupied with chasing after a toddler, you can spend time admiring many beautiful Inuit carvings or enjoy a cup of coffee at the snack shop. There is even satisfaction in simply sitting down and absorbing the special and unique ambiance of a northern airport lounge.

The announcement finally came, and we were now ready to board again – this time, for our final destination, Qikiqtarjuaq. We eagerly got on the small King-Air plane, which smelled strongly of jet fuel and other indistinguishable smells. We found ourselves seats near the window. Our pleasant attendant, dressed in the traditional blue suit, informed us that the flight would first take us to Pangnirtung (approximately one and a half hours), and after a short stop to refuel and pick up more passengers, we would then proceed to Qikiqtarjuaq. Unfortunately, the fog and high winds persisted, and as soon as we landed in Pangnirtung, we were advised that it was not possible to fly to Qikiqtarjuaq due to adverse weather conditions. Therefore, we would have to go back to Iqaluit. Weary from travel and anxious to get settled in our new community, we reluctantly reboarded the plane to head back to Iqaluit.

The following morning, after a good night's sleep at the Discovery Inn, we returned to the airport with optimistic anticipation. Once again, we were greeted by a friendly First Air representative who gently warned us that there was still the possibility that our flight to Qikiqtarjuaq would be cancelled. The winds were certainly milder, and the pilots were eager to attempt the flight. After boarding, I was stricken with a sense of *déjà vu*. I saw the same passengers, pilots, and flight attendant, all sitting in the same seats they had chosen the previous day. After a brief stop in Pangnirtung, we continued on our way to Qikiqtarjuaq. It was only a 40-minute flight, but the mood became solemn as we approached Qikiqtarjuaq airport. The fog was still hovering over the runway, and it was not certain whether or not the pilots would try to land. Providence was on our side. No sooner did we look out the window than we felt the bumps of the landing gear hitting the tarmac. At last – Qikiqtarjuaq.

Outside the one-room airport terminal, community members arrived to greet their families, pick up parcels, or simply watch the excitement. We were approached by a few people who inquired if we were tourists, or if I was the new nurse. The "community ambassadors" were quite surprised to hear that I was the new nurse, and that I had arrived with my husband and son. Several Inuit girls hovered over my son as if he were a new doll, giggling and touching his red curly hair. He was not amused. After loading a van with our backbreaking luggage, we headed off to our unit. Fortunately, all of our supplies and personal effects had been sent about a month before our arrival. Still, we had a lot of unpacking and organizing ahead of us

The Community

Qikiqtarjuaq is located just off the east coast of Baffin Island. Although the island is referred to as "the big island," as its Inuktitut name suggests, it is only 12 km wide by 16 km long. It has a seasonal population of just over 500 people, 95% of whom are Inuit. Qikiqtarjuaq is 513 km north from Iqaluit and about 96 km inside the Arctic Circle. This island is well-known for its traditional Inuit lifestyle, ivory and bone carvings, spectacular wildlife, icebergs, and beautiful scenery. It is the northern gateway to Auyuittuq National Park.

And the Work Begins

The honeymoon period was quickly over. Within a couple of days, we were acclimatized to our new surroundings, and we had established a semblance of order and organization around the house. I was quickly thrown into my work assignment. After a brief introduction to the support staff and a 15-minute orientation of the health centre, I did what I was expected to do: see and treat patients.

During the first few weeks at the health centre, I was a novelty among the patients. I was the new nurse, I was relatively young compared to other nurses, and I even had my husband and son with me. More intriguing for them was the fact that my husband was now the primary caregiver of our son. For most Inuit, especially the males, this is an alien concept. I was quickly accepted into this pleasant little community, and before long, to my deep satisfaction, I became just another household name. I soon learned all the little quirks about our regular patients, such as who got their pills weekly in a dosette, and who were given their pills in bottles, which elders needed home visits, and so on. More importantly, though, I quickly learned the all-important "yes" and "no" in Inuktitut: raising the eyebrows is "yes," while a very quick scrunch of the nose means "no."

Like most other health centres throughout Canada, each day of the week is a different clinic day. For example, Mondays are well-women clinics where women are assembled, and gently reminded about their yearly PAP tests. Tuesdays are chronic disease clinics, when the pills and blood tubes come out in full force. Wednesdays are prenatal and/or family planning clinics. Thursdays are well-child clinics, which generally involve immunizations and crying kids. Finally, Fridays are usually kept open for administration, catching up on charting, ordering drugs and supplies, counting the narcotics, and for anything else that is pending. Generally speaking, working in an Inuit health centre can be anywhere from chaotically busy to painfully slow. Most often, however, it is simply a pure delight.

Being on Call

A community health nurse in a two-nurse health centre is generally on call most of the time. Fortunately, most of the after-hour calls are usually for minor injuries; for viral infections of the ears, nose, throat and chest; for stomach problems, or for other common ailments. When a major accident, illness or tragedy – such as suicide – occurs, it can be very overwhelming, not just for the nurses, but also, and in a more profound way, for the whole community. Almost every Inuit family in this small community has experienced a tragedy in its household, and some have fared worse than others.

Social Life

For many city-minded people, living in a small, isolated community like Qikiqtarjuaq can feel like a cruel jail sentence. For others, it is a much needed escape from the hectic, daily routine of traffic jams, busy time-schedules, noise, and pollution. If peace and quiet, isolation and vast open space are on the agenda, then Qikiqtarjuaq is certainly the place to be. There are beautiful snow-peaked mountains to look at, sunsets over the ocean to admire, and if you are lucky, polar bears, walrus, and narwhal to watch, when they are in season. Besides all of this, there is a marvellous sense of community that develops among families in similar situations. For example, there are wonderful potluck dinners with the teachers and the RCMP, Friday night soccer games at the school, Inuit games and community events, and many other festive activities.

Overall, living and working in Qikiqtarjuaq has been an excellent experience for my family and for me. It has been an opportunity to live in and to learn about a different culture, to work in a challenging yet rewarding healthcare environment, and to create everlasting memories. This is just a glimpse into the world of outpost nursing.

Audrey Steenbeek RN, MScN, PhD (candidate) immigrated to Canada from Malta in 1981. She graduated in 1992 from Mohawk College in Hamilton, Ontario and worked at St. Joseph's Hospital in Hamilton until 1995. She graduated in 1995 from the Post RN program at McMaster University in Hamilton. In 1996, she went to Baffin Island, where she worked in the emergency department at Baffin Regional Hospital and did vacation relief in the settlements. She transferred to the medevac team and stayed until 1998. After moving to Vancouver, she worked in emergency at the Vancouver Hospital and started an MScN at the University of British Columbia. She has done short-term relief in various northern BC communities and occasionally back in Baffin. She is currently in her third year at UBC, working on her PhD in Health Care and Epidemiology. She still lives in Qikiqtarjuaq, where she works as a community health nurse and collects data for her PhD thesis. Audrey and her husband, Jeroen, have a son Ethan.

HOW NORTHERN NURSES ARE MADE
or
HOW I LEARNED TO SURVIVE AND LOVE THE NORTH
Moira MacDougal Cameron

So, this is what happens when one seeks a new direction in life. To think that I said I would go wherever the most challenging job was located. Fine, but Inuvik?

It is January 7, 1974. It is still early in my first day here, and already I know that my former life in Montreal did not prepare me for this. For that matter, neither did the past year in Italy. I told myself that I should be able to make the transition from teaching English in a small community in the South of Italy to being the newly-minted mental health nurse in a small community, north of the Arctic Circle. After all, both are small communities. Swapping the Mediterranean Sea for the Arctic Ocean might be the bigger challenge, but the journey towards wisdom and maturity necessitates an occasional change in direction, right? Also in temperature, or so it seems. And I had been heard to say that all of us should have the strength to cope with anything for a limited period of time. Did I mean with anything, or did I mean *anywhere*?

I already know that the doomsayers who talked of six months of complete darkness are wrong. It is early afternoon and the atmosphere is one of deep dusk, not of total blackness. I've learned that my new *mukluks* are warm, although I do not yet understand how that can possibly be, since my feet are so close to the frozen snow that I can feel every pebble and ridge. I've also learned that *mukluks* are extremely slippery. I discovered this when I decided to pop into the local newsstand to pick up a copy of today's newspaper (which was actually yesterday's, as it was flown in from Edmonton on the same plane that I was on). The clerk merely smiled as I slid through the entrance and stopped only when I grabbed onto the counter. "New in town?" he asked. Then he added, "They didn't tell you that *mukluks* are slippery?"

By now I'm beginning to realize that "they" didn't tell me much of anything. Not completely accurate; "they" did bring me to Edmonton for several days of orientation, during which time I was taught to take and develop chest x-rays and to become familiar with what was known as the TB List. Was everyone in town, and perhaps in the region, positive for the bacillus? Were there not other health problems as well? Considering that I was to be the mental health nurse, I hoped there would be other problems to deal with.

There *were* other problems. The funding for the mental health position was not yet in place, so it was decided that I would join the public health unit, where a vacancy existed. My new colleagues were supportive, and we were all comfortable with the fact that my clinical experience had prepared me for visiting people in their homes, for health teaching, and for addressing the developmental needs of babies and young children. Well-baby clinic was a logical choice for me. Height, weight, growth charts, the Denver Developmental tests, and family planning were all familiar territory. If only someone had told me that when mothers talked about feeding their babies cream, they meant Carnation Milk! This was the only milk product that was consistently available at the Bay. Making formula was based on it. If someone had told me, I wouldn't have described the evils of feeding babies cream to the lovely mother of chubby, healthy, and happy twins. In 1974, the belief was that babies moved on to 2% milk, once breast-feeding had ended. Chubby babies were not in vogue; however, fresh milk was not consistently available and was very expensive, and Carnation did not yet make a 2% product. Health teaching obviously had to be tempered with reality – another missing piece of my orientation.

The recommended feeding guides did not factor in the annoyances that were a natural part of daily life. The availability of fresh and canned foods was dependent on transportation costs, ice roads, and the fact that barges arrived only during summer. The ability to make grocery lists and meal plans for a year was a valuable skill, and one soon mastered, if food costs were to be controlled. As a consumer, I grew pragmatic and learned not to cry "botulism" at the sight of every dented can on the grocery shelves. Once, I even bought Robin Hood flour two years after the contest date had expired. To this day, I still take a pragmatic view of expiry dates.

Subsequent new nurses were saved from the "cream fate" when the guidelines changed, and babies under one year were no longer to be fed 2% milk. Having the ability to learn from my mistakes, I approached the mom who told me about the cream, and I asked her why she had not challenged the advice that she so clearly knew was wrong. She told me that she recognized the lack of preparation on the part of new nurses, and that she had picked up something from me that assured her that I was one who would "make it" in the North – someone who would learn and appreciate this environment. Would that we professionals were equally as understanding!

* * *

The Inuit always seem to give outsiders a chance. Paulatuk was a small community of 110 people on the Beaufort Sea, with no regular plane service, or "sked," as regular service was known. There were no telephones, although there was a radio for emergency contact with Inuvik. There were boats for spring and

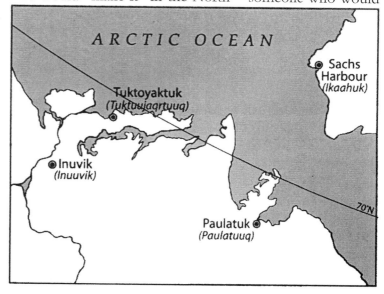

summer travel, and for fishing. Occasionally, people who wanted to leave were able to hitch a ride on a plane that had been chartered for a specific purpose; but generally, when in Paulatuk, you were there until the plane that delivered you returned, usually several days later. As well as the few families who made this community their home, there was a priest who had been with the people for more than 30 years, a teacher at the school that had recently been opened, an RCMP officer who visited periodically, a physician who visited sporadically, and a public health nurse who resided there for three days a month. I became that nurse.

Orientation consisted of instruction in the safe transport of vaccines, what emergency equipment to carry on the plane, and what food to bring. We learned that there were taps and a toilet in the nurses' trailer, although there was no water in either. Thus, I was introduced to the concept of the honey bucket, a name for an object as inappropriate as any I have heard since. I was told that dogs were strictly for work, that they were tethered on short leads when not working, and that I should be careful not to fall in the darkness, as the dogs tended to see anyone on their level as fair game. This was difficult advice since dogs are the same colour as the snow. It was a helpful part of my orientation, although it left me reluctant to leave the trailer, unless absolutely necessary. Fortunately, the invitation to join a local family for a dogteam ride brought back my spirit of adventure.

Also missing from my orientation was the fact that people in Paulatuk generally did not have a schedule to maintain. They ate when hungry, slept when tired, and visited frequently, unannounced, and for long periods of time. On my first night in the community, I made tea for visitors until close to midnight. When the last person left, I washed the cups and prepared for my first clinic at 8:30 the following morning. I worked for the government. In fact, we were all bureaucrats, and regulations stipulated that clinics begin on time. I was ready, though it was not easy to be bathed and made up at that hour, when most of the water supply had been used for the previous evening's cup washing. *No one came.* By noon, still no one had come. I became convinced that I had committed some serious cultural indiscretion and was being punished, but I had no one to ask. If I couldn't identify the problem, I certainly would have no luck in solving it; so I waited.

I needn't have worried. By late afternoon, people began to arrive, mainly moms "packing" babies on their backs, some of them in colourful Mother Hubbards, or the beautiful *amoutis* of the Eastern Arctic, but mainly in down-filled ski jackets (a size too large), and tied at the waist, to keep the child from sliding. On first impression, as they approached the trailer from a distance, these moms all appeared bent at a 45° angle and resembled little old ladies with osteoporosis.

The clinics were busy, with vaccinations, hospital follow-ups, sick kids, and post-partum moms. It was also a time to socialize. During my first visit, I worried about ethics and confidentiality, as private conversation was difficult in a small space. When I heard people sharing, at full volume, the information that I had given so quietly, I realized that confidentiality was my issue, not theirs. Then it was teatime, followed by the midnight washing of cups. For the rest of my visits to Paulatuk, the clinic operated at hours convenient for the community, although I don't think the times were ever changed officially.

* * *

I first viewed the Arctic Ocean when I was sent to relieve a vacationing nurse in Tuktoyaktuk. In the beginning, it was difficult to fathom which part of the seemingly unending expanse of white was ocean, and which was tundra. This was also my first experience of flying in a small plane, and whichever it was, ocean or tundra, it seemed uncomfortably close. It was as though we were flying low over a small city, given the number of oil rigs dotting the landscape. I had to remind myself that this busy scene, with such a density of industry and profusion of lights, was the supposedly "isolated" North.

At that time, Tuktoyaktuk could have been used as a case study of a community in transition – for it was a community in transition. Primarily Inuit, there were seasonal hunters and trappers, as well as regular wage-earners and artists – some who had made a pact with progress and created delicate birds out of antlers, so popular with visitors, quickly and with power tools. Others moved back and forth between Tuk and Sachs Harbour, trapping the white fox, then in high demand, and bringing a high price. The elderly were torn between lifestyles, sometimes able to choose aspects from both modern and traditional, and at other times, feeling disengaged from the familiar.

Later that spring, when television made its appearance, community residents became even more conscious of the discrepancy between traditional and modern life. The school was affected immediately, as kids stayed up as long as the satellite programming made its way through the time zones. It was actually possible to see *The Partridge Family* three times in one evening, because programs were shown again and again. By May, when the sun sat high in the sky all night, and the satellite that brought television revolved, kids at school slept at their desks. I was equally exhausted from sitting up all night to make sure that the 24-hour sun really was just that.

While all of the communities would ultimately be changed by development, Tuk was one of the first to be affected, due to the proximity of oil rigs and the presence of transient rig-workers who travelled from Edmonton to Inuvik, and on to Tuk. These transients brought with them their own social problems, some pre-existing, and others resulting from extended periods away from family and from long hours of work combined with the boredom of camp life. As locals joined this wage economy, they were introduced to the same stressors. Alcohol abuse increased, as did casual sexual liaisons, and violent behaviour. Teenage pregnancy had always existed; now the frequency was increasing, and families were faced with caring for the babies of young mothers, often with no additional resources. The girl-mothers were not financially independent. They lacked knowledge about child-raising and frequently dropped out of school.

Rates of sexually transmitted disease increased. The basic tools of life in the North – guns, knives, and skidoos – became instruments of unhappiness, as they were increasingly associated with accidents and death.

Tuk would not be the only community affected by development. The Mackenzie Valley Pipeline was under consideration, and it was anticipated that its effects would be far-reaching. Industrial workers would be required, and training programs would bring communities sorely needed financial benefits. However, it would create a larger pool of transient workers, both northern and Native. Extra traffic to all communities increased connections between smaller, and more isolated, communities and the larger centres. As awareness of potential social problems grew, so did the recognition that additional supports were required for the nurses in these communities.

* * *

Of the eight communities having nursing stations with resident nurses, four were staffed by a single nurse. Many of these nurses had been in the communities for several years and were comfortable in delivering public health programs in the stations, in the homes, and in the schools. All of the nurses had well-honed, acute-care clinical skills, with sharp problem-assessment and diagnostic skills. While clinic hours could be set and public health activities planned in advance, emergencies occurred, like emergencies everywhere. Women went into labour, babies became ill, accidents happened, and violence occurred on party nights (usually when a chartered plane brought in alcohol, which tended to be quickly consumed). The nurses were expected to respond to all of these situations, and they did. They were also expected to be at the airstrip to meet visitors from zone or region, as well as physicians and visiting personnel from departments such as maintenance and environmental health. They had to feed them and accommodate them at the nursing station, which was also their home. They also entertained and made coffee for transients, whether they were pilots flying medevacs, or lost or ill visitors from the South.

In the absence of veterinary support, the valued pets of friends and colleagues were also sutured and treated for a variety of ailments. A northern nurse cannot survive without a broad range of skills. In present-day jargon, multi-taskers would be an apt description. Those who roll their eyes and express chagrin about expectations not itemized in a job description have never been northern nurses. Still, they should understand that the expression "and other related duties" must have been invented with this group in mind.

What are now known as adventure tours were just beginning. These tours were expensive and appealed to people in an age group older than those who migrated to the North for life or work. They sometimes brought health problems with them and thought nothing of approaching the nursing station for assistance. The station became something of a drop-in centre. When they were not too busy or too exhausted to respond, some nurses found these interruptions of their routine refreshing, particularly when the visitor was a celebrity like Peter

Gzowski, who brought with him a genuine curiosity about how the nurses managed their lives, and who was content to sit and swap stories of life in the North.

Other CBC personnel were not so welcomed, particularly those arriving with preconceived notions that would not be budged. A popular story making the rounds in Inuvik that year was about the journalist who thought that a Japanese-Canadian schoolteacher was an Inuk and interviewed him about his presumed experience of disengagement from his culture. The teacher, heartily tired of southern experts, allowed the journalist to believe what he wanted and fed him what he wanted to hear. The interview was viewed as a success by both the journalist, who returned home with the tale of interviewing a genuine Inuk, and by the teacher, who had proven once again how gullible southern visitors were, especially those from Toronto.

* * *

By the time funding for the mental health position materialized, my orientation was complete. The diversity of problems was indeed challenging. To introduce a mental health program into small communities, where anonymity was impossible, required a creative approach. The Inuit were not concerned whether nurses or neighbours knew they were facing personal problems that required counselling. Usually, it was the transient and white group who were concerned. More than once, I was grateful that the connection with public health had been maintained, as this allowed people to come to the clinic – without being identified as having mental health problems. Sometimes even this connection was inadequate, and I learned not to feel hurt when someone would cross to the other side of the road, rather than speak to me. While I was comfortable greeting clients socially as though we were strangers, they needed to develop trust in the program, before running the risk of being known by the mental health nurse.

At first, I thought, this could become a lonely life. The permanent nurses in the communities, which were then known as settlements, faced a similar challenge. Very few people who lived where there was a single healthcare provider had the option of maintaining complete privacy. Nurses were always aware that they might be required to assume a professional role at any time, and this discouraged a few nurses from forming personal friendships. Those nurses who were able to acknowledge the potential for change in the nature of relationships, and to be comfortable with this, were the most successful – and the most likely to be happy in these small communities. For three and a half years in the Inuvik Zone, I worked with many such nurses.

In my atypical orientation, I learned that the most important thing was this: having the strength to cope with anything for a limited period should not be the goal. That proves nothing other than the ability to persevere. It teaches very little that matters in the long run. Being open to new experiences, and to the people they bring you in contact with and what you can learn from them, is what influences you and accompanies you on the next part of the journey.

Years later, when I lived and worked in Asia, I applied the lessons I had learned from living in the North. I had an occasion to contact a nurse in Iqaluit, regarding a medical emergency experienced by my son, who was a student working for the summer in the High Arctic. After she heard my queries, she remarked that I "sounded like a northern nurse." Apparently, some experiences are so significant that they leave an indelible mark.

Moira MacDougal Cameron BN, MHSc graduated from St. Martha's Hospital School of Nursing in Antigonish, Nova Scotia. She earned her BN at McGill University and her MHSc from McMaster University. She spent 9½ years in the Northwest Territories, where she lived in Inuvik and Yellowknife, and worked with both Medical Services Branch of Health Canada and the Government of the NWT. As the first mental health nurse, and later as a family life educator, she travelled to many communities throughout the Arctic. Her career includes paediatric and mental health positions in Quebec, Newfoundland, and Alberta, and consulting and teaching (nursing) positions in Iraq, Sri Lanka, and Zimbabwe. At present, Moira lives in Calgary where she is a tutor with Athabasca University. She instructs distance students from both Canada and the USA, including some from the Northwest Territories, Nunavut, and the Yukon, as well as senior baccalaureate students in the Mount Royal College-Athabasca University BN program. She also consults internationally on nursing and health care.

SO MUCH FOR TECHNOLOGY!

Barbara Hulsman

Although I have experienced frustrations and time-consuming antics with radio phones in remote regions in the North, I have also had some funny experiences. My first assignment as an outpost nurse was in Fort Franklin, a community of 300 (depending on what government group was doing the counting) on Great Bear Lake at the mouth of the Bear River. This isolated community was halfway – as the crow flies – between Inuvik to the North and Hay River to the South. Inuvik is important to this story, as it was our central medical post. Hay River, on the south shore of Great Slave Lake, was our communication base.

Fort Franklin, like many other small communities in 1969 and 1970, was sadly lacking in communication expertise, especially when you consider that NASA was about to launch a man to the moon. It was the only settlement with permanent nursing staff in the Inuvik Zone that had to use a radio to reach the outside world. The nurses had one of two government two-way radios that were capable of connecting with the outside. The other radios were hams. The Catholic priest had one for keeping in touch with other priests in the area, and for the Native people to chat with their relatives in other communities. The Hudson's Bay Company store and the local airway service had private ham radios, and the band administrator had an NWT one that was solely for the band's use.

Having these radios was great, but seldom did they all work. On any given day, at least one radio was out, and if the weather over the lake was iffy, then none of them worked. Standing on the roof with a bullhorn would have been more effective than trying to relay messages out to our home office. We nurses had to radio south to be connected to the microwave telephone service, north and south of us. So, from Fort Franklin, you radioed to Hay River to be connected to Inuvik, Fort Norman, Fort Good Hope, and so on. Most of the time, it was an impossible task. For reasons of confidentiality, names were not mentioned. Anyone with a $19.95 battery radio could pick up conversations, if the radio had a copper-wire aerial. There was no such thing as privacy in that service.

We had a local community telephone system that was just slightly better than a string between two tin cans – but it was workable. Only the chosen few had a telephone: the Bay store and residence, the priest's house/post office, the band administration office, the administrator's home, and the government school. The local co-op store and residence were connected, as was the local airways service home/office. If we nurses called in an airplane for the evacuation of a patient, people would show up on our doorstep, looking for a ride or asking us to send a parcel out – before we had a chance to close the radio off and get up from the chair. That was called rapid moccasin telegraph.

Needless to say, this was my first encounter with radio communication. The charge nurse was reluctant to relinquish her knowledge of how to use it, so I had to resort to devious means in order to familiarize myself with it. I enlisted the help of the local pilot's wife, when we were alone. The charge nurse was a Dutch lady with northern experience who had not lost her thick accent. When she became excited, even I had difficulty understanding what she was attempting to get across to the listener. If the radio signals were poor, her accent became more pronounced, and her voice rose to the high notes of a screaming match between her and the person at the radio depot in Hay River. On one occasion, I tried to intervene. Big mistake! She was not impressed and told me so. Eventually, she allowed me to take care of radio communications whenever the signals were poor.

Once when she was out for the afternoon home visiting in the community, and I was on duty at the station waiting for the next great emergency, I received a message from the head office of the Hudson's Bay Company. Unfortunately for me, the local store's radio was out and my radio signal was weak. One hour later, I was able to take this confusing message (that was a page long) to the Bay manager. I was sure that I was crazy and that someone had played a joke on me. Each word had to be spelled out to me. For example, alpha for "a", bravo for "b", and so on. The part about the fox jumping up 30 feet and the bear down 20 made absolutely no sense to me. I didn't understand until the Bay manager informed me that this was the price list for the furs he was buying for the company from the local trappers. Everything was in code for their protection from the competition. All I got for my efforts was a thanks, not even, "Sorry we had to bother you."

* * *

The payoff for me came on Grey Cup day. I was on call, so I couldn't join the teachers who were planning to listen to the game. The teachers' am/fm radio picked up signals in Canada. Ours was fancy. We got the BBC in London, England. We also got Moscow and sometimes Calgary, but never, ever Yellowknife, Inuvik, or Edmonton. The Ottawa Rough Riders were playing the Saskatchewan Rough Riders. I was the only easterner in town; all the teachers who were native-born Canadians came from the West. The bragging nonsense was necessary for self-preservation. The game fell on the same day that NASA was to put a man on the moon. Since I was not able to leave the nursing station (boss's rule), I waited for a reasonable length of time before I radioed the Hay River depot. First of all, I wanted to find out who had won the football game, and secondly, I wanted to hear if NASA had been successful in landing a man on the moon. With much repetition and the frustration of at least fifteen minutes of spelling and muttering on my part, the operator finally understood what I wanted. She asked me to hold. After a long, long delay (minus the elevator music), she returned my call, only to inform me that, for administrative reasons, she could not pass that information on to me.

It was three days before the teachers finally admitted to me who had won the Grey Cup. As for news about the moon landing, I had to wait for a pilot to tell me about that. So much for technology!

Barb Hulsman RN, PHN was born and educated in eastern Ontario. She earned her RN from Peterborough Civic Hospital in 1959. After working in hospital settings until 1969, she moved to the western Arctic. From 1973 to 1974, she attended Dalhousie University, where she completed the public health nurse program. She returned north to the mid-Arctic and worked out of Yellowknife. In 1976, she went back to Ontario and worked at the Wikwemikong Health Unit on Manitoulin Island. From 1978 to 1981, she was the Zone Nursing Officer in Sioux Lookout. She spent six months in Fort Resolution, NWT and then returned to Manitoulin Island where she stayed until 1984. Soon after, she moved to London, Ontario to work in occupational health nursing with the federal government. Barb retired in 1998 and enjoys good health.

REBEL SPIRITS SPEAK

Pat Nichols

In the late 1960s and early 1970s, I lived and nursed in one of the larger settlements in northern Canada. For five days each month, I flew into a small First Nations village to provide community health services and to relieve the lay dispenser by providing minor treatment and arranging medical evacuations.

Normally, I stayed in the small two-room health station and, on occasion, I stayed with a couple of teachers. I frequently visited some hippies I had befriended. One day in late February, I was delivered to the landing strip by the regular two-person-plus-pilot aircraft, which sometimes carried more people and a lot of freight, depending on the need. I walked to the health station where I found out the power was off, and it was very cold. I discovered that the teachers and my hippie friends were away. Now what? An Aboriginal mother who lived in a three-room shack with her six children suggested that I spend the night in the Big House. That was the name given by the local people to a large empty mansion in the settlement, which had never been lived in.

The Big House had been built by a prospector who had come from the South looking for gold. From what I'd been told, he had taken full advantage of the Aboriginal peoples' knowledge of the land and their expertise in travelling through remote areas of the country. But he had been negligent in compensating them fairly for their services. The prospector was successful in finding gold. He developed a mine and became wealthy. Local legend has it that he built the mansion to keep his wife from leaving the little village, where she did not like the isolation, and the lack of modern conveniences and "elite" entertainment. However, the beautiful, big house was not enough to change her mind, and she moved to a southern city, leaving her prospector husband behind.

It was a wintry afternoon. With my sleeping bag and a sandwich, I trekked over to the Big House. Since it now served as the location for the school noon-lunch program, it was unlocked. I climbed the stairs where I found a large, clean, and empty room that likely would have been the master bedroom. Fortunately, I was able to turn up the heat, as it was kept on because of the lunch program. Unfortunately, the water was not, so I realized it would be necessary to use a small tin can for certain purposes. I spread my sleeping bag on the bare wooden floor and sat down. I ate my sandwich and did some homework. Soon I decided to make it an early night. I got into my warm flannel pyjamas and wrapped myself in my sleeping bag.

I had been sleeping soundly for about two hours, when I was awakened by strange noises. The room I was in had an empty fireplace, and it was from there that the hideous sounds were coming. At first, I was not alarmed by the screeching, howling, and whining noises, because I thought the teachers had returned and were trying to give me a good scare before inviting me to go to their place. However, the noises became louder. They were intense, prolonged, and frightening. Then I heard footsteps crunching in the crisp, cold snow. If this was a joke, it had gone far enough.

I dressed quickly, ran downstairs and out the door. I saw no one and I found no trace of footprints in the snow. I started walking down the village road, not knowing where I was going, but relieved to be out of that "haunted" house. It was about eleven o'clock. The night was beautiful and calm, except for the dancing northern lights which I could hear clearly in the silence. These were normal sights and sounds in small northern communities. It was so peaceful I almost forgot the sounds of the "ghosts."

Just then, the lone RCMP constable in the village drove up in his truck. Someone had called to tell him that the nurse was walking down the road alone at night. When I told him my story, he offered to take me back to his place. He promised he would check out the Big House with me in the morning. For the rest of the night, I slept soundly in the cozy little shack, secure in the protection of the kind, young constable. He probably didn't sleep as well, knowing that under his roof he had a weird northern nurse who thought she heard ghosts. In the morning, we returned to the Big House to gather my belongings. I felt more secure, but I noticed that my guardian was taking the stairs very quietly, cautiously looking from side to side out of the corner of his eyes. He, too, seemed uncertain. But we heard no sounds that morning.

A few years later, I met the prospector who had built the Big House. When I told him what had happened, he assured me his house was *not* haunted. But he wasn't there that February night, and he didn't hear those sounds. More years passed, and a prominent white member of the community shot the prospector in a bar. It was believed that he resented the prospector's financial success, which he achieved from the time and the effort of the members of the community, without giving them satisfactory compensation or recognition.

At the time this frightening incident happened to me, the way of life and the beliefs of the local people were the same as they had been historically for the majority of indigenous people in North America. They continued to live their lives in touch with their environment and close to the spirits of the natural world. The reason for this attitude was the matriarchal leadership of the settlement. One Native woman in particular, a person with great leadership qualities, had a strong influence on the young people, many of whom are still living there and practising her sacred teachings. To the people of the village, my experience that winter night did not seem out of the ordinary and caused little comment.

FIRST NURSE IN PANGNIRTUNG

Pat Nichols

It was in 1934 that Elsie (McEwen) McKinnon RN and her husband, Dr. Alex McKinnon, travelled on a freight boat to Pangnirtung on Baffin Island in the Northwest Territories. They undertook this adventure because of an urgent request from the Anglican Church, which had a missionary in this settlement and realized the need for medical and nursing care in Pangnirtung. When the McKinnons left Montreal, they knew that their stay in this community would last for at least two years, as these freight boats travelled to the northern communities only every two years.

When they arrived in Pangnirtung, they found many of the residents very ill with what appeared to be diphtheria. Several people had died prior to their arrival. Within a few weeks, they had the epidemic under control, but they had lost a few of the very young and the very old.

The McKinnon's 1929 projector and forty-nine thick glass slides, which showed their time in Pang, are now available for viewing in the Angmarlik Visitor Centre in Pangnirtung. These treasures were left to me by Elsie's niece, following her death. I kept them for several years, but always felt they should be returned to the place of their origin. In April, 2000, a close friend of Paul Okalik, the Premier of Nunavut, transported the projector and the slides from my home in Saskatchewan to Iqaluit. There, he presented them to Okalik, who then carried them on to Pangnirtung (which was his birthplace) where he viewed them with the elders of the community. Also hanging in the Pang Visitor Centre are a letter of farewell and a tribute from the McKinnons to the Eskimos of Pangnirtung, along with a picture of the McKinnons. A visiting nurse had delivered them a few years earlier.

I was familiar with Pangnirtung, where Elsie had been the first nurse. In the mid-1970s, I spent three short weeks there, assisting with the Community Health Representative training program. This was a valuable experience – with interesting, wonderful people – and in a beautiful setting.

Pat Nichols RN, DPH, BScN received her nursing training at the Grey Nuns Hospital in Regina, Saskatchewan. She obtained both her Diploma in Public Health and her Bachelor of Science in Nursing at the University of Saskatchewan, in Saskatoon. Pat spent thirty years with Indian and Northern Health in Saskatchewan, the Yukon, the Northwest Territories, and British Columbia, in positions of hospital nurse, community health nurse, zone nursing officer, and regional nursing officer.

INSTITUTIONAL NURSING IN THE NWT, 1947 - 1978

Sister Marie Lemire

With a nursing diploma in my luggage, I arrived at Aklavik in the Northwest Territories in July 1947. Having dedicated my life in the Order of the Sisters of Charity of Montreal, the "Grey Nuns," my religious and spiritual formation had been well-initiated. My first assignment was to be the director of nursing services at Immaculate Conception Hospital in Aklavik. I was twenty-four years old.

The Journey

The long journey to Aklavik started by train in Montreal, with stopover nights first in St. Boniface, Manitoba and then in Saskatoon, Saskatchewan, with a longer stay in Edmonton, Alberta. These were all cities where the Grey Nuns operated hospitals. The 2000 mile journey across Canada by train opened up for me the vastness of the Canadian West. Memories of those three days are still alive. But I will not linger now on this first trip for me outside of Montreal — except for going to Ottawa. Leaving Edmonton, I was northbound en route to Fort McMurray, Alberta, and then on to Fort Smith, which is close to the southern boundary of the Northwest Territories, and was its headquarters. I was met by my Grey Nun Sisters, whose Provincial House for that diocese was also located there.

Thus began a year of orientation and further religious formation. Through my own reading prior to going to Aklavik, I had learned that it was the most northern post of the Grey Nuns and that the hospital had opened in 1925. I knew that there would be periods of darkness and extremely cold temperatures. I would soon realize that my knowledge was far from adequate to help me face the realities that awaited me at "the top of the world."

The last leg of the voyage was done in a boat called St. Anna, which was operated by the diocese of Fort Smith. It was used mainly for the transportation of goods, food supplies, gas, and travellers. The sisters were given a somewhat exclusive, comfortable cabin.

After leaving Fort Smith, another ten days took me along the winding Slave River to Fort Resolution, on the magnificent Great Slave Lake. The lake could be calm with a far horizon, but it could also be quite menacing when wind and storm literally rocked the boat — and rock it did for two days. We visited Fort Resolution on the south shore of the lake. After a full day, we entered the Mackenzie River and soon arrived at Fort Providence, which was the first mission of the Grey Nuns. They had arrived from St. Boniface in 1867, after 77 days of travelling over land and by water in canoes, to minister to the sick and dispense medication, and to provide nursing services and education.

In early July, after navigating in good weather, we stopped at Fort Simpson where I found an impressive, active hospital staffed by nine sisters. Continuing along the quiet Mackenzie, we passed the Ramparts, the geological marvels of the Rocky Mountains, and went around the rapids. Crossing over the 66th parallel, we reached Fort Good Hope. Finally, after 250 miles, we reached Aklavik on the shore of the Peel River, and our boat was anchored in front of the Immaculate Conception Hospital. People from the community came out to the river banks to greet newcomers and friends, and to welcome visitors. As we approached, I could see the sisters, the Inuit in their traditional garb, and other Native peoples.

The missionary priests, the Oblates of Mary Immaculate, had pleaded with the Grey Nuns' Superior General to send sisters to care for the sick and needy in Aklavik. In the early nineteenth century, the Episcopal Corporation in Fort Smith confirmed a mandate to educate the people of Aklavik, and to provide them with health care on an outpatient basis and through home visiting. As pioneers in the North, the Grey Nuns lived in dire circumstances. By the time I arrived in 1947, there was a hospital, and the North now offered better living conditions, with protection against cold weather. The food, although not varied, was food nevertheless. The hospital proved to be a shock for a young graduate from Notre Dame Hospital, the best hospital with its school of nursing in Montreal, or so I believed. But let me tell you, very humbly, that I survived.

A Long Orientation

My orientation here would last at least a full year, from one summer to the next, for everything in a remote community like Aklavik happened during the open-water period. For the rest of the year, you either lived in the aftermath of the arrival of the boats or, after eight months of snow and ice, you waited with a strong desire for the ice to move down river, in anticipation of the coming boats. Open water brought the excitement of visitors from various companies and organizations with their summer staff of professors and researchers. They were all intrigued by the place (and this was, I hoped, for economic reasons). Around early September, the shores showed the beginning of the icing period. By October, the water route was closed off until June of the following year. During freeze-up, except for the wireless, communication with the outside world by mail, or otherwise, was paralyzed.

In the far North, the days of autumn rapidly become shorter until the end of December. However, above the 66th parallel, total darkness sets in for a full month, beginning with the first days of December and lasting until the second week of January. The return of the sun helped us during the cold days of January because we knew we were heading towards spring. During the coming months, we drew on our inner strength as we anticipated the breakup of the floor of ice which was eight to twelve feet thick. This would allow the Peel River to flow again.

Once Easter was over, I experienced the excitement and emotions of the return of spring. At the end of May, or in early June, the sun shone for about 18 hours a day and the water level of the Peel River rose slowly, but steadily. In May, all the snow melted in seven or eight days, although the ice carpet of the river stayed unchanged and kept the temperature chilly – in spite of the wonderful sun. Ice edges broke loose and remained along the river banks. I remember hearing an unexpected crashing noise, followed by delighted shouts from the patients. Breakup announced our survival of another year. It was my first breakup and what a scene!

Mission Hospital

In 1947, the Aklavik Immaculate Conception Hospital (which has since been demolished) was a 32-bed hospital accommodating 24 to 28 patients of all ages, who required long-term hospitalization for tuberculosis. The other beds were for acute, paediatric, and obstetric patients. There was another hospital in Aklavik, on the Anglican mission grounds. One medical doctor attended both hospitals, as well as serving as the Indian Agent. This agent was a liaison between the federal government of Canada and the Native populations of the area.

The head nurse was the only registered nurse on the day shift; one semi-retired nurse was on duty during the night. The services offered in the hospital included admitting procedures and office work. There was a laboratory, an operating/delivery room and a small radiology unit for diagnostics. TB follow-up was provided for both outpatients and inpatients.

There were ordinary nursing activities, with shifts from 7:30 a.m. to 8:00 p.m. and a rest time in the early afternoon. This rest period, which lasted from 1:00 to 3:00 p.m., was of utmost importance for the recuperation and healing of the TB patients. Silence was observed to allow time for everyone to nap. I was assisted by two other sisters of my community, who were gifted with tremendous kindness and a readiness to serve. Hospital managerial activities were part of the nurse's duties, which is characteristic of small hospital administration in the North. Lay staff were not only of very great assistance for housekeeping, but also for their ability to interpret for our patients. In selecting our personnel, we ensured the presence of representatives of the different Native peoples.

All hospital personnel were expected to help in the fight against tuberculosis which was widespread. The new treatment of TB patients with powerful antibiotics showed good results and hopes were high. Sterile technique was mandatory. This also applied to the 140 or so children present in the adjacent boarding school. A total inspection was done upon their arrival. This included taking their afternoon temperatures (for 15 days) and a chest x-ray. At the time of the annual influenza, each child was watched closely by the hospital staff.

Institutional nursing in isolated areas in the Northwest Territories after World War II was profoundly different from the health care available in large urban areas. This was particularly the case regarding acutely ill patients who required a medical consultation or an examination by a specialist. Transportation to services in the South had to be arranged according to when a plane was available. In our northern hospitals, there was a critical need for more medical and nursing personnel, better equipment, and especially the promotion of nursing education among the Native peoples.

Fortunately, the situation has changed. All areas of healthcare services have shown great signs of improvement. We now have access to outside laboratories, which is facilitated by regularly scheduled planes. Health insurance has improved the financial situation of the hospitals, allowing them to hire lay nurses at competitive salaries. Professional associations for nursing and administrative personnel have been encouraged. Responsibility for the detection, control, and treatment of tuberculosis across the NWT has been transferred to a well-equipped team. The installation and development of the public health station has been a welcome service that has decreased hospital work and encouraged home nursing care.

Nursing Aides

The Rector of the Roman Catholic Mission in Aklavik, Father Sylvio Lesage OMI, asked the Grey Nuns if they would consider setting up a school for nursing aides. He had watched the young girls with nothing to do after completing their grade 8. The idea seemed to be an answer to this teenage situation. This implied the need for space, personnel (already short), sleeping accommodations, and a program. The Grey Nuns provincial council gave it serious consideration and the Department of Education of the NWT put up the funds to get it started.

In 1953, my superior consulted me about the nursing aide project. I was returning from holidays in Montreal and had a stopover in Fort Smith. I was enthusiastic about the idea and was put in charge of this project. It was September 14, and I asked, in my naïveté, "When is this project expected to take shape?" I hoped that she would say, "Next January." Her answer was clear – "In a week or so." My heart skipped two beats. I liked teaching very much, but I equally liked to be well-prepared.

In fifteen days, the empty storage room was painted, a blackboard was installed and a skeleton was hung at the back of the classroom. With a bed and dummy, we were ready to begin. Three other RNs in Fort Smith agreed to give one lecture each per week. I visited with the director at the Nursing Aide School in Calgary to learn about their program. This was a great help.

At last, the program was set up, with a daily balance between lectures and technical practice. The first students were four Indian and two Eskimo girls. They attended classes and worked well. They were dynamic, happy, and successful; their final exams confirmed it. In June the following year, there was a graduation day with white uniforms, caps, medals, and flowers as part of the ceremony. Their graduation was their first public recognition. These nursing aides served in various hospitals in NWT and were greatly appreciated.

The program at St. Ann's Hospital in Fort Smith lasted four years, enough time to convince the Department of Education that the northern students were able to pursue certain careers, provided they received proper preparation. A few years later, the same department re-introduced the one-year Nursing Aide course as part of the vocational training program. The teacher was Sister Julienne Chaillé, another Grey Nun. I was by then at the Fort Simpson Hospital as Director of Nursing and Hospital Management.

Reminiscing

I will recount just a few of the many memories that are dear to me from my time in Aklavik. Learning English was a prime necessity for me. After barely two weeks in Aklavik, Dr. Harvey asked me, "You flew in?" All I could translate was influenza, so I replied, "I have no flu!" When I saw a gentle smile on his face, I realized he had used the past tense of a verb, and I gave a better response.

Years ago, x-rays were often requested. I remember the time a pregnant woman arrived at the hospital from the bush, and an x-ray revealed that she was soon to give birth to twins. As the interpreter explained the coming events to her, she appeared quite surprised. But when the reality of it hit her, she burst out laughing. The doctor and I were perplexed, until the translator told us that she had said, "So funny. I have only one man. I got two babies!"

At the hospital, social life for patients was well-organized, and Christmas time was a peak event. Being short of decorations, we used tin cans which were cut into narrow strips, twisted gently, threaded, and hung as icicles. Even though we used only 25-watt light bulbs, the icicles sparkled and looked genuine. Christmas stockings were the beginning of the fun activities. Early one Christmas morning, I heard a child crying. I was taken aback because everyone else was delighted. Pointing her little finger as she showed me her Christmas stocking, the five-year-old told me, "I have only one side."

Conclusion

This is but a brief account of my thirty-one years in the Northwest Territories. Since I first arrived in Aklavik, living, working, and travelling conditions have greatly improved, and the level of health care there is the same as in other small Canadian hospitals. The Territorial Government has taken over delivery of care on all fronts, and the Grey Nuns have completed their volunteer duties. Mission accomplished!

Sister Marie Lemire OC, SGM, RN graduated in 1947 from the Notre Dame School of Nursing in Montreal, Quebec. Her first assignment as a new graduate was to be the director of nursing at the hospital in Aklavik. She served in the North for thirty-one years. In October 1969, Sr. Lemire became an Officer of the Order of Canada: *"For her dedication as a nurse among the inhabitants of Canada's Far North."* In 1977, she was honoured with the Commemorative Medal on the occasion of the Silver Jubilee of the Coronation of Queen Elizabeth II. In October 2002, Sr. Lemire received the Golden Jubilee Medal of Queen Elizabeth II from the Honourable Lise Thibault, Lieutenant Governor of Quebec.

LETTERS TO ALICE

Marie Skov

Introduction by Anne H. Wieler

When Marie Skov wrote these letters to Alice Smith, Marie was the nurse in charge at Little Grand Rapids Nursing Station, and later, the public health nurse in Berens River, both geographically isolated Aboriginal reserves in Manitoba. Alice Smith was the first Chief Nursing Consultant with Indian Health Services (later Indian and Northern Health Services, and, still later, the Medical Services Branch of Health Canada). Alice and Marie both attended nearby universities in the USA in 1957, and they had a mutual friend and colleague, Dr. Verna Huffman Splane. During this time, Marie applied and was accepted for a nursing position in Manitoba. Subsequently, Alice and Marie became friends – a friendship which endured for many decades.

Marie's letters, written between 1959 and 1961, illustrate the multi-faceted role of the nurse in a nursing station (Little Grand Rapids), the challenge of introducing preventive, non-treatment programs to a community (Berens River), not only to the resident population, but to the other health professionals as well. What also emerges through these letters is the support, both professional and personal, that Alice Smith, in faraway Ottawa, extended to the field staff. Alice was a major force behind the development and success of Canada's Indian and Northern Health Services. Her sincere and constant interest, and her concern for the well-being of all the nurses in the Branch, was widely recognized and deeply appreciated. I feel qualified to say this, because, as a newly-graduated nurse with the Branch in 1954, and until retirement in 1992, I was and still am privileged and proud to count both Alice and Marie as mentors and very special friends.

Anne H. Wieler RN, BN, MPH has worked in several nursing stations and health centres in northern communities and has held various senior positions in Medical Services Branch Headquarters in Ottawa. She was seconded to the "Human Resources for Health" Directorate of the World Health Organization in Geneva, Switzerland and later joined the Canadian Public Health Association's International Health Secretariat on a three-year exchange.

Dear Alice:

Thank you very much for your Christmas card and the colour print. Yes, those were good days that I spent in Ottawa a long time ago. I just love that city. It has been quite a life at Little Grand for the last couple of months, and my personal "batteries" are running a little low. (I borrowed that from J.F. Dulles.)

I finally got tired of my caretaker and fired him. He stayed away drunk for five days, and that was the last straw. One Saturday night, I had a hint that he would not show up to look after our generator plant, so I set my alarm clock for 2 a.m. At 1 a.m., I woke up and realized that the plant had stopped. I marched outside. It was 40 below zero, and the fuel drum was empty – as I thought it would be. Have you ever opened a 45-gallon drum in deep snow, at one o'clock in the morning – in subzero temperatures? Neither had I. If I had not been so mad, I would never have gotten it open. Back in the powerhouse, the diesel generator was getting cold, and it refused to start. I turned different screws and "bled" the ...... thing. Finally it started, but now it ran completely wild, with sparks flying everywhere, and I could not find the screwdriver to stop the "bleeding." Eventually, I found it on the floor. I fixed the motor and got it running smoothly, but what I looked like after that, I will not tell you.

The next day, I hired two men to collect the empty drums for the tractor train and to bring in some wood. The rest I could do myself. The day after that, Dr. Gregory arrived to hold clinic, the tractor train came with 22 drums of oil and took back the empty ones, and the diesel generator was due for a change of oil. My, did I ever long to sit quietly in a concert hall and listen to a Beethoven concert – but that was not possible. I gave the caretaker a chance to come and speak to me, but he didn't show up, so I hired another – the only one on the reserve (and outside) who does not drink. He speaks fairly good English and is willing to work. I have only had him for about two weeks and find that he is not very handy with tools. This afternoon, we were to clean the chimney pipes, and I had to show him how to take them apart and put them back together again.

After this story, you may think that I have forgotten all about patients and public health. This is not quite so. During all of this, I had patients on the ward (at one time, there were three). Home visits have been put off as much as possible. I have been expecting the nurse from England on every plane landing here since February 1, as I was informed she was on her way. On February 20, I called the Winnipeg office and was told that I could expect her in the last half of March. When she has been here for a little while, I will try to get out for a week or so. It may do me and my work some good.

I still hope to be able to go down to Teachers College next January. By that time, I should have around $4000 saved (including about $600 for two months' vacation). It will not be enough; however, by doing odd jobs, I hope to be able to earn at least enough for my room, preferably in International House. T.C. prefers that students start in September, but that is out of the question. I hope they will understand.

Lately, we have had very nice weather. The sun is shining and the snow is melting. We hung our laundry outside yesterday, and it partly dried. I am looking forward to getting the new record system going when the nurse comes up. Since I work on my own here, there is not much time, or peace, for such things.

At the moment, I have a patient on the ward who last year swallowed a spoon at home (the only one they had). Later, she tried to strangle herself on the ward and was shipped out by Dr. Van den Berg. Last Thursday, when she was brought in with a bad cough and chest-pain, I had hoped that Dr. Gregory would take her out. But no, she was prescribed phenobarb to calm her down and whatever else my common sense tells me to give her. I keep track of my spoons, however. It is rather inconvenient to have her here.

I will go to bed now, as my patient is asleep. I hope to see you sometime soon, if not before I go out, then when I do. My best to Verna.

Love,

Marie

Dear Alice:

Thank you very much for your letter, which I received shortly before freeze-up. We are still cut off from the outside world, but hope for a plane next week. I am sorry I have not thanked you properly for the day I spent with you in the office, and in your beautiful home, even though I appreciated so much being with you. Thank you, and please forgive my tardiness.

I have now been in Berens River for two months and have not even scratched the surface of public health. Right from the start, I have been drowned by treatments and home visits to patients. Home visits to the healthy (such as newborns) happen whenever I have time.

The number of cases of diarrhea has been overwhelming. Water levels in the river have been unusually low this year. Often I have found more mud than water in the pail. Getting the population to strain and boil water (or otherwise purify it) every day has proved to be rather impossible, despite my efforts. Countless times, I have gotten fires going and water boiling, while I treated a patient – sometimes scolding the family, sometimes pleading with them to boil the water. After that, the water would be all right for a couple of days, or weeks, and I again would be called to look after another case of diarrhea in the house. I did send water samples for examination, but I never received a report, and I did not press for any, as the cause of the diarrhea was too obvious.

There is one case of "diarrhea" I have to tell you about. I was called out at one o'clock in the morning. An elderly lady came to the door and told me her daughter, Victoria, was very ill. I asked if it was diarrhea, and she confirmed it. Furthermore, her daughter was pregnant and in her seventh month. I took my black bag, and we trailed off along the river to her home, a mile and a half away. When we arrived, the daughter was lying on the bed, complaining of stomach cramps. Her temperature was normal. She told me she was "in seventy month." Since she was pregnant, I could not risk treating her at home. After examining her, I sent one of the neighbours (in cases like this, there are always lots of them around, even after midnight) to get the caretaker and our boat, so we could take her to the nursing station.

In the meantime, Victoria put on some clothing, including a parka and rubber boots. She seemed calm and collected, with no discomfort – until she started to go out to the boat. As she reached the door, she suddenly bent over with stomach cramps and threw herself on the bed. I asked her, in a rather stern voice, to calm herself and get down to the boat. First, however, I examined her, and it is fortunate that I did, because two minutes later we had a beautiful baby, not seven months, but a full nine. Victoria was still in her parka…. That was the most normal delivery I have ever attended. I sent the caretaker to the health centre to get my maternity bag, and an hour later, we left the patient in her home, comfortable, with the baby in her arms. The next day, they were both brought to the nursing station for a couple of days. I am afraid that I am not a good diagnostician.

After the river froze up, the diarrhea tapered off. Now, it is time for respiratory infections. Another serious problem that I have had to deal with has been skin conditions. I have never seen anything like it. Children are literally covered with sores from head to foot. Some of them I have treated on site; some I have sent to the nursing station. The lack of understanding of the infectious nature of these skin diseases, and the fact that people tend not to be overly concerned about them, makes these conditions difficult to treat.

This morning, I went to see a patient with, what I thought was, pneumonia. She had been in the nursing station for three days, and she refused to go back there. I asked her what she had had for breakfast (it was 11 a.m.), and she said she had not eaten anything yet – as there was nothing to eat in the house. There were three little children around her bed. Her husband had gone to his traplines. I walked over to her parents, who live a hundred yards away, and urged her mother to make some porridge. I took the boiling pot, sugar, and milk back to my patient. I waited until she and the children had eaten, and then I sent the oldest girl back with the pot. I am almost sure that the grandmother now looks after them.

Dec. 3, 1961

So far, I have had the best co-operation with the sisters at the nursing station, although I have to be a diplomat, and I work very slowly to get some of my "new" ideas incorporated there. Some of their methods I do not approve of, and they may have the same opinion about some of mine. As time goes by, I hope that, together, we can improve the health condition on this reserve, for it is badly needed.

I remember one night when I was called to see a patient. I did not know where she lived, so I went first to Stan the caretaker's place. Not finding him at home, I continued on my own, to the place where I had been told the patient lived. It was a cold night. The bush trail was snow-covered, and the moonlight shone through the trees. The wind whistled in the dry grass, and dogs (or were they wolves?) howled in the distance. As I passed a cabin on my way, I saw a man leave, unsteady on his feet, heading towards the neighbours – probably to continue some kind of celebration. I knew the family and the house; I knew that it was dirty and neglected, and that it was the same for the little one-and-a-half year old girl, who was the only one left of their three children. No light came from the house, but behind the window, I could see a woman standing and I could hear her singing a weird song in the night. The whole thing was so very sad. I could have cried right there on the path. I eventually found my patient at the end of the trail.

She had a badly swollen hip, caused by a number of infected sores on her buttocks. It took a week for her to recover.

I am grateful every day that I am allowed to experience this life. One can be mad at it or laugh at it, be sorrowful over failures, and exhilarated over victories. It all adds to the sparkling mosaic of this life. A life, which is rich in colors, both bright and dark, but great in its effect, when one looks back.

Dec. 10, 1961

I have not yet had any regular clinics, such as well-baby or prenatal. I feel that I first have to know the people and their homes, before I can give them intelligent guidance in a clinic. It will take time before they get used to coming here when they "are not sick." As it is now, I have to be satisfied when they come with their children on the days that they feel like it. I have to get used to prenatals showing up the day *after* I have asked them to come. And I know that I will not see them again until I go and ask them, yet another time, to come back to see me. It is a slow procedure, but it may work out well in the end.

This has been a letter long in the making. Christmas is not too far off, so I will end my epistle by wishing you a blessed Christmas and a happy New Year. Thank you so much for the year gone by.

Sincerely yours,

Marie

Marie Skov RN, BScN, MPH(A) was born in Denmark on February 16, 1914. She graduated as a nurse in Sonderborg in 1938, and later earned a diploma in Public Health Nursing. She came to Canada in 1955. In 1961, she completed her BScN at Columbia University in New York City. In 1967, she earned her Masters in Public Health Administration at the University of California in Los Angeles. When she retired from Health Canada in 1975, she returned home to Denmark.

Editors' note: Marie informs us that she borrows at least one book in English every week, in order to keep up her English skills.

NURSING ON THE HIGH SEAS

J. Karen Scott

Northern nurses have always been in high demand for nursing aboard ships. I had worked in remote areas in Canada's North. Since I had my degree in nursing and I had attended one of the early versions of the nurse practitioner courses in Toronto, I qualified for the position of Chief Medical Officer aboard the Canadian Scientific Ship Hudson. M.J. (Bunny) Hayman, who was the Regional Occupational Health Nurse for the Atlantic Region of Health Canada, had been looking for northern nurses. The Hudson and the Canadian Coast Guard ships were basically isolated posts because they were seldom in port with access to medical support.

Good nursing skills and sound medical judgment were essential; otherwise, the ship might have to be diverted to a port for hospital care for a single ailing crew member. This would result in the loss of valuable ship's time. Being able to sort through a problem on your own, knowing how to take a medical history, and being capable of providing immediate first aid would buy you time to assess whether or not you had a major or a minor problem to deal with.

If you have worked in the North, you know what it's like to be on duty, or on call, 24 hours a day. That is what is expected of nurses at sea, because you are often the only medical person aboard. You understand the importance of knowing how to find what you need in medical reference texts and of always being ready, in the event of an accident or an illness.

My most exciting season aboard the Hudson was a trip around the North American continent. During our nine month trip, we would log more than 34,000 nautical miles (approximately 38,700 road miles) – or one and half times around the equator. The ship's scientific computers used a modified form of Julian date in which the days of a particular year are numbered continuously from 1 to 365. They also used Greenwich Mean Time which was necessary to avoid confusion, since the ship travelled through many times zones. Some scientists wore two watches: one with computer time, and one with ship time.

Julian Day 40 – 106: February 9 to April 16, 1981

I met the Hudson in Sorel, Quebec, at the start of my third season on the ship. It was during the ship's last week of refit, in preparation for her circumnavigation of the North American continent. She was being reconfigured to carry special hydrographic launches that were needed for the Beaufort Sea phase of the cruise: the main purpose of this adventure. Because of ice conditions, ships could get into the Beaufort earlier from the West and could leave later going east, which allowed for more working time. This was the reason for taking the long route to the Beaufort.

The Hudson, a diesel-electric driven ship, is used for multidisciplinary oceanographic and hydrographic research work. Built in 1963, she has a Lloyd's Ice Class 1 hull. Her length is 90.4 m overall, with a 6.3 m maximum draft. She has a full speed of 17 knots and a cruising speed of 13 knots. There are four permanent laboratories aboard and two computer system rooms. She also has a hanger and a helicopter landing deck.

For this trip around North America, the ship's time was to be divided into three sections. The first was the East Coast (from Dartmouth to Puntarenas, Costa Rica), with the chief scientists coming from the Bedford Institute of Oceanography (BIO). The second or West Coast section (from Puntarenas to Resolute Bay in the Northwest Territories) was divided into two phases. During the southern leg, the scientists based at the Institute of Ocean Sciences (IOS) in Sidney, on Vancouver Island, would conduct oceanographic, geological, and geophysical studies. The primary mission of the northern phase of the West Coast section was to conduct a hydrographic survey in the Beaufort Sea, with a full complement of hydrographers and a specialized crew coming from the IOS. The final section of the circumnavigation brought back the East Coast scientists from BIO, as we travelled from Resolute Bay back to the Hudson's home base in Dartmouth, Nova Scotia.

* * *

From the dockyard in Sorel, Quebec, we travelled down the St. Lawrence, through the ice flows, past Quebec City, en route to the Bedford Institute of Oceanography in Dartmouth. As the scientists on the ship were not yet working, I felt more like a tourist than an on-duty nurse, which I would be for the entire voyage once we left BIO. From the ship's deck, I shot about 30 frames of the activities of the Quebec Winter Carnival and the spectacular scenery along the St. Lawrence, only to realize I had no film in the camera. Lesson learned early.

At the Bedford Institute, there was more than the usually frantic week in port, in preparation for a trip. All the West Coast oceanographic equipment had to be loaded into the forward hold, for use after the stop in Costa Rica. While this was going on, the BIO scientists loaded their scientific equipment, computers, and workshops for their section – which was from Halifax to Costa Rica. In the midst of this organized confusion, the ship's stores arrived. Lined up on the pier were trucks loaded with milk, meat, fresh and frozen vegetables, soup, and other basic necessities such as buckets and mops. The beer truck waited in line with all the others.

Meanwhile, I began the series of typhoid injections which were required for the southern cruise. I gave the first during the day, and many crew members had serious side effects. When it was time for the second injection, I waited until the crew headed for their bunks. This worked much better. I also had to chase down those elusive final staff and crew lists, to make sure that tetanus and polio shots were up-to-date, while reminding people to bring suntan lotion and hats. Since the heat was expected to be intense for the southern part of the trip, sleeping bags were in order for camping out on the upper deck. I had worked out my drug order on the final cruise the previous year, and it was waiting for me on our arrival in Dartmouth.

With the press conference over, the bon voyages said, our ship's whistle (which had been used on the Centennial Train in 1967) blew the first four notes of *O Canada* and the Hudson was under way. It was with a great sigh of relief that a relative semblance of order returned to my life, and the rhythm of the Hudson was restored to normal. As we sailed out of the Bedford Basin past Halifax Harbour, we all stood on the deck, mentally saying our good-byes one more time. When we passed Chebucto Head, the last point of land, we were alone at sea, this time heading south toward the Panama Canal, on the first leg of our long journey around the North American continent.

* * *

Since this is a book about northern nursing, I will focus mainly on the northern section of the trip; however, it is interesting to make some comparisons to nursing in the South. Early in my days on the Hudson, I became aware of the dramatic difference in my workload when we were in southern waters. For instance, in the heat, every scratch became a festering wound, which had to be attended to immediately; whereas, in the North, a little soap and water would normally solve the problem. However, no matter where we were, dental and mental problems were my greatest challenges, as they wouldn't go away with basic first aid intervention – which was the case with minor accidents, cuts and bruises.

The stress of the heat in the South caused a greater number of emotional problems; whereas, the isolation of the North triggered fewer and less severe reactions. Sometimes a person would start to lose control; then everyone became worried for their own safety. The stressed-out crew member had to be evacuated from the ship, as his problems became the problem of the entire crew.

As the nurse on duty, I always felt better when I knew precisely where the ship was. In the North, we were most often in sight of land. On the bridge, the officer of the watch would have his navigational charts in front of him, and I could get a sense of just where we were in the universe. If there was a blank sheet with no land reference (as was often the case), I felt uneasy. I needed to know where we were.

* * *

Food poisoning was something I never had to deal with in the North, but on this trip I had two serious cases of crew members becoming severely ill from eating food purchased from street vendors on the north side of the Panama Canal. This happened in spite of my warnings to everyone: do not drink the local water, take no ice in your drinks, and avoid eating any food while ashore. One crew member (who did not follow my directions and had to be evacuated from the ship) was later diagnosed with amoebiasis. He left with someone who could not handle the stress of the heat and another person who had a knee problem that was exacerbated by the constant motion of the ship. I was able to care for the second man with food poisoning in the sick bay. Controlling his high fever posed a real challenge. Because he couldn't keep ASA or acetaminophen down, I had to resort to tepid baths in the sick bay tub to cool his body. The temperature of the ocean water was perfect for this procedure. At this point, we were equidistant between Puntarenas and Acapulco – two days sailing time each way, and thus four scientific days lost. The captain chose to divert the ship to San Jose, Guatemala. Air Force personnel and customs officials toting machine guns escorted medical attendants aboard. They flew the sick crew members to Guatemala City, where they were handed over to the Canadian Embassy. After further treatment, they returned to Canada.

Another public health situation we never had to deal with in the North was the potential for rat infestation. One night after dark, while we were tied up in Puntarenas, the dock became alive with the huge, fat rodents. The local fellows laughed at the small rat guards on our shiplines. The gangway was then put on weighted pulleys, which kept it about five feet above the dock, when it was not in use, to avoid invasion by the rats.

Heat prostration made life difficult for some at sea. In the area of the Costa Rica Dome, where there was no wind and the water temperature was 89°F, the crew's quarters were unbearably hot, so the crew took their sleeping bags to the upper deck. In preparation for being on display for the Scripps Institute of Oceanography in San Diego, the crew painted the Hudson. (Scripps was considering chartering the Hudson the following year, and we wanted her to look her best.) The heat was intense and the paint baked, while the seamen fried in the sun. I met with the crew several times to discuss signs of dehydration, avoidance of heat prostration, and sunburn – and basically how to survive in this extreme climate. In Puntarenas, Costa Rica, we had an impossibly short turn-around time when the East Coast phase of the trip ended and the West Coast scientific staff from the Institute of Ocean Sciences at Patricia Bay came aboard. I sat in the shade outside the sick bay and monitored people wilting in the heat, as they hauled freight from the forward hold to their respective labs. I would stop them, check their skin turgor, tell them if it was time for a break, and send them for a cool drink in the officers' lounge.

A few days later, when several crew members complained of severe stomach cramps and diarrhea, they blamed the cooks for trying to poison them. However, our food came from the same galley, and no scientist or officer became ill. I went looking for the cause, only to discover that the ice machine in the crew's mess was the culprit. It was immediately shut down and sterilized. A larger scoop was provided, and the crew was lectured about keeping their bare hands out of the machine. Problem solved.

* * *

Despite the problems with the heat, the crew seemed happier during the southern portion of the trip, perhaps because they had more time for recreation than they did in the North. For a change of pace, we had Sunday cookouts on the flight deck, using barbecues that the engineers made from oil drums. Various small swimming pools helped people relax and cool off. One pool, actually a big fiberglass fish tank that was on the main deck outside my cabin, was shattered in a storm off Bermuda. After we lost that pool, the crew made another one out of canvas and set it up on the helicopter deck. It leaked, but it served the purpose. The air conditioner in the officers' lounge worked; unfortunately, the one in the crew's lounge was not very efficient. The pool was the only relaxation that gave the crew any relief from the heat.

The pool also contributed greatly to our mental health. The ship was so fully loaded on this trip, however, that there was no place to put other recreational equipment that we had the following year, when a long, cold trip was planned for north of Iceland to the Barents Sea. We were expecting icing conditions, so all excess equipment was removed from the decks of the ship. As a result, the hangar became available. At my suggestion, the ship's captain budgeted money for exercise bikes and other recreational games such as darts, basketball, and badminton. (Try hitting a badminton bird on a rolling ship. It really tests your dexterity.) The exercise bikes were in the machine shop for repairs so often that the engineers started riding them down in the engine room. Eventually, they began to join the rest of us in the hangar. As a result of this, the engineers (and others) started coming to the sick bay to have their weight and blood pressure checked. In most cases, there was great improvement. I also tried out several salt substitutes, to find which one tasted the best. After that, there was always a bottle on every table.

Another bonus of having access to the hangar was that the crew could listen to their boom boxes at full volume – well away from the sleeping quarters. This was not a luxury they had in their cabins, where noise was not allowed because people were sleeping at all hours. Almost immediately, the number of requests for antacids dropped dramatically. Instead of going through a case of antacids every ten days, which normally happened, only two cases were needed for the season. It was wonderful for everyone's mental and physical health.

Whether we were in the hot waters off Costa Rica or in the icy conditions of the Beaufort Sea (where we were headed), safety was the number one concern for the entire ship's complement: one individual's inattention could endanger the lives of the rest of the ship's personnel. I counselled regularly to that effect and was constantly vigilant for signs of carelessness that could have serious consequences. No one wanted to get sick or injured at sea due to negligence or stupidity. It was interesting to watch the peer pressure.

Julian Day 107: April 17

After a ten-hour stop in Acapulco on Good Friday to pick up some parts for a winch that had broken down, we headed north, our *O Canada* whistle blowing as we left the harbour. There was a dramatic temperature change. Everyone shivered, only to find that the mercury was still at 85°. Next morning, the arthritic club met in the sick bay to compare joint pains: hands, knees and hips. We were all stiff. There was a toxic level of analgesic balm in the air. I checked blood pressures more frequently and readjusted hypertensive medications back to Halifax dosages, as the temperature cooled off.

Julian Day 129 – 186: May 9 to July 5

After a three-day stop in San Diego, the rest of the trip north to Canadian waters was uneventful. We stayed at the Institute of Ocean Sciences in Patricia Bay on Vancouver Island long enough to off-load thousands of bottles of water samples. During this time, I arranged for medical appointments for some of the crew members. Then we headed down to Yarrows Graving Yard, to have the first stage of repairs done on one of the four diesel-electric engines.

The term "graving yard" goes back to the old days of sail and ships of oak. According to Michael Jones, the Deputy Harbour Master in Toronto, the term "to grave" means to clean and "pay with pitch," the ship's hull. A ship would be beached and careened (rolled on its side for cleaning or repairing). When careening went by the board, the Yarrows Graving Yard had to diversify, and it expanded into other ship repairs.

While the Hudson was in the Yarrows shipyard, I spent the week arranging more doctor appointments and medical clearances for the northern phase of the trip. I sent these crew members to a doctor at a Victoria clinic, recommended by National Health and Welfare. I discovered that the clinic was in a church basement, and it had a regular cliental of hippies. Although the crew was not impressed with the doctor's rather informal surroundings, they thought he was great.

From May 15 to June 8, I went on leave while the ship worked around Vancouver Island. I returned to Victoria, batteries recharged and ready to go. The following day, I travelled to Port Hardy with the scientists from IOS to meet the ship. At this time, we had a third change of command.

Had the weather been better, and not just "extra-wet British Columbia," the scenery we passed travelling south on this section of the west coast, between the island and the mainland, would have been positively gorgeous. As it was, we saw a lot of fog, mist, and low-lying clouds wrapped around trees, bush, and mountains, on both sides of the Inside Passage. All my slides look as if a double-gauze filter had been placed over the lens of my camera. Geologist Dr. Chris Yorath from the IOS made the whole trip through the fog memorable, with his comments over the ship's public address system about the geology of the area, supplemented with interesting Native history. This was Haida country. (By the way, Dr. Yorath got the nickname, Dr. Bang, by being part of the team that created the largest non-nuclear explosion that blew up Ripple Rock – the greatest hazard of the Inside Passage, where many ships had previously gone aground.)

The ship's scientific cargo from the work around Vancouver Island was off-loaded at the Institute for Ocean Sciences in Patricia Bay; then we moved back to Yarrows Graving Yard for the second part of the engine overhaul. Relocating from one pier to another created some logistical problems for me, since the crew members who required follow-up medical appointments (that had been initiated while we were in Patricia Bay) were now 30 miles away in

Victoria. Fortunately, the assistant marine superintendent from the Bedford Institute of Oceanography had a rental car, which I was able to use to take them back and forth to the doctor.

* * *

In Victoria, I had an opportunity to see the Pacific Princess, television's *Love Boat*. What stood out was its singular lack of visible rust. At one point, the Hudson and the Pacific Princess were both tied up opposite each other, at a concrete pier in front of the Empress Hotel, near the centre of Victoria. The Hudson had to be moved there because the engineers wanted to run up the engine (which had just been repaired), and they needed a mooring strong enough to hold the lines. Had this been done in the Yarrows Graving Yard, it was likely that great sections of the wooden dock would have come away, along with the lines – and who knows where the ship would have landed. When compared to the Pacific Princess, our Hudson looked like a rust bucket – but we all loved her.

Julian Days 187 – 228: July 6 to August 16

The hydrographers were busy with last minute arrangements at Yarrows in Victoria: they prepared the hydrographic launches and installed the special computers. As well, they attended to the myriad details that were part of this intense operation. Their mandate was to chart a ten-mile-wide corridor, 170 miles long in the Beaufort Sea, which would guarantee safe passage for the deep-draft supertankers, tentatively scheduled to traverse the North after 1985. When the American supertanker, Manhattan, had tried to cross the Northwest Passage, it almost went aground on the first unknown underwater pingoes in the Beaufort Sea. Eventually, 274 underwater pingoes were discovered and charted. Common only in the Beaufort and on its southern shores, pingoes resemble frost heaves which rise abruptly from the ocean floor. They are a hazard to navigation, because the water in the Beaufort Corridor is very shallow.

As the Hudson progressed north and west towards the Aleutian Islands, the fourth engine was put on line because of the strong tides and currents. When we crossed the Arctic Circle on July 14, King Neptune (the Captain, with the appropriate crown) and Queen Neptune (Chief Engineer Jim Rippey, wearing a floor mop wig and queenly attire) held a special ceremony on the hangar deck for those of us crossing for the first time. The next week, we slowly worked our way north to Point Barrow, Alaska, then southeast through the ice towards Herschel Island, where the first of four ARGO navigation stations had been erected. Herschel Island is a very old whaling station, later used by the RCMP for the St. Roch, which patrolled the Northwest Passage in the early 1940s.

On July 22, Captain Fred Mauger, the ship's permanent master, affectionately known as "the old man," resumed command of the Hudson. He had been on leave from Panama until now. Captain Mauger was an expert not only in Arctic navigation, but also in the ship's research capabilities in the North. Because of our trust in his leadership, we were far more relaxed and confident, which made my job as nurse much easier. I was then able to spend more time observing the crew and the scientific staff at work.

In the Beaufort, we had two, sometimes three, helicopters coming and going. They brought extra coxswains and hydrographers to work in the launches. To calibrate the four ARGO navigation stations with the on-board computers, test runs had to be done. Once the four hydrographic launches began to survey the Beaufort Corridor, the pace of activity aboard the ship never let up. When the hydrographers were not running their set grids, Denis Foley of the Atlantic Geoscience Centre surveyed the sea bottom acoustically. Work never stopped.

Two mechanics worked the night shift, making necessary repairs to the launches, to keep them in first-rate order. Because of the large numbers of trees and dead-heads from the Mackenzie River, many propellers and driveshafts had to be replaced during these overnight sessions. Perhaps because everyone was so busy, no one had time to get sick. When they weren't working, they were sleeping. With the twenty-four hour daylight, the whole ship danced with activity around the clock. As the four-hour shifts in the launches set off from and returned to the Hudson, I was available on the deck to meet each two-man team – to make sure they had no health concerns before going on or off duty. During this hydrographic phase, their hours were my hours.

* * *

These were the early days of satellite navigation. I was fascinated by the state-of-the-art electronics the hydrographers used, and the efficiency and accuracy of their work. The four launches worked out from the Hudson, five miles on either side, running hydrographic lines

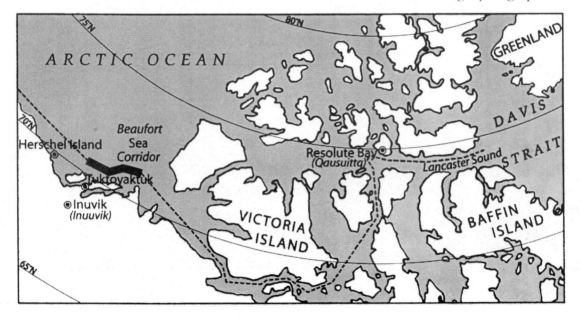

back and forth, in a set pattern. When the ship reached zero on the matching computer on the bridge, the launches appeared right on schedule, as if out of nowhere, even if there was fog. However, no amount of planning could predict ice or rough weather. Although we were lucky with the ice, the weather was erratic. When the wind picked up, recovering the launches was a dangerous task. At times, I was on deck while the ship's master and the chief hydrographer made decisions as to when the launches should be called back to the ship. The safety of the men was always the number-one priority. With so much going on, I was excited to be part of this project. This phase of the Hudson's circumnavigation was never dull.

Julian Days 229 – 246: August 17 to September 3

On August 17, to give the hydrographers a change of pace when the weather was too rough for the launches to work, Tony O'Connor, the chief hydrographer, recovered three current meters. They had been dropped through breaks in the ice from a helicopter a year earlier, each held in place by an old steel railway wheel. The area was now open water. With written instructions in hand, on how to electronically release the current meters, Tony carefully proceeded step by step, as the oceanographer back in Patricia Bay had explained to him. When a meter hit the surface, he was as excited as a new father. As the second and third meters surfaced within a hundred feet of the ship, Tony was absolutely euphoric. What made this especially interesting for the captain and the two senior hydrographers was that they had found a new application for their hydrographic computer technology. Hudson crews had previously picked up many current meters, but never with such speed and accuracy.

* * *

During our Beaufort time, there was only one serious accident. It happened when a hydrographer loosened a radiator cap in a launch. It blew off, releasing boiling fluid which shot up the inside of his left arm up to his neck and caused extensive second degree burns. He had the presence of mind to shove his arm immediately into the icy sea water. This prevented some of the possible side-effects of such a burn. He could have gone into shock. Unfortunately, because we were working at the mouth of the Mackenzie River, the water in the Beaufort was full of silt. When I met the hydrographer on his return to the Hudson *after* his shift, he told me that he had had a small accident. By this time, two huge blisters had formed: one from his wrist to his elbow, and the other from his elbow to his upper arm. In the sick bay, I ran copious amounts of cold water over the affected areas, in an attempt to get rid of the silt. He claimed that it didn't hurt, but he agreed to take a pain reliever – if that would make *me* feel better. In the fridge, I had an old jar of Flamazine cream, which I applied generously to his arm. Then I added Jelenet gauze squares, followed by "combination pads." To secure everything in place, I wrapped the entire area from his wrist to his shoulder with cling bandage. I put his arm in a sling and sent him on the next helicopter to Tuktoyaktuk, from where he would go on to the hospital in Inuvik.

Once word got out that the injured hydrographer was going to Inuvik, he had requests for T-shirts and "Tuk U" certificates. The Captain asked if he would cash a Bedford Institute cheque for ship's incidentals. I had a limited supply of Flamazine and cling bandage, so I asked him to get more. He was examined at the hospital and re-bandaged. After he had done all the shopping and errands on his list, he arrived back at the ship, both arms loaded, and with the bandages hanging off his arm. The doctor's instructions for me were to carry on with the treatment that I had initiated, as the burn had been sealed by the blisters with no sign of infection. By the end of three weeks of treatment, with bandages changed twice daily, and another trip to Inuvik, the new skin had formed nicely. I was pleased with the outcome.

* * *

A week after this accident, I flew into Tuktoyaktuk with a crew member who was showing signs of stress. When we arrived at the nursing station in Tuk, I informed her she would have to leave the Hudson and go home for a rest. I did not want to tell her on the ship, as I was afraid there would be a problem in the helicopter, and that is the last place you want someone getting upset. Before we left the ship, I arranged for her roommate to pack her clothes. Although she slipped in and out of reality, she was fairly calm at the nursing station. Later, we dropped her off at the Polar Shelf base.

The Polar Shelf stations in Tuk and in Resolute Bay coordinated all of the scientific projects during the summer in the North. They had daily radio contact with scientists out on the land and at sea. While I was with the stressed-out crew member at the nursing station in Tuk, I took the opportunity to call Dr. Donald MacDonald, my Health Canada backup in Halifax. I needed to report on these two incidents and to bring him up-to-date, in the event of anything untoward happening, and in case he might receive an inquiry about either incident. His secretary informed me that he was at a meeting, and had left instructions not to be disturbed. I told her that she had to get him to the phone – because this was an emergency. Furthermore, my helicopter was waiting. When I got back to the ship, I put the crew member's luggage aboard the helicopter, which was returning to the Polar Shelf station at Tuk, where she was to spend the night before heading home.

* * *

As a nurse working alone in an isolated outpost, or on the high seas, mental health for me meant being able to get CBC Radio or Radio Canada International on shortwave. The Caribbean network of RCI was great, until we got too far west and lost contact from Panama to Washington State. Along the west coast, we could get various relay stations, such as Prince Rupert. Then it was over to radio stations from Alaska and American News from the Lower 48. Now that we were in the Beaufort Sea, CBC from Tuk was on twenty-four hours a day in English, with news initiating from various time zones across Canada. This was because of a strike at CBC. We could hear *The World at Eight* from Halifax (this made the engineers happy, because they could keep up with Atlantic news), Toronto, and Calgary. I was pleased when CBC rebroadcast W.O. Mitchell's *Jake and the Kid* stories. Another bonus of the CBC strike was that we could hear favourite programs, such as Alan McFee's *Eclectic Circus*, before its usual midnight time. A real diversion for some of us, as we travelled in and around the ice floes, was listening to the Royal Wedding of Prince Charles and Diana, Princess of Wales, on Mackenzie Radio from Inuvik on July 29, 1981. When the mail finally arrived, after a long postal strike, there was a great rush for *Time* and *Maclean's* magazines to see pictures of the wedding.

* * *

By the end of August, the hydrographers had completed 51% of the proposed shipping corridor survey. Had the weather been better, we might have finished the task. However, as the month progressed, the weather deteriorated and by August 28, it was snowing. Just to transfer fuel from the barge, which had come down the Mackenzie from Norman Wells, took four days. With the fuel barge having only a six-foot draft, it pitched and rolled in the extreme. For safety reasons, the weather had to be just right before we could begin. To stabilize the two vessels, we tried going into the ice. By the time the Hudson was steady in the ice, and the barge was moving into place, the ice had been blown away by the wind. This procedure had to be repeated several times before we were successful.

The next few weeks were full of disappointments and frustrations for the hydrographers. There was some confusion about icebreaker support once we left the Beaufort. With this in mind, and with the memory of a horrendous trip across the Northwest Passage by the Baffin a few years earlier, Captain Mauger felt that to be on the safe side we had to leave the Beaufort earlier than mid-September, as had been planned. The Ice Observer came aboard with charts showing Prince of Wales Strait blocked, and ice along the Prince Regent Sound area, west of Resolute. With great regret, we left the Beaufort on September 3.

Julian Days 247 – 250: September 4 to 7

Once we left the Beaufort, we lost the radio signal, and then I was back again to Radio North on short wave – when I could get it. The programming was normally quadralingual, but because of the CBC strike, it was entirely in English. The best part about being anchored off Resolute Bay was CBC radio and television. The sense of isolation you experience, when you're unable to get any radio signals, tends to evaporate when you have contact with the outside world. There was a gap from Nanisivik, halfway down Baffin Island, until CBC's European Network came in on shortwave.

One Saturday afternoon, we were tied up in Nanisivik where they received CBC Montreal. Because there was medical support ashore, I sat in the armchair in my cabin, and sipped Valpolicella while I listened to the opera at full volume. The crew knew, when serious classical music was playing in *her* quarters, this nurse preferred not to be disturbed – unless there was an emergency. This was the one and only time during my four years aboard the Hudson that I was able to relax and enjoy the Metropolitan Opera broadcast from New York. Much to my frustration, but to the delight of the crew, Mackenzie Radio played mostly country and western music at this time slot while we were in the Beaufort.

From the Beaufort Sea, the Hudson travelled along Amundsen Gulf, Coronation Gulf, through Dease Strait, along Queen Maud Gulf, north through Victoria Strait to Larsen Sound, and then past Peel Sound to Resolute. With the sun shining and the water smooth as glass, the scenery was out of this world. The crew continued to be in good health, so different from when we were in the heat of the South.

Anchored offshore, when we reached Resolute, were the Canadian Coast Guard Ships, the Franklin and the Pierre Radisson. The following day, along came the third ice-breaker, the Louis St. Laurent. The Coast Guard had not been able to guarantee us icebreaker support for this part of the trip, and yet here were three of their vessels, off Resolute. For this reason, we had left the Beaufort Sea early. The West Coast hydrographers now had time to do East Coast survey work at the request of the Bedford Institute. Because there was too much ice in the Viscount Melville Sound area, west of Resolute, we did the second section requested by BIO, at the east end of Lancaster Sound.

The last week of September, we were anchored off Resolute again, moving freight ashore in a sling under the helicopter. One positive aspect was that we had radio and television to break the monotony. Because of the shore ice, we couldn't run our usual launch shuttle, and those who wanted to get to a telephone had to hitch a ride in the chopper. Since Resolute had little to offer at that time of year – beyond a telephone – no one complained about there being no formal shore leave. During the fifteen minutes I spent at the airport, I managed to get a call through to the National Health and Welfare nursing station. The nurse there was busy with three people who were about to be medevac'd. She told me that she had been on her own for several months. I wanted to invite her out to the ship, but I wasn't sure how I was going to get her back to the station that evening, because the helicopter would have finished for the day by the time dinner was over. Since the telephone line I tried in Toronto was busy, I was back aboard in no time.

At Resolute, we had a change of scientific staff. The hydrographic freight was transferred ashore – to be flown back to Patricia Bay in British Columbia. The IOS personnel left and the BIO scientists and technicians took their place. We were back to BIO scientific work. When we left Resolute, we lost our CBC radio signal one more time.

Julian Days 285 – 287: October 12 to 14

One hundred and three days without a port call is rather extreme. Yet that was the time we spent on board the Hudson between Victoria and Godthab, Greenland – without a crew break. There were few complaints, as the options were either Resolute Bay or Arctic Bay (Nanisivik). We had stopped at Arctic Bay, which was a mine site, to pick up some heavy equipment that couldn't be brought aboard from Resolute. We were *all* ready for Godthab.

From a medical viewpoint, Godthab was the busiest port call I'd ever had in my four years aboard. I administered first aid to people who had fallen down stairs or off ladders, and I sorted out the crew after a night of burning off excessive steam. The result was that three of the crew were sent back to Halifax. I reached my limit with one of our cooks, who had struck the chief officer. Another seaman had aggravated his fellow crew members sufficiently that he was put on the "endangered list," and sent home. A third crew member tumbled down the stairs incurring a fractured wrist, which I splinted before I sent him off to the hospital and then home with the other two. Had he not been so relaxed going down the stairs, he would have broken his neck.

A reception was held aboard the Hudson for the local dignitaries of Godthab. The President of Greenland, recently elected following independence from Denmark, came along with his entourage. Everything went well until one of the science students brought his video camera into the lounge. He wanted to film the Hudson officers with formal attire on; however, the President thought it was a political ploy. He and his delegation left immediately. Two days later we found out why. They did not want to be seen socializing with Canadians, because it would compromise the delicate fish-quota negotiations which were in progress at the time.

* * *

After leaving Godthab, the ship was very quiet, and we were content. All the troublemakers had left. The worst that we had to contend with was the weather. The sky was overcast, and the seas were grey and rough; rain poured down in sheets, and visibility was poor. When weather permitted, the scientists took core samples of the seabed; otherwise, they towed the magnetometer to record the changing magnetic pattern of the underlying rocks. They also closely surveyed a grounded iceberg, using the side-scan sonar. The iceberg scowers were of interest to oil companies who were considering the possibility of laying a pipeline from the oil rigs to an onshore storage location. "Scowers" are trenches left on the ocean floor when an iceberg rolls and is dragged along the bottom in the Labrador Current. With the technology of the time, a pipeline would probably not have stayed intact for long, because icebergs could easily have ripped it out.

* * *

Dental problems were among my greatest challenges, and they happened mostly in the North, when we were away from port for long periods of time. During the course of the 1981 cruise, I had six serious dental problems to contend with. Most were caused by excessive decay and lack of preventive maintenance. Two people had wisdom teeth cutting through their gums; another two had abscessed roots, which caused facial swelling. Unfortunately, the people with cavities also had low pain tolerance and a great fear of dentists, so they had put off seeking dental care for as long as they could. All they wanted were 292s. Since we were away from our home port of Dartmouth, I insisted that their problems be attended to, if they wanted to continue sailing on the ship. When we were in a foreign port, we always had an agent who would quickly find a dentist, a doctor, or a hospital for me to access. In a Canadian port, I was on my own, with some help from Health Canada – or the yellow pages of the phone book.

I could handle the burns, I could look after falls off ladders or down flights of stairs, and I could contend with diarrhea and fever in the South; but the dental and mental problems of the crew would not go away as easily. There was no quick fix.

* * *

Working as a medical officer on a ship was comparable to working in a small, isolated community such as Grise Fiord on Ellesmere Island, close to the same latitude as the magnetic North Pole – with a few variations. In Grise, depending on the northern lights, I would have direct radio contact with doctors in the hospital in Iqaluit; but on the ship I had to use a telex system. My messages were sent to the Queen Elizabeth Hospital Emergency in Halifax via Coast Guard Radio Medical. This was a service provided to all ships at sea, around the world. The messages had to be written in plain (not medical) language because they often went through the Coast Guard stations of various countries, depending on the location of the ship. The emergency doctors in Halifax were familiar with the Hudson; they also knew me, my expertise, and my limitations. I had spent a week there before sailing for the first time, and in the following years, I always made a point of checking in to say hello. They also knew what basic drugs I had aboard. The radio operator on our ship was my link to the medical world. At Grise, your voice-transmission radio signal might be down for days, depending on the weather and the northern lights. With the satellite communication that is available today, it is much easier.

In my experience in remote northern communities, when someone needed to be medevac'd, the "moccasin telegraph" informed the whole community. The "Hudson telegraph" was even faster. The difference with a high seas medevac was that when someone had to be transported from the high seas to a hospital, everyone stopped working and went with the patient. Whereas a medevac from a remote community might be delayed because of weather, in the case of the Hudson, the actual medevac might take longer – depending on the location of the ship. In either situation, the main priority for the nurse was to stabilize the patient, until a plane could get into a community or the ship could reach the closest port.

The Radio Medical replies were an invaluable backup to my nursing work on the ship. Sometimes, we had to be creative because time required for a medevac might mean the loss of a major portion of the scientific work aboard. On an earlier cruise, our radio operator put out an All Points Bulletin for verbal assistance about a serious problem. I wanted a second opinion. He found a Polish cargo carrier only four hours away, with a Russian doctor aboard and a Polish-American tourist, who could act as a translator. The two ships rendezvoused. Five languages were spoken around a terrified patient in the sick bay, who only began to relax when I gave him the nod that he was in good hands. The doctor was able to solve the problem in short order, and within four hours, we were back at our original working site, as opposed to four days if we had gone into port. Radio Medical from Halifax was also of great assistance to me, while we were in the South.

Having worked on nursing stations in the far North at a time when there was no radio, TV, or newspapers, I knew what that kind of isolation could do to you. On the Hudson, we had short-wave radio, and, if lucky, even some TV – if we were close to a settlement. Every afternoon and evening, a movie was shown on the VCR. It was great escapism. At one time, we had all the *Pink Panther* films which were very funny. The stations now have phones, TVs, and email. Apparently, email is available on the Hudson, along with satellite telephone communication, and sophisticated navigational systems. Personal computers were far off during my time aboard. Only the labs and navigation centres had computer systems, which then were so huge they took up entire rooms.

Julian Days 308 – 309: November 4 to 5

On November 4 in St. John's Newfoundland, I finally had another port call where I was off duty, for at least a day. The chief mate, who managed to put his back out from coughing on toast crumbs at the breakfast table, was sent home the next day, and another chief mate arrived from BIO to take his place. From St John's, we headed southeast towards the Azores, to recover another set of current meters that had been put in place earlier in the season by our sister ship, Baffin. Once we hit the Gulf Stream, we had two glorious days in the heat. For the first time since Good Friday, the previous April in Acapulco, I was able to be on the deck without wearing my parka.

Julian Day 319: November 15

After a very successful voyage around North America, the CSS Hudson sailed into the Bedford Basin and the Bedford Institute of Oceanography with only our regular ship's foghorn blowing. By the time we had reached Acapulco, the *O Canada* whistle had lost its third note. Somewhere in the Beaufort, someone had tried to play it on the holiday weekend in August, and it was promptly ordered to be disconnected by Captain Fred Mauger.

My experience as an outpost nurse certainly made my work aboard the Hudson much easier than if I had come straight from a hospital setting. During my time aboard, I used all the public health, occupational health, medical diagnostics, and psychological skills that I had honed while in the North. By this time, I had very good diagnostic instincts: I could look at someone and know what was happening medically. The Hudson had lost only about 12 to 14 hours in a nine-month trip for medical purposes, and that was in the southern portion, when we diverted into San Jose, Guatemala. I was able to hold on to any other problems until the next port of call. In hindsight, I realize that the stopovers in the South were too short. A twenty-four hour break in port was not long enough for a crew on an extended cruise such as this one. Without my background as a nurse working in remote areas of the North of Canada, I would have found the work on the ship far more stressful than it was. I knew I had good survivor skills.

The four years I spent as Medical Officer aboard the CSS Hudson were my Outward Bound experience – and the best years of my professional life. Being able to handle any problems that came my way gave me tremendous self-confidence. Nevertheless, I realized that I had to move on. I transferred back to Toronto as the occupational health nurse at the Revenue Canada Taxation offices where I took boot-camp training in union/management and staff relations. When it was time for the Hudson to sail the following year, I found myself pacing in my apartment, wishing that I was on board. Nursing on the high seas was the most exciting time in my life – and it still stands out as the highlight of my career.

J. Karen Scott RN, BScN graduated in 1963 with an RN from the St. Thomas Elgin General Hospital in St. Thomas, Ontario. In 1968, she earned her BScN from the University of Windsor. She completed the course for nurse practitioners in 1975 at the University of Toronto. She worked in the Sioux Lookout Zone in Ontario, during which time she was seconded to Povungnituk, in northern Quebec. As the Chief Medical officer aboard the CSS Hudson, she spent considerable time in Arctic waters. On her return to Ontario, she worked as the Occupational Health Nurse at Revenue Canada Taxation in Toronto. She later transferred to Yellowknife, NWT, as the Regional Occupational Health Nurse. After further studies at the University of Alaska in Anchorage, she moved to Prince Edward Island as the District Office Nurse for Veterans Affairs Canada. Karen has retired and now lives in Oakville, Ontario. This is the second collection of stories about the North that she and her friend, Joan Kieser, have published. Her story "My Best Christmas Ever: Povungnituk, 1975" appears in *Northern Nurses: True Nursing Adventures from Canada's North*.

The author wishes to thank Tony O'Connor, Clive Mason, and Kevin Robertson who read her story for scientific accuracy.

Dr. Shirley Marie Stinson OC, AOE, Honorary Northern Nurse

Citation on being named an Officer of the Order of Canada

She has raised the profile of nursing in Canada and contributed to improved standards of patient care around the world. Her pioneering efforts to establish nursing research as a respected field of study led to one of the first Masters and Doctoral in Nursing Programs in Canada. Founding Chair of the Alberta Foundation for Nursing Research, she has worked to promote the study of advanced clinical nursing practice, theory and research, and brought this view to other countries. Professor Emerita at the University of Alberta and Adjunct Professor for Life at the University of Calgary, she is a mentor to generations of young nurses.

Eleanor Wheler going on
a home visit (1939)

Eleanor Wheler and friend

Lowell DeMond
enjoying retirement

Kathleen Mary (Jo) Lutley in
Great Whale River (1962)

Martha Aldrich and Tops van
Vliet (summer, 1980)

Tops van Vliet on an outing near
Coppermine

Little Grand Rapids Nursing Station staff
(Martha, Tops, Walter Moar, Jemina Keeper) with Dr. Eng

The Nanuk Clinic: a Quonset
hut used by the x-ray survey
team (Cambridge Bay, 1956)

Kay Dier (right) with Pearl Morlock, the
nurse who replaced her, at the entrance to a
packing case home (Cambridge Bay, 1956)

Kay Dier checking a new puppy at a packing case home (Note the
chimney protruding from the snowbank in the background.)

Julie, Mrs. Mackenzie, Maureen Dauphinais, and Hilda "Tacky" Doran (1951)

Mackenzie River breakup in Norman Wells (1951)

Hilda Doran and The Band in Norman Wells (1951)

Norman Wells ambulance crew (1951)

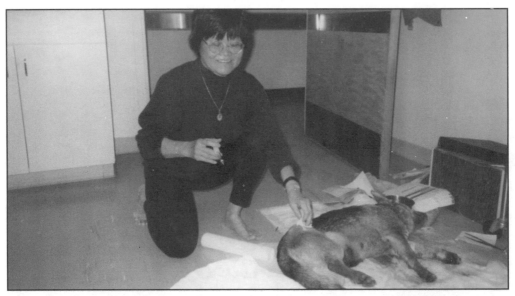

C.J. Reed performing "other related duties" (Pangnirtung, 2001)

Heather Thomson and Katie in Attawapiskat (Nov. 2004)

C.J. in Auyuittuq Park (2001)

Constable Matatall and Peyton (in car seat) picking up new baby, Caleb Rockel, in the RCMP Suburban (2001)

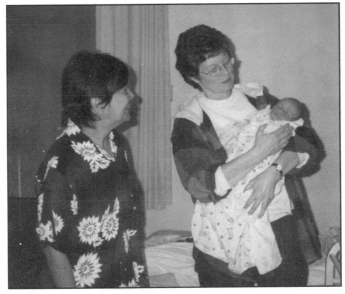

Nurses Linda Crawford and Alida Silverthorn with Caleb (2001)

Dale, Cecilia and Caleb Rockel in Uranium City (2001)

Hazel Booth in treatment room of the nursing station

Matt and Hazel hugging Morris the Moose in snow shelter following the rescue

Ildiko Luxemburger with firefighters

Firefighters at lunch in their northern-style mess tent

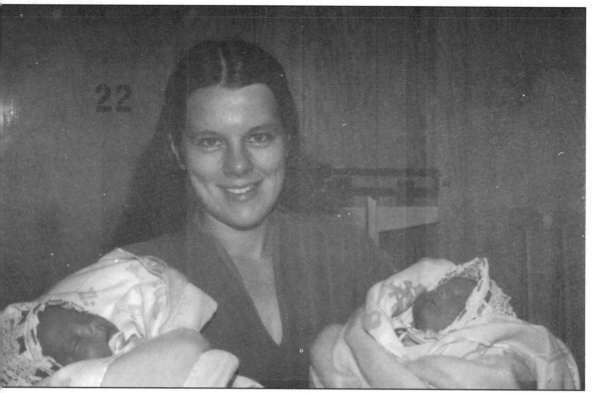

Janet Cross with the twins (1981)

The twins at their "walking out" ceremony

Janet Quananack (named after
Janet Cross) carrying her
cousin, Elaisha Quananack in
her amouti (2000)

Pat Nichols with baby (who is now a
220 lb auxiliary RCMP)

Barbara Bromley in Yellowknife

Anne Pask Wilkinson

Vera Roberts receives the Order of
Canada from Governor General,
Jeanne Sauvé (1987)

Celebrating the retirement of Alice Smith

Standing (left to right): E. Casselman, P. Laurin,
M. Skov, H. Williams (at very top), H. Ferrari,
A. Wieler, A. Smith, B.L. Trimmer, P. White.
Kneeling: M.J (Bunny) Hayman, H. MacDonald,
J. Neuman, C. Keith, J. MacDonald

Cay Keith and Verna Huffman at Mile 777 of the Alaska
Highway in the Yukon (March, 1969)

Verna Huffman Splane celebrating her ninetieth birthday

Photo by Mone Cheng

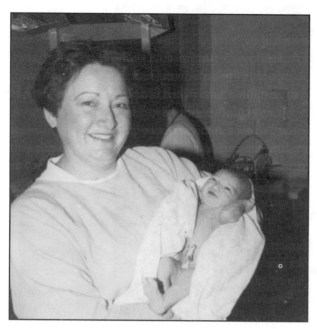

Sue Pauhl with Adrienne (Inuvik)

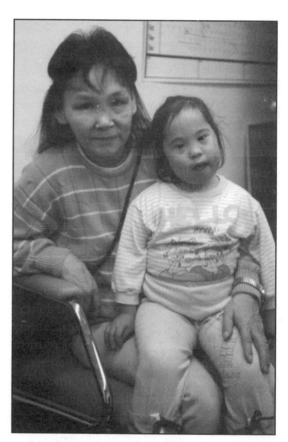

Mary Louise Elias, a favourite of the nurses at the hospital in Inuvik, with her grandmother, Margaret Klengberg

Sue Pauhl with good friend, Theresa Aklunark

Christine Egan, during her early
nursing days, with baby in amouti

Sr. Marie Lemire (standing), after
receiving the Commemorative
Medal for the Queen's Golden
Jubilee from the Honourable Lise
Thibault, Lieutenant Governor of
Quebec (2002)

Sr. Marie Lemire teaching student nurses at
St. Ann's Hospital in Fort Smith (1954)

Regina Pastion (right) accompanied by her daughter, Gladys, after receiving the Commemorative Medal for the Queen's Golden Jubilee from the Lieutenant Governor of Alberta, the late Lois Hole (centre) in 2002

Joanne Smith (standing at left, middle row) and Regina Pastion (second from right, middle row) and staff at Hay Lakes Nursing Station (1994)

Thomas Richard (Coxswain), J. Karen Scott (Chief Medical Officer),
William Gray (Quartermaster) aboard CSS Hudson in 1982

Postcard sent from CSS Hudson

The nine-bed Makkovik Nursing Station
(1969)

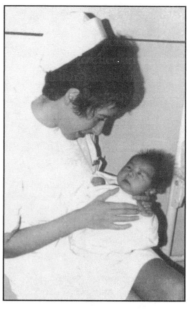

Eleanor Lindsay's patient in
St. Anthony, NL

Eleanor at the radio telephone

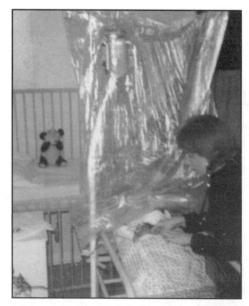

Eleanor attending baby in makeshift
oxygen tent

Chris and Kelly Lemphers in Old Masset, Queen Charlotte Islands
(late 1970s)

Sonya Grypma, looking for the white flag during the row-a-thon

Elizabeth (MacLaren) Sperry

Angela and John Sperry, children
of the North

Rev. John Sperry, having just returned from a spring trip,
holding his daughter, Angela

Honda garage (or igloo) with snow machine
inside (Whale Cove)

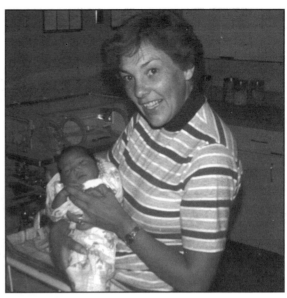

Mary Flowers Wesko with baby Nancy in
Whale Cove (1973)

The Whale's Tail (Whale Cove)

Mary building igloo on winter survival
course in Churchill, Manitoba (1974)

Ettunga, the McKinnon's right hand man in
Pangnirtung (1934 to 1936)

Dr. Alex McKinnon

Elsie (McEwan) McKinnon,
first nurse in Pangnirtung

The photos on this page were reproduced from glass slides which are presently in the Angmarlik
Visitor Centre in Pangnirtung

TOPS AND ME

Martha Aldrich

Tops (Antonia Hendrika van Vliet) was born in Ermelo, Holland on April 1, 1925, the only girl in a family of eight siblings. She inherited her name from her mother who was also called Tops. In the early 1950s, she came to Canada, shortly after completing her nursing education which included one year of obstetrics. While awaiting Canadian registration, she spent a year working on the IV team at the Ottawa Civic Hospital. In 1956 she went to Newfoundland to work for the International Grenfell Association at the hospital in St. Anthony. It was here that I met Tops. We became good friends and continued to work together for the next 24 years.

I grew up in Quebec and graduated from the Sherbrooke Hospital in 1951. A year later, I took a one-year course in teaching and supervision at McGill University in Montreal. Then I worked for three years on the teaching staff of Sherbrooke Hospital. This was long enough to convince me that teaching student nurses was not my cup of tea. I saw an advertisement for nurses to work for the Grenfell Mission (as it was called then) in Newfoundland and Labrador. I applied for a job and was soon on my way to St. Anthony, where I got to know Tops – and where we stayed for five years.

The only road at that time was from St. Anthony to Cook's Harbour, so travel was mainly by boat or plane in summer, and by plane, dog team or snowmobile (not skidoos, which came later) in winter. For part of this time, Tops was nurse in charge of the hospital. She took over when Phyllis Baird left. I worked for a year in the operating room and then moved to general duty. There were few registered nurses, and the hours were long; but the work was challenging and satisfying (in spite of the pay which was $1000 a year, plus room and board). The staff was like a family, and we got along amazingly well. There were opportunities to learn and do things not ordinarily expected of nurses. We also travelled to nearby communities. Some of these trips were to administer polio vaccine which had just become available. Tops and I soon discovered that we shared a liking for this type of nursing.

When we decided to leave St. Anthony, we went to work in a small hospital in Kemptville, near Ottawa. After less than a year, however, we were on our way north again, with Medical Services Branch of the Department of National Health and Welfare in outpost nursing stations.

See "Tops and Martha: Legends of the North" by Rick Tremblay in *Northern Nurses: True Nursing Adventures from Canada's North.*

In October, 1962, Tops and I arrived at the nursing station in Sandy Lake, Ontario, north of Sioux Lookout, on the last plane before freeze-up. The first night we were there, a baby was born. In the two weeks it took for the ice on the lake to freeze thick enough for planes to land, two more babies were born. During this time, a baby died and a small child had to be admitted for treatment of convulsions. (I will always remember Johnny Fiddler.) Our experience in Newfoundland had prepared us for what was required of us here. It was imperative that two nurses working and living in such an isolated place should be able to get along together, both on duty and off. Tops and I were good friends and we shared our different areas of expertise. In difficult situations, we were able to compromise, if necessary, and come up with the best possible solutions. For toothaches, which were a frequent complaint, I did the freezing and Tops did the pulling. She delivered the babies and started the IVs, while I filled out forms and wrote the reports. We both became quite expert at suturing.

In Sandy Lake, there was a strong chief and council who invited us to their regular meetings. We relied on them for help on many occasions. The priest, Father Bignami, showed movies, a popular entertainment. The council sometimes punished people for misdeeds by barring them from the movies. It seemed to work quite well. Almost every week, there were square dances which we enjoyed attending. I even had a regular partner — a man whose wife didn't dance, and she didn't mind my dancing with him.

After three years in Sandy Lake, we were encouraged to transfer to another place, or go to university to study public health nursing. We chose the latter and took a one-year course at the University of Toronto, finishing in 1966. The people in Sandy Lake, and especially the chief at the time, Tom Fiddler, wanted us to return there. However, because Medical Services recommended that all nurses regularly move on to another station, this was not approved. So we moved to Little Grand Rapids in Manitoba.

* * *

In Little Grand Rapids, we had many memorable experiences. The community was across Family Lake from the nursing station and the Hudson's Bay store, so it was necessary for people to travel by boat to get nursing care and supplies. I soon learned how to operate an outboard motor. In spite of repeated instructions from our supervisor, Marie Skov, that we were not to use the boat unless the janitor was with us, we certainly made good use of the boat for both work and pleasure — without him. Fortunately for us, Miss Skov was unable to visit us very often.

We were always welcome to attend the drum dances that were held frequently in Little Grand Rapids. They took place in one of the homes, which sometimes consisted of a single room. In one corner, two or three drummers would be seated at the drum. Around the stove (which was usually in the centre of the room) the dancers would shuffle in time to the drumming and the singing that accompanied it. Both adults and children participated. It always seemed to be quite dark, smoky, and warm.

During the time we spent in this community, the first landing strip was built, and we saw the first plane, a Twin Otter, land on it. One spring day, the pilot of a DC3 who was planning to land on the ice called in and asked us to go outside. When he flew over, we were to look up and check to see if his landing gear was down. It was – and he landed safely. In both Sandy Lake and Little Grand Rapids, communication with the outside world was by two-way radio, which had limitations. If signals were not good, the radios did not work at all. Because we were often asked to give weather conditions to incoming planes, we had to learn how to estimate wind speed, visibility, and ceiling, and how to measure the ice thickness.

* * *

From Little Grand Rapids, we wanted to go farther north. So in 1970, we asked for a transfer to Tuktoyaktuk, close to the Beaufort Sea in the Northwest Territories. While we were in Inuvik, (on our way to Tuk) we bought cross-country skis. Cross-country skiing was becoming popular, largely due to the success of the Firth twins, Sharon and Shirley, from Fort McPherson. It was here that we met Dr. Elizabeth Cass, ophthalmologist extraordinaire, an experience not to be forgotten. I will always remember her boxes and boxes of files, and her remarkable memory of individuals, their eye problems, and their names. One day a patient asked her how old she was. (We had heard that she never told anyone her age, so we all listened attentively.) In her reply, she asked the woman (whose name I have forgotten) how old *she* was. On being told, Elizabeth said, "Oh, I am older than you are, dear."

* * *

For various reasons, we spent only one year in Tuk. In 1971, we left for Kugluktuk (Coppermine) in the Central Arctic and we stayed there for seven years. Both Tops and I took the nurse practitioner course at the University of Alberta in Edmonton, but at different times. We enjoyed the people of Kugluktuk, the work, and the area. By this time, we had our own small boat and motor, which we often used to go exploring. A favourite place was Bloody Falls, a short distance up the Coppermine River. On our days off, we would leave a sign on the door of the nursing station telling people where we were going. If we were needed, someone would come for us. This happened only a few times, and then only for real emergencies. Alcohol was a problem in this community, as it had been in Tuk. It was flown in from Yellowknife and some was made in the community. I tasted the local home brew – only once. To me, it was horrible.

The Arctic Summer Games were held in Coppermine during our time there. We attended the planning meetings which took place preceding the big event. It was decided that those coming to the games would have to be housed in tents and provided with bathroom facilities of some sort. As people did in most homes in Coppermine, they would have to use honey buckets and would need a place for washing their hands. (A honey bucket is a pail with a plastic bag inside, which is changed as often as is necessary, then put outside to be picked up and taken to the dump.) At one meeting, I suddenly heard Tops' voice volunteer us (the nurses) to look after the honey buckets. That meant changing bags and looking after hand-washing supplies. There had been several cases of infectious hepatitis in the community, so this task was important. And who better to do it than the nurses! It turned out to be quite a job, as it meant checking honey buckets – and there many of them – for the tent people and for people in some other locations, at least three times a day. We put the full ones on a wagon parked nearby. That summer, we never heard of anyone getting hepatitis as a result of being in Coppermine. An added note: I took part in the blanket toss at the games which was quite an experience and lots of fun. Although I was not very good, my picture appeared in the NWT Explorer Guide.

* * *

In most of the communities where we worked, a council ran local affairs. One of these communities had a local health committee. Because it was vital to have a good relationship with the council, we often attended their meetings. If we had a particular problem with something or someone, or if we wanted to promote a new project, we could take it to the council and usually come up with a solution or a plan.

Tops and I spent considerable time in the schools. We knew that getting along well with the teachers was important: teachers and nurses had to be in agreement about certain things. It was an opportunity to check the children for health problems and to give immunizations. In one village where it seemed as if every man, woman, and child had head lice, we set up a community-wide program to get rid of them. The bigger hurdle was getting permission from parents to cut their children's hair, if it was necessary. The boys were no problem, but mothers were reluctant to have their daughters' long, beautiful black hair cut off. Eventually most of them agreed. Tops cut the boys' hair, while I did the girls' hair. We did not eliminate the problem completely during the four years we were there. Nevertheless, I like to think that things improved. In spite of my precautions, I even caught a few lice myself.

In another village, where scabies was quite prevalent, the nursing station became a public bathhouse. The treatment for scabies included washing their bedclothes, as well as the clothing they wore. However, most homes did not have hot and cold running water. I don't know how the women did it, because they had to carry water from the river and heat it on the stove. We used the situation to promote the idea of getting either a public bathhouse, or running water in the homes. With both head lice and scabies, one of the complications is impetigo, which can be serious, so prevention was most important.

* * *

In 1978, we transferred to Pannirtuuq (Pangnirtung) on Baffin Island where Vera Roberts was the Zone Nursing Officer. Tops first went to Igloolik for several months. She was much better at relief work than I was, and if one of us had to do it, she always volunteered. The months I spent in Pangnirtung, before Tops got there, were quite difficult for me, but things improved with the arrival of Mary Barton, a nurse from British Columbia who was doing a six-month term. We became friends, and still are. The three of us made a good team. But, alas, Mary left when her six months were up.

A memorable moment for me occurred while I was in Pang. A man came to the nursing station asking to see me. He wasn't sick, he assured me. He had a present for me. I could see nothing in his hands, so I asked him what it was. He announced, "I have quit smoking!" I was very pleased because nearly the whole population of Pang were smokers, and several people died of lung cancer while I was there. I had spent a lot of time trying to convince them that it would be a good idea to quit. This was a wonderful gift for me.

* * *

Part of our reason for going to Pangnirtung was to hike in Auyuittuq National Park one day. We had read about the park and we talked to people who had hiked there. We did a lot of walking and cross-country skiing around Pang. Then in August of 1980, we decided go to Auyuittuq. We flew to Qikiqtarjuaq (Broughton Island) and continued by boat up North Pang Fiord to the park entrance. From there, we would follow the Owl River to Summit Lake, and then the Weasel River to Pang Fiord, where we would be picked up by boat, and would return to Pangnirtung. The first night we camped at an emergency hut close to the park entrance. The next day we hiked to the Owl River, which we had to cross. The only way to get to the other side was by wading through the water. We camped there, planning to ford the river early the next morning, when the water would be at its lowest level.

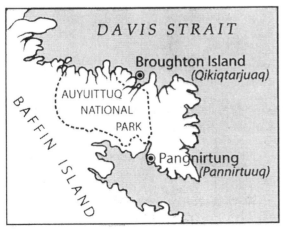

It was while we were crossing the river on August 13, that the accident happened, the accident that claimed Tops' life. The river was rock-strewn, quite deep in places, and swift-flowing. Tops led the way. Before we had gone very far, she lost her footing, fell and was swept downstream – around a bend and out of sight. I watched, helplessly, knowing that if I went on, the same would happen to me. Tops was a strong swimmer, and I hoped and prayed that this would save her. It was not to be. I got back to shore, and although I scrambled along the bank, back and forth several times, I could see no sign of her. Then, as quickly as I could, I made my way back to the emergency hut. I activated the radio, praying that it would work, and called the park office in Pangnirtung. They answered immediately and arranged to have a helicopter (which just happened to be in the community) fly in with Pat Rousseau, one of the park wardens. Before they landed where I was, they had already located Tops. But she was beyond help. I was flown back to Pang, and the helicopter returned to recover Tops' body.

The next few days were surreal. Tops' brother, Paul Van Vliet, the only one of her brothers living in Canada, arrived within days. Also, my sister, Doreen Irving, from Moncton and Margrit Ramel, a good friend from Yellowknife, both came. I don't know how I would have gotten through those days without them. Mike and Margaret Gardener, Vera Roberts, and all the people of Pang were very supportive. Our friend, Tops, is buried amid beautiful surroundings in the cemetery in Pangnirtung

* * *

It was not always smooth sailing in the places where Tops and I worked, but the good times certainly outnumbered the bad. From early on in our days of nursing in the North, we were aware that prevention was more important than treatment. We understood the necessity of good prenatal care, immunizations, well-baby and preschool checkups, even though treatment always seemed to get more attention.

After taking some time off following the death of Tops, I continued to work for Medical Services until 1990. I was stationed in Rae-Edzo and Fort Simpson, both in the Northwest Territories, and in Kashechewan in Ontario. Perhaps the highlight of my whole nursing career happened in 1982 when Jan Stirling, a highly-respected public health nurse in Yellowknife, and I each received an honorary life membership in the Canadian Public Health Association at their conference in Yellowknife.

And to this day, I still cross-country ski.

Martha Aldrich RN, Dip.Ed, NP graduated in 1951 as a registered nurse from the Sherbrooke Hospital School for Nurses in Sherbrooke, Quebec, where she worked for a year. In 1953, she received her Diploma for Teaching in Schools of Nursing from McGill University in Montreal. She was a science instructor for student nurses at Sherbrooke Hospital for Nurses. She was with the International Grenfell Association in St. Anthony, Newfoundland from 1956 to 1961 and then at the Kemptville District Hospital in Ontario. In 1962, Martha joined Health and Welfare Canada and worked at the nursing station in Sandy Lake, Ontario. In 1966, after completing a one-year Diploma Course in Public Health Nursing at the University of Toronto, she worked in Little Grand Rapids, Manitoba until 1970. In the NWT, she worked in nursing stations in Tuktoyaktuk and Coppermine. After completing the nurse practitioner course at the University of Alberta in 1974, she worked in Pangnirtung, Rae-Edzo, and Fort Simpson. In 1982, Martha received an Honorary Life Membership in the Canadian Public Health Association. She worked in Kashechewan, Ontario until she retired.

FRIENDS

Sharon Irvine

The Birth,

at Grenfell Mission,
an easy delivery,
deft hands meeting unbendable strength,
drawn by. . .
Who knows? – but friendship born of
mutual skills and adventurous appetites:
A team.

In Between,

an open kinship, always room for one more:
Indian, Inuit,
pilots, nurses,
doctors, dentists, drunks,
and
a painter.
Easy camaraderie: sharing families, troubles,
the dissonant harmony of the North.
A paper trail of connections
from Sandy Lake to Kashechewan.

Time together; time alone:
gardening, sketching, sewing, camping.
And always the work: healingandteaching:
tragic, funny, frustrating.
Keepers of the secrets and the faces.
Etching their way into the archives of the North.

The friends are Martha Aldrich and Tops van Vliet. The poem was written after the tragic death of Tops. See "Tops and Me" in this collection.

Death,

at Owl River: a glacial stream, running swift and silty.
An uncertain step on the rocky bottom and. . .
frantic anguish on the banks, around the curve;
screams into the wind.
So much lost.

So much gained.
Two women who laughed and cried and endured
for twenty-four years, over thousands of miles.

A gift.

Sharon Irvine has spent the last 41 years in the Northwest Territories and admires those who live and work in the North. She is a retired school teacher who loves to tell stories in both prose and poetry.

REGINA'S SPECIAL AWARD

Joanne M. Smith

In the summer of 2002, I received a phone call from my regional nurse manager who asked my opinion on nominating Regina Pastion* for the Commemorative Medal on the occasion of the Queen's Golden Jubilee. We collaborated on the application. We had to provide the reason for the nomination, in the form of a short narrative – which was not to exceed 40 words. It read:

> *Regina has worked as a Community Health Representative (CHR) for over 28 years. She increased the importance of health in this community with a strong and significant emphasis on immunization of infants. Prior to her dedication and passion to increase immunizations, the coverage was extremely low; today it is well over 90%.*

In fact, Regina had been dealing with the health needs of the community (First Nations Reserve) of Assumption, Alberta, since the early 1960s. Although she was thrilled to receive the medal, she feels the most important result of her years of service was a healthier community.

In the early years, the remoteness of Assumption made it a challenge to look after the sick. All of the health care was done in the homes. As the only means of transportation was either by horse and wagon, or by foot, these visits took time. Regina visited all of the families to find out about their health issues and needs. When the doctor and nurses came to the community, Regina was their translator. She would provide them with a list of the people that they would need to visit, she would give them the background history of the patients, and then she introduced them – so that both parties felt comfortable.

Regina tells us that there was a feeling of mutual respect between her and the people she served. "Because I liked them," she says, "there was real good communication with the people." However, the children of the community were not impressed when they saw Regina and the nurse coming to do immunizations, and usually they ran off and hid. She says that she would sometimes have to haul kids out from under beds, or even out of the bush. According to Regina, the biggest hurdle was overcoming the misunderstanding of the importance of proper health care. A great many of the medical conditions at that time, such as lice, scabies, and impetigo, were a result of a lack of running water and poor sanitation. Today, we see very few cases of these conditions.

* * *

---

* "Regina's Story," a profile of Regina Pastion, also by Joanne Smith, appears in *Northern Nurses: True Nursing Adventures from Canada's North.*

But back to the saga of the Commemorative Medal. The nomination was sent off. Nothing was heard until early in December, when I received a phone call from the office of the Regional Director General of Alberta. His secretary informed me that Regina was to be in Edmonton on December 13 to receive her medal. She had already left for the day, so I was unable to tell her the news until the next morning. Needless to say, she was thrilled. She was to be allowed two guests, and I was honoured to be one them. Her other guest was her daughter, who lived in Edmonton.

* * *

I made travel arrangements for the two of us. We were both going down the day before, but on different airlines. Assumption is 115 km from the nearest airport, which is in High Level. I was flying out at 6:45 a.m. I chose to go to High Level the night before and spend the night in a motel, so that I wouldn't have to worry about the driving conditions at five o'clock in the morning. Regina's flight was at 11:00 a.m., also on December 12. I had arranged to pick up a rental car in Edmonton, and I told Regina that I would meet her at the airport when her flight arrived. Both Regina and I were to stay at the Westin Hotel, which is quite close to the Shaw Conference Centre where the award ceremony was being held. I got into Edmonton by 8:30, picked up my car, did some running around, and then went to meet Regina at the airport.

I arrived a little early and settled in to wait for her. Several flights came in, but there was no sign of the plane from High Level. When I inquired at the desk, I was told that it had been cancelled due to freezing rain in High Level. They didn't know if the evening flight would go or not. Regina was booked on it *if* it happened. I called the nursing station on my cell phone and let them know what was going on. I spoke to Gina and asked her to make sure that Regina went back in for the evening flight. Gina assured me that she would take care of it. Then she called me back to say that she couldn't find Regina. She had not come back to Assumption, and she wasn't at the airport. The taxi had dropped her there, not realizing that the flight was cancelled.

We started to make contingency plans. The 11:00 plane the next day wouldn't get her to Edmonton for the ceremony. The early one that I had taken would get her there on time, but it was booked for the next morning. Gina made tentative plans for a charter flight, if necessary. Meanwhile, attempts to locate Regina were unsuccessful. I met the evening flight with my fingers crossed. Would she be on it? *She was.* I breathed a sigh of relief. When there had been no flight, she had caught a ride to her sister's place near High Level, where she had spent the day. She had taken a taxi back to the airport, in time for her trip.

* * *

The next day, all decked out in our "dress or business suit," as directed, Regina and I went to the Conference Centre, where we met her daughter, Gladys. There was a rehearsal for the recipients, before the Lieutenant Governor came to present the medals. Finally, the big moment arrived. The Honourable Lois Hole, Lieutenant Governor of Alberta, was ushered to the front, accompanied by her aide de-camp. The names were read out, along with a brief reason why each person was receiving the award. Regina's citation was essentially the same as the original narrative that we had sent in along with the nomination, back in the summer. As each name was read, the person proceeded across the stage and received his or her award from the Lieutenant Governor. As Regina's award was presented to her, the Lieutenant Governor said, "It is on occasions like this, I am glad to be the Queen's representative, so that I can bow to people like Regina." And then, she did so.

After the award ceremony, Health Canada employees were taken to a side room for a group photo with Anne McClellan, the federal Minister of Health. Following that, there was an opportunity for Regina and her daughter to have their photos taken with the Lieutenant Governor. Regina stayed in the city with Gladys for the weekend, while I flew back that evening. It was a day to remember – as it was my birthday as well.

* * *

For several years, Regina kept telling us that she was going to retire in the summer; but as summer got closer, she would change her mind, and say, "Just one more year." However, in August of 2003, she finally decided that this was the time. She had had a tough year, with several losses in her family, and she was feeling tired. August 30 was her final day.

We made plans for her retirement party, which took place on October 6, 2003. Several dignitaries from the Head Office in Edmonton, including Don Leduc, our Zone Director, flew up for the event. The festivities were scheduled to start at 10:00 a.m., and we were all ready to go – except that the guest of honour was missing. Finally, at about 10:40, we called her. She said she wasn't sure what time it was to start, but that she would be right over. One of the members of the local RCMP had agreed to don his red serge for the occasion and escort Regina to the stage. There were many presentations and awards given to her. Following the ceremony, there was a community feast which was well-attended.

Although Regina is officially retired, she still comes in as a volunteer on "doctor day" to help the clinics run smoothly. We are very glad to have her around. The nursing station just isn't the same without her.

SNOWBUNNY

Joanne M. Smith

It was a blustery night in March, the kind of night when all northern nurses go to bed saying a little prayer that they will not have to go out before morning. It was the mid-1980s and I was working in Jean D'Or Prairie, Alberta. Our station was in two separate buildings, approximately 150 feet apart. Going out for a call meant putting on your parka, Sorels, and mittens. Because we did not have an intercom system, the patients came to the door of our trailer and either rang the doorbell, banged on the door, or opened the door and yelled. The doorbell was a recent addition, and not everyone was aware that we had one. (That is another story.) There were very few telephones in the community, so most patients arrived without advance warning.

Around 3:00 a.m. on this particular night, there was a knock at our trailer door. I answered and found a man standing there. He said, "My wife, he's sick." This meant she was about to deliver her baby. (When I first heard this statement, I was confused; but I soon learned that, in the Cree language, there is no gender differentiation.) He said his wife was waiting in the car. They had been on their way to the nursing station when their car had run out of gas. I ran to the station, grabbed the always-packed maternity bag, and hurried to the government Suburban with the husband. I knew that his wife had short labours and that she had a habit of waiting at home – just to be really sure she was in labour. At least one of her five kids had been born at the nursing station, and the doctor who visited the community had teased me, saying that *I* would be delivering her current baby.

I followed the road that the husband indicated. We could see the car up ahead, but suddenly he told me that I should turn down another road. Actually, it was a trail – not a road. Although there were skidoo tracks off in that direction, it had not been plowed. I shifted into 4-wheel drive and forged on. As the headlights pierced the blowing snow, I could see two people ahead of us. One was lying in the snow, and the other was standing beside her, clad only in a short-sleeved blouse.

I quickly sized up the situation. Apparently, the man's wife and her mother had decided to walk to the nursing station after the husband had left. On the way, the baby had decided it was time to enter this cruel, cold world. Grandmother had delivered the baby, taken off her coat and wrapped the baby in it, then placed her between the mother's legs. She had not yet delivered the placenta. I sent the husband back to the vehicle to get the maternity bag, so that I could cut the cord and get the baby out of the cold. By this time, the nearest neighbour had come out to see what was going on. We placed Mom on the stretcher and loaded her into the Suburban. Then I discovered we were stuck in the snow. The husband and the neighbours piled out and pushed. Eventually, we got the car moving and drove quickly back to the nursing station. I hurried the grandmother inside – she was wrapped in a blanket and carrying the baby. The men carried the mother in on the stretcher. It was quite comical to see them struggling to get their moccasin rubbers off, while still holding onto the stretcher and trying not to flip Mom off in the process.

After I got the mother and baby into bed, I asked the men to fill hot water bottles to warm them, especially the baby. The men headed for every sink in the station to run hot water. They hurried back with the bottles and backed into the room, so that they wouldn't see the mother in bed.

After I made sure the patients had warmed up, I called our taxi (also a Suburban) to take us to the hospital in Fort Vermilion. We put the patient on a gym mat in the back and I rode there with her. On the way to town, I had the taxi driver translate for me, and I asked the grandmother if the baby had cried right away. She said, "Yes, baby cry, baby cry!" I thought to myself, I'll bet baby cried – going from a +37° tummy, to a –20 ° snowbank. (The baby was probably thinking, "Let me back in!") When we arrived at the hospital, the doctor met me with, "I told you so!" I said that I couldn't take credit for the delivery. All I did was scoop everyone out of the snowbank.

And what has all of this to do with a snowbunny? The family name of the newborn baby was Wapoose, which translates as "rabbit." Because of that, my staff gave the baby girl the nickname of Snowbunny.

Joanne M. Smith, RN, PHCNP, BScN graduated in 1982 with her degree in nursing from the University of Windsor, in Ontario. She completed her Primary Health Care Nurse Practitioner certification in 1996 at the University of Western Ontario in London. She currently works in Assumption, Alberta. Joanne's story "Northern Nursing Observations" appears in *Northern Nurses: True Nursing Adventures from Canada's North.*

HE'S ALWAYS RIGHT

Joy Pritchard

It was a beautiful, late spring morning in Spence Bay. Mike Hewitt* gassed up the skidoo, and I packed the sled for a day trip fishing. Many times, I had said to and about Mike that he was like a breath of fresh air when he came to the community. He was always funny, always willing to try to fix anything – sometimes succeeding – and very intent on getting us out of the nursing station.

It was Angela Poole's turn for a weekend on call. I wasn't really interested in going fishing, as I detest fish. But Mike insisted it would be good for me. He drove the nursing station skidoo. He refused to drive Angie's and my Elan, Skidoo's baby snowmobile. I hated riding on the sled, for it was very uncomfortable and really rough going over the late spring terrain, with exposed rocks and puddles of icy water.

Not soon enough for me, Mike thought he had found a good fishing lake. How would he know, I wondered. He parked the snowmobile beside a nice little island, got out the axe and crowbar, and took off to dig a hole in the ice. Meanwhile, I unpacked the polar bear and caribou skins, and a rug, and laid them on the dry land. I took out a book and some munchies, removed my mukluks and socks, rolled up my jeans, and using my parka as a pillow, basked in the intense spring sunshine. *Heaven on earth.*

For what seemed like hours, I could hear Mike chopping and digging. I called out, "Any fish yet?" No answer, so I looked up. There he was, stripped to his bare chest and red as a lobster from extreme activity. I called out again, "Have you reached water yet?"

"The only water in this hole is what's dripping off my nose!" was his reply. (And many of you will remember Mike's nose.)

He dug six holes that day, but caught no fish. He was right about a couple of things, though -- that I would enjoy the day out in the fresh air and that it would be good for me. Don't you hate it when someone is *always* right?

---

* Mike Hewitt was the Zone Nursing Officer for the Mackenzie Zone in 1973. His story "My First Solo Flight" appears in *Northern Nurses: True Nursing Adventures from Canada's North*.

WE SHOULD HAVE PATENTED THE THING

Joy Pritchard

I was returning from my fourth medevac since arriving in Spence Bay in the early 1970s, when I had a chance to talk to Ruth Sutherland, who was the nurse in charge in Cambridge Bay. We always had to stay one night in Cambridge.

Ruth's many years of experience in the North, and her rather stern countenance, always made me feel a bit intimidated. I was still pretty green and, honestly, I didn't have a clue about how to run a nursing station. I finally plucked up the courage to ask Ruth, "Ah, Ruth, do you ah, do you do um, home visit?" I felt stupid and it didn't help that Ruth looked at me as if to say, "You twit, of course we do home visits. They are only the most important part of our job!" She didn't say that, of course, but said, "Yes we do, don't you?" And that was the end of the conversation. Dinner was ready. She had made a sumptuous feast of pork chops, mashed potatoes, peas, carrots, and a great dessert. All the meals Ruth made when I passed through Cambridge were terrific.

When I got back to Spence Bay, Angela and I began working on a home visit program, which became a masterpiece. Not one program category was missed. Not one child, not one elder, not one person was omitted from this work. It accounted for every home, every office, every store – well, the Hudson's Bay – and the school. We even included the churches, community meetings, and the newly formed health committee. It was wonderful.

You might ask, "Did it work?" Yes!

It was a monthly calendar. Every program was given a different colour. For example, high-risk infants were red, pregnancies were pink, TB and chronic disease were black, the elderly were green, and so on. And we listed every family and family member, group, agency, and business. We figured out how frequently we needed to visit each person, and then put the appropriately coloured pin in the day the visit was to take place. After the visit and the charting were done, the pin was stuck in a column at the end of each week. We'd check regularly to see if we had done all the visits, and if we hadn't – nothing is foolproof because there would always be medevacs, holidays and relief in another community – we would place the pins in for the next week.

I think it took longer to create this piece of art than to do the work, but it helped. We became very familiar with all the families and the community, and we began doing an enormous amount of health promotion. And at the end of each month, I could count up the coloured pins to do statistics.

We should have patented the thing!

"HOW MANY SLEEPS TO THOM BAY?"

Joy Pritchard

Aiola said he would take me to Thom Bay, where a film crew from England was making a documentary about a young English explorer. On Thursday night, I packed the *komatik* (sled): two polar bear skins, two caribou skins, a down sleeping bag, a huge box of food, chocolate bars, and extra gas. Aiola checked my skidoo and gassed it up for me. I laid out my long underwear, two pairs of wool socks, my *kamiks* (seal skin boots), seal skin mitts, down parka and wind pants, a wool toque and a scarf, and I was set. Angela Poole was very jealous because I was going "on location," but it was her turn to take weekend on call.

At 8 p.m., Aiola hadn't arrived, so I called him. He said, "Not going."

"What? ... Why?"

Then he said, "Ask my brother." And he hung up. Aiola has *eight* brothers!

I called the youngest brother. "I'll take you. Be ready by 10." At 11 p.m., I called him and he said, "Not going."

"What? ... Why?"

"Ask my brother."

I called David, one of the older brothers, and he said, "I'll take you."

"Are you sure?" I asked.

"Yes. I'll be there at midnight." And he was.

We drove all night. It was about minus thirty, but there was no wind – except the wind rushing past as we raced and bumped along over the ice. I pulled the scarf over my nose so only my eyes were exposed, and they were crusted with icicles. I could feel my nostril hairs stiff with ice and began to wonder if we would ever get there, wherever "there" was. The night was clear like twilight, with just a hint of orange on the horizon, as the sun struggled to greet the day.

About eight in the morning, we arrived at David's camp and found all his family sleeping soundly in the tent. "Sleep," he said. I crawled into the tent with my sleeping bag and snuggled in amongst David's many children. Blissfully warm, I fell asleep.

The film *How Many Sleeps to Thom Bay?*, directed by Graham Hurley, was produced about thirty years ago by Independent Television Northampton, UK. It won best foreign film documentary in England. To the best of the knowledge of the author (who played the part of a nurse in the film), it is no longer available.

When I awoke, David was making tea on the Coleman stove. Everyone else was up and had gone fishing. We had tea and pilot biscuits, and eventually I asked if we should get going. "Not going," he said.

"What? ... Why? Why did you bring me here only to tell me we're not going on?"

"Can't take *kabloona* (white) woman over the ocean," he said.

"David, you already brought me here. I'm already on the ocean. Besides, I promised the film crew I'd be there and they're depending on me."

"See those mountains over there?" he said, pointing with his tea mug. "They're black, very far. See those mountains over there?" pointing into the haze. "They're blue, soooo far. That's where we go."

"I don't care how far it is. I want to go. Please, David," I begged.

"OK."

We drove along at a good clip, when suddenly David stopped. He indicated for me to stop, and be quiet. He slung a rifle over his shoulder and crouched behind what looked like a white kite. What was he doing, I wondered. We were somewhere on the Arctic Ocean and he was going to fly a kite! Suddenly, a sound coursed through my body. I thought the ocean and the sky had split. What was that? I soon discovered that David had shot a seal. He pulled it out of the ice-hole, strapped it onto his sled and we were off again. Not a word passed between us.

We continued for hours. I couldn't see David anymore, but I could hear his skidoo. I should run out of gas pretty soon, I thought. Just then, my skidoo began to sputter. I looked around. My sled was gone.

I'd been told never panic – and *never* leave your skidoo if it breaks down. So I waited. I'd also been told: don't get too physical; keep moving, just enough to stay warm, and don't sweat; you will become hypothermic very quickly with a layer of ice all over your body. So I waited. I had plenty of food and matches. I would have had the Coleman, but... I had no sled. I wondered how long it would be before David realized I was not behind him.

It warmed up and the sun shone, as only the Arctic sun can shine. I took out my sunglasses, for I would need them. I remembered that the Inuit use eyewear made out of caribou antler or whalebone, with tiny slits. Snow-blindness would only have added to my misery.

The expression "other world" had meaning for me at this point – because it truly was otherworldly. The horizon was indistinguishable in all directions and shrouded with fog that wafted over the ice. White everywhere, not a whiteout though, because I could see myself and the skidoo – but not my sled. The white defied description, like white on white; white that was the palest blue, ethereal, and amazingly beautiful. I thought that it must have been a very calm night when the ocean had frozen because it was flat, like a skating rink. Silly things you think of when trying not to be scared to death. I recall thinking: I'm a minute speck in this Arctic expanse, almost nothing in the universe. And what's a girl from Down Under doing on the Arctic Ocean anyway … beside a dead skidoo?

Finally, I could hear the skidoo (actually an Arctic Cat). "Here he comes! Thank God!" But he didn't stop; he just whizzed past. I waited. He came back. Without a word, David hooked up my sled, gassed up my skidoo, and we were off. I now understood a fundamental of the Inuit language: it is only necessary to speak of things that are not obvious. Of course, I felt stupid. But more than that, I realized how fragile I was and how dependent on this one human being. I also knew a greater power was marvelously present and probably enjoying my adventure.

We seemed to drive forever. I wondered how David knew where to go because everything looked the same to me. The mist-like fog clung to the ice and obliterated all form. We changed direction slightly and went toward what appeared to be an incline from the ice rink ocean. We entered a maze of ice and zigzagged, bounced, strained, and bumped through ice tunnels, over moguls of jagged ice, through interminable time. I was tired, cold and hungry. My whole body had been tense for hours, and I was already feeling the next-day stiffness. I was light-headed and mesmerized by the monotony of struggle, and I kept wondering if this would ever end.

Then suddenly we were there. We burst onto the "beach" and there was the film crew and their camp. I have never seen four extraordinarily good-looking men roar with such delight and disbelief when they realized we were not a figment of their imagination or a mirage. Bear hugs and kisses from all four, and I loved being me.

I had many extraordinary adventures during that amazingly short weekend, but they will have to keep for another time. So, how many sleeps to Thom Bay? Just one!

Joyce (Joy) Pritchard RN, SCM, BEd earned her RN at the Tamworth Base Hospital in New South Wales, Australia. She studied midwifery at the King George V Memorial Hospital and the Royal Prince Alfred Hospital in Sydney, also in NSW, Australia. At the University of Alberta in Edmonton, she did her clinical training. Later, at the University of Calgary in Alberta, she achieved her Bachelor of Education. Joy was the nurse in charge in the Spence Bay Nursing Station in the early 1970s. She lives in Edmonton where she is currently working at Alberta Health and Wellness as the Provincial Coordinator for Human West Nile Virus Surveillance. She is a sessional instructor at the Faculty of Nursing at the University of Alberta. Joy has a beautiful daughter, Katie; a wonderful son-in-law, Shawn, and two grandchildren, Jaeden and Biala.

THE FLAG BEARER

Sonya Grypma

Late one Sunday evening, a young boy knocked on my door and told me that his grandmother had a headache. He seemed so distraught that I grabbed my nurse's bag and followed him down the gravel road to his house. I had lived on Dolphin Island for over a year and knew most of the 500 residents. But I didn't know Angie* or her grandson.

The island is off the north coast of British Columbia, not far south of the Alaska Panhandle, and accessible only by boat or seaplane. In the 1980s, when I was in this community, there were only two phones in the whole village. One was at the one-nurse station where I worked and the other was at the school. There was only one vehicle, a pickup truck. Villagers travelled to and from other communities by fishing boat. It took about ten minutes to walk from one end of the community to the other.

I found Angie sitting on her couch, clutching her head. Her living room was already lined with concerned relatives who had been notified of the crisis by the ever-present citizens' band radio. I reached for the blood pressure cuff and crouched in front of her. I took mental notes of her symptoms. Suddenly Angie's left arm and leg jerked straight out. Her eyes widened in fright, and she slumped over, unconscious. Was it a stroke? A seizure? My heart raced when I realized there would be no way to get her to the hospital to get the care she required. It was too dark for the medevac helicopter to land safely.

As I bemoaned our limited options for treatment, family members helped to lift Angie onto a stretcher. "Nurse," said a relative, as they slid the stretcher onto the bed of the pickup truck for transport to the nursing station, "the Coast Guard ship is docked at the float. Maybe *they* could take her to town." Unbelievable! A Coast Guard ship? I had never seen one in the village before. Sure enough, the village school had invited them for a visit. The crew generously agreed to carry Angie, her son, grandson, and me to the mainland, some forty miles east. For six anxious hours, I kept vigil perched on a crate beside Angie's stretcher as the ship sailed toward the sunrise.

It was daybreak when an ambulance met us at the town dock. As we arrived at the emergency room, I was startled at the swiftness with which Angie was whisked away by the medical team. How abruptly my responsibility ended! I catnapped on a hospital couch and then caught a morning seaplane flight back to the village. Before I left, the physician told me that these kinds of symptoms in an otherwise healthy 64-year-old were "ominous" and that he had

---

* Pseudonym

arranged for Angie's immediate transfer down south to a major Vancouver hospital. It was weeks later – and only by chance – that I learned of Angie's outcome . . . .

* * *

Six weeks after Angie's crisis, I left the village for good. I had already shipped my belongings to the mainland, and I would now follow by kayak as part of an annual row-a-thon fundraiser. A female friend and I joined a group of twenty village men for our 4 a.m. departure. By taking turns paddling in streamlined ocean kayaks, my friend and I hoped to keep up with the fishermen in their bulkier canoes. While one of us paddled, the other rested in one of the escort boats.

There was something very satisfying about leaving that mystical, ancient Tsimshian community in the dark. We sat level with the ocean, surrounded only by sounds of paddles lapping the water and the hum of the escort boats' engines. Later in the day, we watched seaplanes flying overhead. They dipped their wings in greeting, as they carried villagers from the island to the town for a celebratory post row-a-thon feast.

After ten long hours, we spotted the shoreline. We were mistaken in believing we were almost finished. My friend and I got into our kayaks for the last leg of the trip. Minutes stretched into two hours as we paddled parallel to the shore towards town. We felt exhausted and discouraged as we realized the town dock was still miles away. But then a small group of onlookers began to cheer us on from a lookout spot on the shore. A little further on we saw them again – a small band of people cheering and honking, and waving a small white flag. They drove from point to point, recognizable because of their omnipresent white flag.

The dock was jam-packed when we finally arrived. As someone helped me out of my kayak, I heard my name, "Sonya! Over here!" It was uncharacteristic of the villagers to call me by my first name. Turning towards the voice, I saw that the elderly woman who addressed me was the flag bearer, for she was still waving the white flag – or rather, a white plastic grocery bag tied to the end of a cane. It was Angie! She needed the cane because she was still recovering from life-saving emergency surgery she had undergone six weeks earlier in Vancouver for a brain aneurysm.

Sonya (Visser) Grypma RN, PhD (candidate) graduated in 1986 with a Bachelor of Nursing from the University of Calgary in Alberta. Her work as a northern nurse with Health and Welfare Canada triggered an ongoing interest in intercultural nursing. Sonya has worked as a public health nurse in Calgary and Lethbridge. She has volunteered on international nursing projects in Uganda and Guyana. She has taught courses in community health nursing and transcultural nursing, most recently at the University of Lethbridge. In 2001 she graduated with a Master of Nursing (intercultural focus) at the University of Calgary. Sonya is presently a doctoral candidate at the University of Calgary where her research is on the history of Canadian nurses in China from 1888 to 1949.

MRS. O'FLAHERTY OF MANOR FARM

Eleanor R. Wheler

In his book *Whistle Stop Dentist: On the Ontario CPR Dental Car 1931 to 1935*, David C. Brownlow, tells about the Dental and School Cars which travelled the railways and visited small isolated communities throughout northern Ontario with a dentist, a teacher, and a public health nurse on board. Brownlow, whose father was a dentist on one of these cars, spent his first two years on the trains.

He writes, "The public health nurse provided assistance to the dentist, making a preliminary review of the children's overall health and dental hygiene, and advised the dentist accordingly. Unlike the dentist who did most of his work on the Dental Car, the nurse would often go off into the community and individual homes to carry out her checking of people's health. She also provided healthcare instruction and treatment for minor ailments."

Eleanor Wheler was one of those nurses referred to in Brownlow's book. Her story, which follows, was originally published in *The Canadian Nurse, April 1933, Vol. XXIX, No. 4* and is reprinted here with minor changes with permission.

After walking two miles and a half up the tracks to see the five children who are attending the Canadian Pacific Railway School Car, I walked on another mile to see the mother of three of the children who are so eagerly pursuing their education. They are getting instruction one week out of every five, and study at home the other four weeks. These children had given their address as Manor Farm, so I was expecting a rather up-to-date establishment. However, since I had followed their directions, and since they had told me that theirs was the last house for eight miles, I decided that I must be approaching Manor Farm, when I saw a low shack built of logs with the bark still on them, and the chinks filled up with clay. From the tiny chimney, a spiral of pale smoke rose to the sky. Tucked into a corner of the rocky hill behind the house, were the barn and chicken coop, also built of logs, but of a more careless type of construction.

I knocked at the door, and the woman who opened it jumped as if terrified at the sight of a stranger.

"Good morning, Mrs. O'Flaherty," I said, "I am the nurse from the Dental Car."

"Come on in, Nurse. You're welcome, sure. I've never seen a stranger here for so many months that the sight of you nearly took my breath away. But I'm glad to see you, Nurse; I am that. I've been here for twenty years and I've never had a nurse to see me before. It was good of you to walk a way out here. Three miles it is from the village, Nurse, and it's been near two years since I walked out to the village, Nurse,— "

"How are you feeling, Mrs. O'Flaherty?"

"Oh I'm fine. I've never been sick a day of my life for twenty years, Nurse, not since we came to this country. My husband's a beautiful provider and we never want for a thing. We're CPR, Nurse, you know, and we can have everything we want."

"Your teeth don't look very good, Mrs. O'Flaherty. Do they never bother you?"

"No, Nurse, my teeth are fine. They never bother me at all, at all. I've only six left, and they don't just meet. But they are far better than the false ones my husband got from the dentist. He never gets no enjoyment out of his food at all now, and I can eat anything with mine and I've never no rheumatism, nor nothing like that, so why should I part with these six good teeth, Nurse"?

"How is your digestion? Can you chew your food properly, Mrs. O'Flaherty?"

"Sure, Nurse, my digestion's fine. I never have a pain nor an ache. But my husband's a beautiful provider. We even have a ricer for the potatoes, Nurse. We never want for a thing."

"When I was examining Mary— "

"Yes, Nurse, what did you think of Mary, Nurse? She's my baby. Eight years old she was this fall, you know, and I guess she'll always be the baby now, for I'm fifty-two this year. She is the last of eight of them, all away now but the three at school, and all doing well, Nurse. Three boys in the Government camps, one girl in a situation at Winnipeg, and maybe you have heard of Maggie. Her it was that married the teacher, Nurse. Just turned seventeen she was, and I never thought she would do so well for herself as to marry a teacher. You'll have the pleasure of meeting them when you go to the second stop on the line. To think of our Maggie marrying the likes of a school teacher — "

"And about Mary, Mrs. O'Flaherty — "

"Yes, what do you think about Mary, Nurse? You know it's the first time ever a nurse has looked at them, and I've been here twenty years. Next year we get a long service pass, Nurse, anywhere from coast to coast. Won't it be grand to travel, Nurse? Twenty years I've lived in this house and I've never been more than thirty miles away."

"I thought that Mary looked very thin, Mrs. O'Flaherty. What do you give her to eat?"

"She gets the best food we can get, Nurse. Why, we have fresh pork and potatoes twice every day. My husband's a beautiful provider. We even have a ricer for the potatoes, Nurse, and oh, it makes them beautiful."

"Have you any other vegetables?"

"No, Nurse, we don't like anything else so well as potatoes, Nurse, and we can't get carrots and cabbages and them things to grow and we haven't had a cow this two years, Nurse, so I guess the children don't get enough milk to drink. Our cow died, Nurse, but we are going to get another next fall, and they drink lots of this canned milk in their tea and coffee, Nurse—"

"But, tea and coffee, Mrs. O'Flaherty, are not—"

"Yes, they get all the tea and coffee that they can drink, Nurse. My husband's a beautiful provider. We even have a ricer for the potatoes, and it does make them beautiful, Nurse."

"Milk and fresh vegetables—"

"All right, I'll do anything to oblige you, Nurse. It's the first time ever a nurse has come to see us, and I'd like to do anything I can to oblige you, Nurse."

"It's the health of your children that I am thinking about, Mrs. O'Flaherty. If they eat the right food—"

"I'll tell my husband what you say, Nurse. He's a beautiful provider, Nurse. I'm sure I don't know why the children don't get fatter."

Feeling that the topic of food was not getting a proper audience, I thought I would try another subject.

"I noticed that Mary had a great many nits in her hair, Mrs. O'Flaherty, but the boys—"

"We never had such a thing in our lives until the children went to school in the village; that was three years ago, after we were burnt out with the fire, and I've never been able to get rid of them since. She gets her bath every Saturday, and I wash her hair every week and fine-comb it, but it never seems to get a bit better. If the boys get them, we clip their hair right off short; but with Mary, she's my baby, you know, Nurse."

"If you would mix equal parts of coal oil and sweet oil – I shall leave you a copy of the directions and I am sure that with a little work you can get rid of them in a few days." And I explained the treatment at greater length, without more than a dozen interruptions.

"While the Dental Car is here, Mrs. O'Flaherty, don't you think it would be a good idea for the children to come and get their teeth—"

"Yes, Jimmy's bothered terrible with the toothache; but he stands it like a man, he does, Nurse."

"His six year molars are quite gone, Mrs. O'Flaherty. There is nothing left but the roots."

"I never complain about *my* teeth, and I've only six left, but a better six than they are I have yet to see, and sure, Jimmy can get on with the mouthful he's got, but I'll send them down to the Dental Car tomorrow, Nurse. I'll do anything to oblige you; it's the first time ever a nurse has been here, and I've been here twenty years."

"Proper food will help the children's teeth, too, Mrs. O'Flaherty. Don't you think you could get some vegetables and whole-grained cereals sent in from the store in the village?"

"I'll do my best to oblige you, Nurse. We might be able to send Jimmy in with the dogs. I've really no trouble to clothe the children, Nurse. Some rich women in Ottawa send the grandest things for the children to wear to school: sweaters and socks and mitts, and even pants for the boys and skirts for the girls, and what do you think was in the box they sent this Christmas, Nurse? A red dress and a green, and both in the finest satin. My eyes just sparkled when I saw them, Nurse, and I thought: My! How fine I would have looked in that twenty years ago. But I am too old to start wearing satin now, Nurse. I have never worn a satin dress in all my life, but I thought how pretty Maggie would look in them two satin dresses, her that married the teacher, you know, Nurse; so I sent them on to her, and she says she feels just like a princess, Nurse."

I saw that the sun was setting, so I said I would really have to start for home.

"Well, I am glad you came, and I am sorry you can't stay for a bite to eat, but maybe you'll walk out again, Nurse. I would like you to tell me more about the children, and I'll try to oblige you and do all that you say, Nurse, and the next time you come perhaps the children will be fatter. My husband's a beautiful provider; why we have a ricer for the potatoes and everything. We never lack nothing. I'm awful glad you came, Nurse. You've a long cold walk. It's twenty below now, and with the sun down you will have to walk fast to keep warm. Goodbye, Nurse, goodbye. I'm awful glad you came."

As I walked home, I thought about Mrs. O'Flaherty and her husband who was the beautiful provider and their little log house with the floors of rough planks and the homemade beds and stools and table, and I wondered if the few words that I had been able to get in were worth that long, cold walk. But don't you think Mrs. O'Flaherty has been provided with another subject of conversation? Can't you just hear her say,—

"I have been here twenty years, and I never had a nurse come to see me before, but one day a nurse walked three miles just to see me, and when she started for home it was twenty below, and oh, the fine talk we had. That was the year Maggie married the schoolteacher. What a fine match she made!"

Eleanor Reesor Wheler RN, DPHN was born in Pittsburg, Pennsylvania on October 17, 1900. She graduated in 1924 from the Toronto General Hospital Training School for Nurses. After further education, she became a public health nurse in northern Ontario. In 1945, she moved to Prince Edward Island where she continued her public health nursing career. She resided in Fernwood and Bedeque, PEI, with her life companion, Elaine Harrison. She loved animals and the sea, and she appreciated all the arts. She played the violin and recorder, painted, hooked rugs, and wrote many stories and poetry. Eleanor died in Charlottetown, PEI on December 27, 1996.

DESPAIR AND JOY

Margaret Hamilton

"**N**urse! Come quick! Kenneth's gone mad!" The bearers of this news were two young boys. I immediately ran for my bag and hastily followed them on the dirt path that led to Kenneth's tent. He had been brought into the village from his trapping line where friends had stopped to see how he was getting along. To their surprise, they had discovered that his camp had burnt to the ground. With difficulty, they found him and brought him home. Not surprisingly, Kenneth was very disorientated and agitated.

When I examined him, I thought about tubercular meningitis and was concerned about the spread of infection among the members of the community. It was arranged that his wife and small children would stay in a nearby cabin with their elderly neighbour, Sarah. There were many offers of help to sit with Kenneth to attend to his needs, and to feed him when he was rational, and to protect him when he was not.

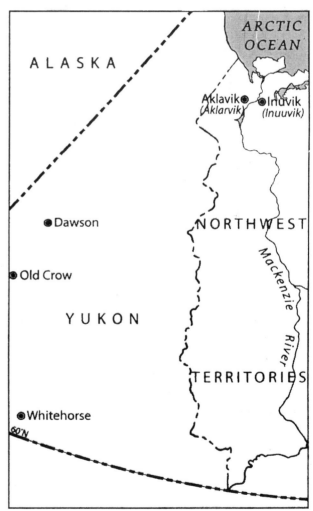

Having notified the RCMP of the situation, we had to wait for the appointed time to use the ham radio which was operated by a small generator at the barracks. We were in Old Crow in the Yukon. Aklavik and Dawson City were the nearest communities with a doctor. What caused us further delay was the fact that the Department of Transport only listened for radio transmissions on a special frequency from Old Crow between 7 and 7:30 p.m. It was Aklavik that was first able to get a doctor to the radio station. After we discussed the situation, arrangements were made for a plane to come the next day to evacuate Kenneth to hospital.

Throughout the night, men took turns looking after Kenneth, and women came with food and drinks for them. They observed a limited kind of "barrier nursing" – they washed their hands before entering and leaving the tent. The adults who cared for him came from households without small children.

The following day we looked for the plane, but the weather was dreadful, with pouring rain and low clouds. Since Old Crow did not have an airstrip, the river was the landing field. What made matters even worse was that a plane coming to Old Crow had to carry enough fuel to fly both directions, because there was no supply of aviation fuel in the community. This added to the problems. In order to save fuel, the pilots were obliged to fly through Rat Pass, because flying over the mountains would use up too much fuel. For ten days, we waited for a plane to come.

The weather remained dull, and it was raining when a plane finally arrived. We were surprised to see Dr. Elizabeth Emily Cass getting off. She was an ophthalmologist who had previously visited Old Crow, and who wanted to see three patients. The plane was to leave in half an hour. A neighbour was sent to find her patients and direct them to the mission/nursing station. Our log cabin overflowed with people. Kenneth's brother turned up and asked us not to send Kenneth away. He said that he was too close to death. It was a difficult time for his brother and his family. If he were to live, however, he would need more care than we could give him. Amos, a wonderful handyman, was asked to convey Kenneth to the plane.

Weeks passed before we had news of Kenneth. Through the RCMP, we learned that he had received excellent treatment in Inuvik. He was later taken to the Charles Camsell Hospital in Edmonton, where he had surgery for a tuberculoma. Several months later, when he returned to the village, he was given a warm welcome. His friends helped him build a new log dwelling for his growing family.

Margaret Burt Hamilton, RN, SRN, SCM graduated as a registered nurse from Southend on Sea General Hospital in England in July, 1949. She studied for the first part of her certification as a midwife at Middlesbrough Maternity Hospital in Middlesbrough, Yorkshire. She received the second part of her certificate at Thorpe Coombe Maternity Hospital in Walthamstow, England. In September 1951, she graduated as a certified midwife.

HELP FROM THE SKIES

Reverend John R. (Jack) Sperry

Isolation, an historic feature of life in the Arctic, has always been a heavy burden on northern nurses, especially for nurses of a bygone era. Prior to satellite telephone service, radio communication was always an encouraging factor – particularly when the atmospheric conditions were congenial. Advice from a southern doctor on a difficult case was always more than welcome. However, in dire emergencies, the need for a physician or surgeon, on hand to take charge, could not be exaggerated.

This was especially emphasized on the Arctic Coast, when spring was on the way, and the ice on the rivers and lakes was beginning to break up. In the 1950s, the bush planes that flew into Coppermine (Kugluktuk) were fitted with either pontoons for open-water landing or skis for solid ice landing. When there was neither water nor ice suitable for landing, it was a bad time to require professional medical assistance from the South.

* * *

In the spring of 1953, these problems were put to the test. Constable Victor Cormier, one of the two RCMP detachment personnel, had recently returned sick from a long, dog-team patrol to the North in severe weather conditions. He was taken to the nursing station, where he was quickly found to be suffering from pleurisy, a serious condition of the lungs, which would require speedy professional attention. Consultation by radio verified serious concern in the South, but landing conditions prevented any possibility of a rescue by plane. An appeal was made to the Canadian Forces, who responded with urgency, which resulted in help arriving from the skies. The excitement among the people of Coppermine made the coming event momentous. How could a doctor arrive by airplane when it couldn't land?

Early in the afternoon, a Dakota aircraft flew over. The whole community, the Native families and everyone else, cleared a stretch of ground between the few buildings, and they watched as the first marker-parachute floated down. Presumably with an eye to the wind, they dropped a second chute, with a large Red Cross on the panoply, and delivered a large trunk of medical supplies.

The main event followed. A huge, white parachute floated down, with a man swinging underneath it. It was the doctor himself, Squadron Leader Wynn. The second arrival was Corporal Strachan of the Airborne Regiment. There they were, both hastily trying to furl their chutes. If they had they not done that, the jump-master in the aircraft would have assumed an accident had happened and he would have descended himself. We did give them help – but only after we had taken our share of photographs.

Once they disentangled from their parachutes, the team was taken to the nursing station to attend to the sick constable. The necessary procedures were followed and not long after, a verdict of steady improvement and eventual health added to our gratitude for the entire operation. The early attention and consultation by the nurses over the radio, as well as all their assistance throughout, made them both necessary partners – even if they didn't have to jump from an airplane in the process.

Within a week, the Coppermine River disgorged itself of ice, and a float plane could land. The rescue team left for the South with the recovering constable – the close of yet another dramatic Arctic rescue.

Reverend John R. Sperry CM, CD, DD was born in England, and served in the Royal Navy during WWII. After he came to Canada, he graduated from King's College at Dalhousie University in Halifax, Nova Scotia. He moved to Coppermine in 1950 and served there for 20 years. His late wife, Betty, spent much of her time doing relief work at the nursing station. While working in Yellowknife, he became the third Anglican Bishop of the Arctic. In 2002, Bishop Sperry became a Member of the Order of Canada. His citation read:

He has been dedicated to the people of Canada's North for more than 50 years. Starting in the Missions of Coppermine and Fort Smith, he went on to become Bishop of the Arctic for the Anglican Church of Canada. Working throughout the Northwest Territories, Nunavut and northern Quebec, he was especially sensitive to the needs of the Inuit population, respecting their culture and way of life. He learned their language, translated their prayer books and lived as they did, often travelling by dog sled. He continues to minister to others within health and volunteer organizations in his community and as Chaplain of the Canadian Forces Northern Region.

MEMORIES OF AN ARCTIC MOTHER

Angela Sperry Friesen

For fifty years, my mother, Betty Sperry, spent an active life in the North. In June, 2001, at the age of 78, she passed away. She was born Elizabeth McLaren in1923. She took her nursing training in England, which included graduating from the London Homeopathic Hospital as a State Registered Nurse (SRN). She later studied for her midwifery qualifications and graduated in her State Certified Midwifery designation (SCM) at the Queen Charlotte's Hospital, in London, England.

In 1947, my mother enrolled in Emmanuel Missionary Training College where she studied for three years. In 1951, at the request of the Anglican Church, she spent a year in the northern settlement of Aklavik in the Northwest Territories, at the Anglican Mission Hospital. In 1952, she travelled with Bishop Marsh to Coppermine (now called Kugluktuk) where she married Reverend John Sperry. Betty Sperry took on a new role as a nurse on call and she also participated, alongside her new husband, in the missionary work in Coppermine, until 1969.

* * *

There is a story about her during that time that I remember well. One day, as I stood by the kitchen sink in our mission house in Coppermine, I watched Mum dashing around in the kitchen with her parka on. She pulled a pair of scissors, some heavy string, and some Kleenex from one of the kitchen drawers. When I asked her what she was doing, she explained quickly that she had to go "outside" (a northern term for going south, which included Yellowknife). She had to escort a woman who was expecting a baby. She was taking the scissors, string, and Kleenex, just in case the baby arrived early, while they were on the bush plane flying out. Mum didn't think this would really happen. However, she took the extra items – a desire to be prepared – as she hurried out of the house to get to the plane.

I was quite young at the time, so this intrigued me. I was especially interested since I knew that when it came to nursing habits, our mother was of the old school of thought: anything used in a delivery would have to be sterilized. But not in this case. Mum was in a rush and a little anxious. I too became excited.

Whenever our mother carried out her "on call" nursing duties, my brother John and I were left at home with Dad to take care of us. Some time later, a message got through to the nursing station in Coppermine that the baby had indeed arrived on the plane, and that both mother and infant were well. We, as a family, were delighted. When Mum arrived home from the trip, she related the whole story to us. She couldn't emphasize enough how calm the mother had been about giving birth on the plane. The mother seemed to have had no concerns, and the way Mum spoke about it, the delivery had been smooth and almost painless. Since the little girl was born in flight, her parents named her Angel, because the word for angels, in the Inuinaqtun bible, means "messengers with wings." The little angel had certainly arrived into our world with wings.

* * *

Another story about Mum goes back to the 1950s, when she and Dad lived in the first mission house – one that was built in 1929. Mum was faced with delivering a breech baby, and Dad was to be her assistant. In this case, delivering the baby would not be as smooth and easy as the birth on the bush plane. This mother was in considerable pain.

When a woman was about to give birth, the custom with the people in the Coppermine area was that the spouse would be, deliberately, otherwise engaged. My parents had been married for only a few days when my father was recruited to assist in this delivery. He admitted, at the time, that he too would have been much happier being engaged in another aspect of mission work. However, he did what Mum told him, and he shared some of the distress of the mother. Nevertheless, it all went well. The whole event attested to Mum's midwifery skills, skills that were practised alone, sometimes with her husband, and in a mission, instead of in a modern hospital like the one in Aklavik.

Angela Sperry Friesen was born and raised in Coppermine in the 1950s. She remembers well her years in the North with her parents, Rev. John and Betty Sperry. Angela and her husband, Doug Friesen, and her father, John Sperry, still live in Yellowknife. They are true Northerners.

FROM GLASGOW TO CANADA'S NORTH

Ann M. Connelly

At the Glasgow airport in September of 1980, I said goodbye to my parents and to Scotland. I was leaving to nurse for a year in St. Anthony, on the tip of the Northern Peninsula of Newfoundland. The jumbo jet journey was a blur. I cried the whole way. This was unusual for me, as I had often travelled alone to unfamiliar destinations. I now believe that I knew I would never be back to Scotland on a permanent basis. In the twenties and thirties, many of my relatives had gone to New Zealand, Australia, and the USA. None of them had returned to their homeland. In those days, they could only communicate by letter. Logically, I knew I would never be in this situation, but somehow it felt as if my life was changing.

After I had seen a newspaper advertisement about nursing in Canada, I had made inquiries. It was a big decision. I had worked for five years in a job I liked, I had bought an apartment, and I was enjoying my life. However, the thought of doing something different was always in the back of my mind, and I decided to do something about it. I attended an interview in London, during which I was shown some slides of the St. Anthony area. I would be working for the Grenfell Regional Health Board, as a public health nurse. The interviewer gave me a list of items I should take with me. Since there were no stores and no ways of getting everyday things, she suggested I should take items like toothpaste, soap, and stockings. She had obviously never been in Newfoundland. Who ever wore stockings? Had she never heard of the Sears and the Bay catalogues?

* * *

It was foggy when we arrived in Gander. I quickly recovered my composure – I was to catch the Grenfell Mission plane to St. Anthony. I cleared customs and recovered the one piece of baggage I had been allowed. I made inquiries about getting the next plane, but was told that it was grounded by fog. I wondered: what now! I knew no one and only had traveller's cheques with me. I managed to phone a contact in St. Anthony, who told me to wait at the Holiday Inn. The next day, I met a woman who was waiting for the same plane. She worked at the Bay store, and her husband was the plane mechanic. We ate together and explored the town.

On the third afternoon, the fog cleared and we set off. I was unprepared for the journey on the nine-seat plane, as I had never been on such a small aircraft. Little did I know that over the years, this would be one of the bigger planes in which I would travel. Flying out over the Atlantic, and then over trees, trees and more trees, I wondered what I was getting myself into. It seemed like the end of the earth. At St. Anthony, we were bundled into a van to be driven into town. Although it took only fifteen minutes, the trip along the gravel road from the airport seemed unending. My nursing supervisor met me and took me to the apartment that I was to share with two other nurses who worked at the hospital. After we picked up some basic food, I was on my own.

On my first weekend in St. Anthony, I realized how small it was. What a contrast to Edinburgh with its culture, its many museums, art galleries, and facilities – not to mention friends. My first purchase was a radio for news, entertainment, and music. I discovered the CBC, and I have been a fan ever since. As in many small places, people in St. Anthony clubbed together and entertained themselves. Before long, other nurses invited me to join them for meals, parties, and sing-along gatherings. Crafts were popular with everyone. Having knitted for years, I soon learned how to knit the special patterns unique to Newfoundland. I even learned how to bake bread and attended carpentry classes.

Each week, I drove along a gravel road to visit eight small communities: St. Lunaire, Griquet, Noddy Bay, Gunner's Cove, Hay Cove, Quirpon, Straitsview, and L'Anse aux Meadows. When driving was not possible, I travelled by skidoo, and occasionally, by boat. Winter conditions were frequently treacherous, with huge snowdrifts making it impossible to see more than a few yards. Nobody could get through until the plow and the grader had cleared a path. When getting back to St. Anthony was impossible (as it often was), I would have to stay with a family in one of the communities. After a few months, I grew to love the place and the people. As a result, I ended up living and working in St. Anthony for three years – two years beyond my original contract.

There was one event from my years in St. Anthony that I will never forget. In December of my second year in the community, a client asked if I would nurse him at home. Sam was dying, and he wanted to be near his family. I agreed and I was provided with a bed in a nearby house, so that I could visit him several times a day to give him medication, and make him comfortable. Family members cared for Sam. However, they needed help with some of the more technical procedures. I saw him as late in the evening as possible, and then went off to my own bed. They tried not to disturb me in the night, unless the situation became unmanageable. During this time, my normal duties went on as usual. By the third day, I was becoming tired; but I decided to continue.

In the middle of the fifth night, Sam died peacefully with his family present. They sent for me, so I was with him at the end. I removed the catheters and prepared him for viewing. To my surprise, two men came into the room with a homemade coffin. They asked me if I would put on his best suit. I somehow managed to do this with the help of a male relative, and together, we placed him in the coffin. It was a very emotional time for the family. It was for me, too, because I had become attached to all of them during Sam's last days. This happened just before Christmas. You can imagine how I felt on Christmas morning, when I received a parcel with a note from Sam, that said, *"Thanks for everything."*

After my time in St. Anthony, I worked for what was then called National Health and Welfare. From 1983 to 1985, I was the public health nurse in Rae-Edzo, which is northwest of Yellowknife in the Northwest Territories. Rae and Edzo are two villages eleven kilometers apart. When I was there, the school and an eight-bed cottage hospital were in Edzo, despite the fact that most people lived in Rae. Nurses, teachers, and local people who worked at either the school or the hospital lived in Edzo. The public health nurses shared the government car. I lived in Edzo, but regularly went back and forth, as I worked in Rae at the public health office and the clinic, which was in the same building. I was also the school nurse. Rae had stores, a church, band offices, social services, and an ambulance. The sick were transported to the hospital in Edzo by ambulance or by skidoo when the lake was frozen. Mostly, patients just arrived by any means possible.

As part of my job, each month I had to fly into Lac La Martre, Rae Lakes, and Snare Lake. One of the journeys to Rae Lakes, north of Rae-Edzo, proved to be more than I expected. The plane was chartered from Yellowknife. Since it cost the same for two people as for one person, my friend Sr. Barbara got permission to accompany me. (Sr. Barbara was a nurse at the hospital in Edzo.) We drove to Yellowknife in her car, full of equipment and supplies for the two-day expedition. At the airport, we transferred the supplies to the plane, and set off for Rae Lakes.

Although it was snowing in the community, we managed to land without incident. We unloaded the supplies and made our way into the nurses' quarters, which were at the back of the band office. They consisted of a room with a bed, a couch, a stove, and a fridge. The clinic room was separate, and people waited for treatment in the corridor. We unpacked and I set up for clinic. Sr. Barbara went to visit the priest, who was often in the community, while I worked in the clinic all day. I made lists for the doctor who was coming to the village the following day, with the environmental health officer. This was to be a day trip for them. By evening, the snow was becoming thicker, and Sr. Barbara and I wondered if the others would be able to land as scheduled.

Next morning, the snow had stopped but it was very dull. The plane made it in as expected, and the doctor and the environmental health officer (EHO) immediately set about the jobs that they came to do. Shortly after their arrival, however, the snow started again. By mid-afternoon, the snow had begun to blow around, and it was obvious that we would be unable to take off. The doctor, the environmental health officer, and the pilot had brought only their lunches with them. We had enough food for ourselves, with a little extra in case there were delays. We pooled what little we had and managed to eke out a meal. Sleeping arrangements were interesting. The doctor decided to sleep on the clinic table; the pilot settled down on the floor in the corridor, and the EHO grabbed the bed – which left the two-seat couch for Sr. Barbara and me. We slept fitfully, head to toe, in our heavy winter sleeping bags.

The following morning, it was obvious that we would not be travelling that day either. The doctor and I did some home visits, while the others hung about the clinic. The priest, Fr. L'Amoreaux (who was probably an Oblate of Mary Immaculate from France), came over later in the day to invite us for a caribou supper. What a great feast we had! After supper, the priest produced a Scrabble board, and we played Scrabble and more Scrabble. Another crowded night. We awoke to more blowing snow. Although Fr. L'Amoreaux had lots of caribou in his freezer, we did not want to clean him out of his supplies completely, so we made a dish with rice and other bits and pieces of food. Scrabble tournaments were set up between tending to patients, and we all got to know each other better.

By the fifth day, when the weather had finally cleared, we were very ready to leave. The pilot decided that he could take a chance, so we all piled into the plane and set off for Yellowknife, and home. We arrived without event. Sr. Barbara and I headed straight to the nearest restaurant, where my order included a large coffee. Fr. L'Amoreaux, who had thoroughly enjoyed his visitors, had beaten us all at Scrabble, hands down. Sr. Barbara, who had only been given two shifts off work at the hospital to travel with me, had much time to make up. While I was able to put it down to *just* another trip as a public health nurse.

* * *

One summer, between terms at university, I worked at Rae for eleven weeks. The small cottage hospital in Edzo had been shut down in 1985, and a nursing station had been built in Rae. There were six staff at the nursing station when I arrived. However, as holidays came along, this number was soon reduced. I had been assigned there before, as the public health nurse, but this time I was to do both public health and nursing station work.

Rae is not far off the road, where it turns south towards Yellowknife, just past the North Arm of Great Slave Lake. Accidents often happened on this narrow, gravel road. One evening when I was on call, five hysterical, injured men turned up at the door of the nursing station. They had been in a car accident on the Rae road and had somehow managed to carry one of their friends to the nearest habitation. They had been driving all day from Edmonton to Yellowknife and had diverted into Rae, to get some gas. It was obvious that they had been drinking en route. The rest of the nursing staff were immediately called as backup. As luck would have it, a doctor was in the community for a few days.

We all set about caring for this group of men. Each nurse took a patient, while the doctor went from one to the other and assessed the problems. Two nurses and the doctor worked on the man who had been carried in. However, it soon became apparent that he had died. To calm the others down, we decided not tell them about their friend – until their own needs were assessed and treated. They continued to ask about his condition, and they became belligerent when we would not let them see him. We patched and sewed up several wounds, took x-rays, applied bandages, and generally cleaned the men up.

Once the situation was clear, we decided to tell them about their friend's demise. They immediately went berserk. They pulled off bandages, threw chairs, and hit nurses. One of us managed to reach the phone and got through to the nearby RCMP attachment. After what seemed like forever (but was only a matter of minutes), three officers arrived with guns drawn. They obviously were called from off duty, since all but one came over in sweats and assorted street clothes. They brought order to the situation and escorted the four men to the police station where they spent the night, before being transferred to Yellowknife. The police inquiry began the next morning, and the body was removed to Yellowknife. None of the staff was injured. Nevertheless, it took us quite some time to clean up the mess and to recover from our night of excitement.

* * *

Working within the government system in the South is difficult once a nurse has worked in an isolated community. I am happy to have found a job in the Victoria area which gives me some autonomy. Nursing in the North is not for everybody, but those who like to work with different "rules" often find it hard to return to the status quo.

My original year of adventure has now grown into 24 years of working in Canada. After much thought, I became a Canadian citizen in 1990. Scotland will always be at my core. I say it is home when I'm in Canada; but when I'm in Scotland, I consider Canada as home. To take on citizenship of another country is not an easy decision – even if you love the country and are happy to spend the rest of you life in it. My journey from the northern tip of Newfoundland to the southern tip of Vancouver Island, where I now live, has been both interesting and worthwhile, and it has had its share of adventures.

During the days when I had both parents still living in Scotland, I went back every second year, with Mum and Dad visiting Canada on a regular basis. After Mum died, Dad came by himself to spend summers here. Now that he is unable to travel, I go to Scotland every year to visit him. I still have relatives and friends in Edinburgh and in the Glasgow area. In retrospect, I have no regrets about my decision to make that first move, despite my early anxiety. My initial instincts seem to have been proven right.

Ann M. Connelly RN, BScN, CHTP graduated from Glasgow Royal Infirmary as a registered nurse in 1970 and earned a certificate in psychiatric nursing in Edinburgh, Scotland in 1972. After a course in midwifery, she trained as a public health nurse at Queen Margaret College in Edinburgh. She also received a certificate as a field work teacher which allowed her to teach public health students "on the job." In 1980, she came to Canada and worked in Newfoundland, the Northwest Territories, and British Columbia. In the meantime, she earned her degree in nursing. Since then, she has obtained her Certified Healing Touch Practitioner and Reflexology certificates. She continues to work as a public health nurse, using holistic knowledge both on and off the job. Ann presently works in Victoria, BC, for the Inter Tribal Health Authority on two Native Reserves.

OVER THE FENCE

Janet P. Cross

It was a day to remember, a day I can never forget – even some 23 years later. It was August of 1981 and I was living on the island of Moose Factory in northern Ontario. Life was good, life was even great, and as head nurse of the obstetrical ward at Moose Factory General Hospital, I thought I had seen it all. We had an active unit with approximately 350 deliveries a year. And some of the most adorable babies ever born. Most of our patients were either Cree or Inuit, and as nurses, we were delighted to be their caregivers.

On this particular day – a rare day off for me – my pager rang, so I called the hospital to receive my message. I was stunned. A patient who was in labour was on her way by Twin Otter from "up the east coast" of James Bay. What we heard third-hand was that a foot could be seen. The next message was a request to meet the aircraft in Moosonee which is on the mainland, on other side of the river from Moose Factory. My initial reaction was "Help!" but then I said to myself, "Let's go." Thankfully, the transport isolette was ready. With our paediatrician and with as much equipment as we could carry, we headed for the ride across the river. Once in Moosonee, we were whisked to the airport to await the arrival of our mom-to-be. We hoped and prayed that she still *was* a mom-to-be and that she hadn't delivered on board.

The plane landed without incident, and within minutes we were attending our patient. We quickly learned that she was already the mother of eight. Had I known this fact earlier, I would have been much more uneasy as we waited for her to arrive. The baby's foot was indeed trying to make an entrance into the world first. But to my sheer delight, it was moving, and *that* was a beautiful sight. At this stage, we decided it was best to head directly to the small clinic in Moosonee and deliver the baby there, rather than attempt the trip back across the river to the hospital, in the event the delivery occurred in transit. Two of the clinic nurses were ready and anxious to help, so we set up. I was the appointed midwife. That was all right with me, as I had attended many deliveries on my own since arriving in the North. However, I was not quite prepared for what was to come.

* * *

The little foot began to turn mottled and swollen. It appeared that the time had come to meet the owner of the little foot. Breech deliveries constitute only about 3% of births, which means that the number we attend in a small hospital is very few per year. And this would only be my second breech delivery, solo. Statistics aside, the fact that eight babies had already paved the way made me feel better. The urgency of the situation was first and foremost in my heart and on my mind.

The isolette stood ready and the paediatrician was prepared. With a few pushes and manoeuvers (thank goodness for my photographic memory of the chapter on breech birth), a baby girl joined us. She gave a little cry and was passed off to the waiting doctor. What happened next shocked us all. As I attempted to deliver the afterbirth, something that was critical because bleeding had started, I put my hand on the mother's abdomen and discovered something unusual: waiting to join his or her sister was another baby. We were about to have twins in our care, unbeknownst even to the babies' mother. This baby, baby "B" as she became known to us for the time being, was delivered head first after rupturing her mother's membranes – and with a little help from Mom.

We now had two little baby girls in one isolette. Both were breathing on their own, but they were too small for comfort, and both started to display signs of respiratory distress. Mom was as well as could be expected, having just survived an unnerving plane trip, delivered two babies, and added more to her family than expected. She smiled, thanked us, and inquired as to when she could go home.

* * *

The trip back to the Moose Factory hospital by Hovercraft was an experience in itself. With twins in respiratory distress, a new mother who was at this point bleeding more than was acceptable, and a nurse who, by now, was in distress, the trip was even more interesting and harrowing. We were welcomed with much fanfare, as the whole island of Moose Factory had already heard the news and was out in full force to herald our arrival. A quick ride by ambulance from the dock up to the hospital was the last leg of our journey – or so we thought.

* * *

It had been several hours since I had received the call and we had left to meet the plane in Moosonee. Now it appeared that the babies would need to be looked after in a larger hospital than the one we had in Moose Factory. Our nursery was not equipped for long-term care of fragile, premature babies. Nor did we have the extra staff to look after them around the clock. Ordinarily, we medevac'd all newborns in need of special care to Kingston General Hospital via charter air flights. And that is what happened next. I found myself on my way back to the airport in Moosonee. I escorted the twins to Kingston on another leg of a journey that seemed to have no end. Between ensuring that their IVs kept running and trying to keep them breathing, it was a trip I never want to repeat. As long as the babies were sucking, I knew they were breathing, so my little fingers came in rather handy.

On arrival in Kingston, we noted that the air terminal seemed desolate and dark. It was after midnight and the airport was closed. There had to have been an oversight on someone's part. In the meantime, we had to get to the hospital, which meant we needed an ambulance. The pilot had radioed the hospital for one, and now we realized that the gates of the airport were closed. And locked! I suppose northern nursing prepares you for almost anything. It took only moments to decide that we would have to carry the isolette through the long grass and pass it over the fence to the ambulance crew. We did just that, and the babies' journey continued.

* * *

In the interim, we found someone to gas up the plane, and we travelled back home to Moose Factory. The mother was anxious to hear about her baby girls, and we were eager to tell her that they had arrived safely. Meanwhile, the twins began to make a terrific transition to city life in the hospital in Kingston. Before long, they were back at our hospital, thriving and ready to make the trip home to their settlement, and to the rest of their family.

It was, indeed, a day (or two) to remember, and a delivery that will always stand out for me. Over the years, I have kept in touch with the twins and their mother. In fact, I was invited to their "walking out" ceremony, which is held when the children begin to walk and go outside the tent by themselves, dressed in ceremonial clothing. To have been a part of such special times in the lives of those precious little girls has been a privilege.

Janet Cross BScN graduated in 1974 with her BScN from Queen's University School of Nursing in Kingston, Ontario. Immediately after graduation, she worked on the obstetrical ward in Moose Factory in northern Ontario. She stayed until 1977, when she transferred to the General Hospital in Frobisher Bay, on Baffin Island, for a brief stint. Following that, she returned to Moose Factory General Hospital as obstetrical head nurse until 1981. During those years, Janet spent several weeks at nursing stations in Povungnituk and in Salluit in northern Quebec. Those were times when she had some of the most enriching experiences of her career, both professionally and personally. Janet has since worked in Winchester and in Ottawa, Ontario, in the field of maternal and newborn care.

NURSING IN THE SATELLITES

Barbara Bromley

During the early sixties, public health nurses in Yellowknife reached satellite communities in various ways – from canoes and dog teams to snowmobiles, bush planes (either on skis or floats), and cars. We were responsible for Yellowknife and several outer communities: Snowdrift (now Lutselk'e), Trout Rock, Wool Bay, Dettah, and Fort Rae – the only community with road access. The only Inuit settlement we looked after was at Pellatt Lake, 170 miles north of Yellowknife.

Dettah

The trips to Dettah were among my favourite. It is a Dene village just across Yellowknife Bay on Great Slave Lake. To get there in the winter, we travelled about 4½ km by dog team on an ice road, or sometimes on one of the first big snowmobiles. In the summer, we went by canoe because in the 1960s there was no road. We usually depended upon the Chief, or another resident of Dettah, to pick us up and bring us back. On our arrival, we always went first to the Chief's house in order to pay our respects. We would ask if we could hold a baby clinic and also see any others who were not well. The Chief's wife was expecting us and had the teapot on. Moccasin Telegraph told the people we were there and ready to see them.

In the baby clinic, we weighed babies and did immunizations. We encouraged breast-feeding, which was easy to do in those days, because getting into town for canned milk was not a simple matter. We treated impetigo, coughs, earaches, head lice, infected mosquito or other insect bites in the summer, and frostbite in the winter. During these visits, we were able to carry out an immunization program and do TB tests, because it was a time when people got together.

It was also a good opportunity for the women of the community to bring out their handicrafts: their beautiful beaded or embroidered, bleached-white caribou or moose-hide moccasin slippers, gloves, and low-cut boots. Public health nurses snapped up these articles – they were always great for gifts, as well as for our own use.

An interesting time to go to the villages, particularly Dettah, was Treaty Day. It always took place near the first of July. The RCMP liked to have a nurse present, along with other government officials, and we would go out in canoes to this event. After the treaty money was presented to the people, the Chief would say a few words, and then there would be a tea dance with Dene drummers, followed by a feast of caribou stew, boiled fish, and bannock. Everyone – elders, parents, children, RCMP and government personnel, nurses and visitors – joined in the

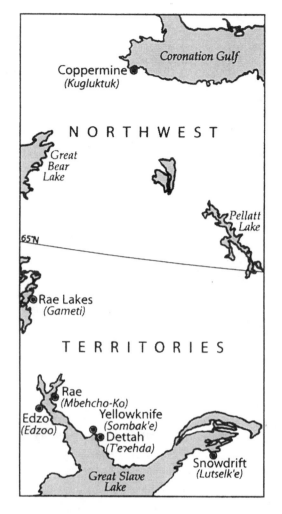

dance. It was held on the rocks and mossy, open space in the village. Afterwards, we all enjoyed the country food.

Wool Bay

One trip I remember well was to Wool Bay, a few miles east of Dettah, where only one or two families lived. Judith Marlow had just had her seventh child, a lovely baby girl, in the local municipal hospital (a 42-bed cottage hospital built by the Red Cross and the federal government in 1948). When Judith was ready to leave, it was early spring and the ice was breaking up. Although the ice was firm further out, it was not safe for planes to land near the shores of the lake. We chartered a small plane to take her home, and I went along to check out the rest of the family. It was a very short trip – takeoff, ten minutes in the air, then landing. We were met by the baby's father, who came out in a canoe which he pushed onto the ice, near where the plane had landed. Then we paddled to shore.

The other children stood waiting outside their small log cabin. They were smiling, immaculately clean, and in their Sunday best. The girls wore dresses and the boys wore white shirts and black pants, the oldest one holding the youngest in his arms. They were very excited and anxious to see their new sibling. (I recall that it brought tears to my eyes.) Dad had the kettle boiling, and I had a quick cup of tea, but the pilot was anxious to get off the "iffy" ice as soon as possible. I often see Judith, the mother, in the grocery store or walking up from the Old Town. Now a proud Grandma, she always has a big smile and warm handshake when we meet. And she always calls me "Nurse."

Pellatt Lake

Visits to Pellatt Lake were always interesting. Only six to eight Inuit families lived there; they had moved down from the Coppermine area. (There is no Inuit settlement at Pellatt now, as the people have moved back to the Arctic coast to Kugluktkuk, which was formerly called Coppermine.) Pellatt was really a lovely place. Some of the families were related, but it was just a very close-knit community. The men always seemed to do well with their hunting and trapping, and the women made practical and beautiful *mukluks*, as well as slippers and parkas.

Jim McCauley, a game warden who had a cabin in Pellatt, was often our contact. One day, we got a call from him, telling us that an Inuit named Jack had had an accident. He was building onto his cabin when a lengthy two-by-four slammed him across the bridge of his nose. I'm not sure how this happened, but Jim said that Jack had a swelling as large as a golf ball, right between his eyes, and that he was in quite a lot of pain. The doctor in Yellowknife thought he should be brought out. I contacted Ptarmigan Airways, and we started out. Another Inuit from Pellatt Lake was waiting to go back home, so he came along with us.

The weather wasn't great – turbulent, with heavy clouds. About an hour into the flight, the passenger seemed to be quite restless. When I asked him if he was all right, he just grimaced and didn't answer. Shortly after, he tapped me on the shoulder and said, "Pee." I didn't understand at first. Then he pointed to his crotch, and to the door, and downwards, as if he thought we should land. I told him we couldn't land, as there was no lake below us – but the pilot would not have stopped for him anyway. He continued to get frustrated, and I felt him moving around a lot in his seat, which was just behind mine. Not long after, he seemed to settle down. So I sat back to enjoy the rest of the flight.

About forty-five minutes later, we landed at Pellatt Lake. The pilot had barely got the plane tied up, when the passenger jumped out on the float, wearing one rubber boot and carrying the other one very gingerly with both hands. He teetered on the float, turned the boot upside down, and poured his pee into the lake. Now we know what to do, if we really need to "go" while flying in a small plane.

Jack, the patient we came to see, did have a large bump between his eyes. By now, it was more the size of a baseball. There was not much I could do for him, except give him some medication to ease the pain and apply a cold pack. Then we got him back to Yellowknife for more medical attention.

Snowdrift

On our trips to Snowdrift (now called Lutselk'e), we witnessed the most beautiful scenery. The tall, red cliffs along the larger islands were magnificent. Snowdrift, another settlement we had to reach by plane, is at the east end of Great Slave Lake. We used the Hudson's Bay manager's house there as a clinic. The manager, who also acted as a lay dispenser, contacted us if there were any health problems or accidents, and he was always helpful in letting the people know when we would be coming in. Even so, we usually had to round up the families whose babies needed immunization and those requiring TB checkups and other medical attention.

One of my trips to Snowdrift remains very memorable. In early spring, just before breakup time, I had gone out on a routine clinic day. We had to land on the ice across from the wide bay that leads into the settlement. The bay itself was open water, and the small planes were still on skis. When we arrived, one of the Dene came by canoe to take us in. The clinic usually lasted five or six hours. Just as I started packing up my equipment after I finished the clinic, I heard a scream outside. We rushed out and found a young girl holding her hand – with blood spurting out of her fingers. Apparently, a group of kids had been playing tag around a pile of 45-gallon drums. The girl had grabbed the edge of a drum, just as some others had slammed it towards her, and her hand had been squashed between the two drums. The tops of two of her fingers had literally popped open. My concern was that they had also been broken. I managed to apply pressure bandages, and using tongue blades, I strapped a sort-of-splint on. But I knew I'd have to take her back with us to Yellowknife for treatment.

When we came out of the house to get into the canoe, we found, to our horror, that the wind had come up, and the ice had drifted back and plugged up the bay. There was no way a canoe could get through to the plane. The only thing we could do was walk around the bay to the plane, a distance of more than a mile. As we struggled through the bush, the pilot and I helped the girl. It was a painful hike for her. The only relief she could get, besides the 222s I had given her, was from keeping her arm up fairly high – tough to do when going through wet, boggy land and spruce trees. She was brave. There was not a tear as she struggled along to the plane. We had a great pilot who made a safe and quick trip home. The girl had three broken fingers and needed several stitches. Whenever we talk about our experiences in nursing outposts, the brave girl from Snowdrift often comes to my mind.

* * *

Not long after this incident I resigned from Medical Services. Following the sudden loss of my husband, Peter, I had to take over the family business: a hardware and mining supplies store. After I had spent seven years in the business, and my youngest son had turned 18, I decided I wanted to get back into my profession. At a round table conference with my four children, I realized that each of them had a desire for their own career – other than in hardware. We decided that we should sell the business, but retain our building, which had been under construction when we lost Peter. Everyone agreed that I should go back to nursing.

I took the very first Registered Nurses Refresher Course offered in Yellowknife by the Northwest Territories Registered Nurses Association. After I successfully completed the course, I returned to community nursing as Coordinator of Home Care for the City of Yellowknife: a new field for public health nurses at the time. I continued in this work until I retired. I still volunteer. I drive homecare patients to appointments and do "other related duties." I especially enjoy keeping in touch with other nurses.

Barbara Bromley CM, BSc, RN worked intermittently as a nurse in Yellowknife from 1948 to 1963. From 1965 to 1967, she was nurse in charge at the Yellowknife Health Centre. When she lost her husband, she took over his hardware business until 1975. Later, she became coordinator of the Home Care Program at Stanton Yellowknife Hospital, a position she held until 1982. Barbara Bromley has received many awards for service, including the Canada Volunteer Award in 1989 and The Order of Canada in 2000. The citation for the latter award reads:

> *She is the quintessential Volunteer. Active in her community, this registered nurse was the first in the city to speak out as a proponent for the elderly, and is a founding member and director of the Yellowknife Association of Concerned Citizens for Seniors. Whether volunteering at the hospital or with the local Scouts, she is always generous with her time. Deeply committed to the city's residents, she has been a caregiver, activist, organizer and, most importantly, a friend to many in the community.*

Barbara's story "Early Days in the NWT" appears in *Northern Nurses: True Nursing Adventures from Canada's North.*

MY STUPID LITTLE APPENDIX

Lowell R. DeMond

During the winter of 1955-56, I was enrolled in a federally-sponsored program in meteorology. The surface weather part of the program was given at Malton Airport (now known as Pearson International), and the radiosonde technician section, which included observing and reporting data on the upper atmosphere, was given at Toronto Island. I was expected to write my final examinations in April. If successful, I was to be posted to Sable Island, Nova Scotia, for a month and then to Moosonee, Ontario, for eleven months. If I proved to be a valuable employee during this probationary year, I could expect a tour of duty in the High Arctic. This is what I wanted — because the pay was good. In isolation, there was no opportunity to spend money, and I was saving for college.

The spring airlift to the then four joint Arctic weather stations with the United States: Mould Bay, Isachsen, Eureka and Alert took place in April. One of the radiosonde technicians at Mould Bay had to be evacuated, so a replacement was required. No experienced person was available. I was recommended by the training school and was asked if I would like to go. Of course, I said, "Yes!"

At the Radiosonde Training School on Toronto Island, all of the 32 radiosonde sites in Canada were marked with thumbtacks on a map. Every student knew of the High Arctic stations, and they were sought after, mostly because of the pay. These stations were indeed isolated, the most southerly of the four being only 800 miles from the North Pole. The station personnel consisted of four Americans and four Canadians: one cook, one mechanic, two radio operators, and four radiosonde technicians. The officer in charge (OIC) was a Canadian radiosonde technician; the executive officer was American, usually a radiosonde technician.

Every student also knew two other important things about these stations. First of all, mail delivery was promised only four times a year: during a spring and a fall airlift, and during a summer and a Christmas airdrop. Secondly, you had to stay healthy, as there was little hope of medical evacuation if a person got sick at a time when no airlift was scheduled. This was especially true during July and August, when the snow had melted and the airstrip was muddy, and also from November until March (which included the dark period), when the airstrip was snow-covered.

* * *

On April 23, 1956, I left Toronto by train for Montreal. I spent the night in Montreal, and on the following day, I started my journey to Mould Bay. I was excited about getting underway, but I was also a little anxious, since I had never flown in an airplane.

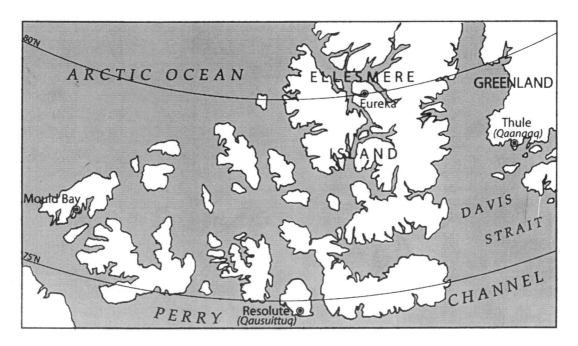

My flight to the Arctic in a North Star aircraft took me to Ottawa, Winnipeg, and then north to Churchill, Manitoba, where I spent the night. The next day, I flew to Resolute Bay on the southern shore of Cornwallis Island. Resolute Bay was, more or less, a hub station for the four outposts. Oil and other supplies were delivered there by icebreaker during the summer months and then flown to the outposts during spring and fall airlifts. Resolute Bay had twenty-four hours of sunlight, and the airlift to the outposts continued on an around-the-clock schedule.

On Thursday, April 26, I climbed on board an RCAF C-119 aircraft, also known as a Flying Boxcar, for Mould Bay. My flight was uneventful, but I still have vivid memories of it. The crew of five was up in the cockpit. I was assigned a seat by the bulkhead in the cargo bay, and directly behind me were two rows of barrels containing aviation fuel. Each row of barrels had a chain around it, and I wondered just how secure these were going to be during takeoff and landing. I began to feel a little nervous and very much alone.

About fifteen minutes after takeoff, the crew chief came down the ladder and invited me to join the others. I was overjoyed with this invitation and gladly accepted it. Once I was in the cockpit, I was introduced to the crew and made to feel welcome. They offered me a little bench between the pilot and co-pilot, and coffee was served. It was a noisy but a pleasant environment. I remember the only two colours I could see when I looked out the windows – the white of the snow and the blue of the sky.

The captain was curious as to why I would want to spend a year in an isolated place like Mould Bay, and he said he didn't envy me. The other members of the crew agreed with him. They liked tall trees, tall buildings, and tall women, and Mould Bay had none of these. When the station came into view, the captain circled around twice, giving me a good view of my future home. I can still picture the tiny orange buildings below. Then we lined up with the airstrip, set down, bounced a few times, and came to a halt. We taxied to the parking area, where I counted four men, two bulldozers with sleighs, and a couple of dogs.

The station staff knew I was arriving on this aircraft. They were pleased to be finally getting a replacement for their member who had been evacuated, so their workload could be reduced. They were expecting someone with Arctic experience, who could easily fulfill the role, and who could work independently. This was the way it always was. A greenhorn, directly from the training school, never got that far north.

When the rear doors of the aircraft were opened, I saw one of the station staff coming toward me. He introduced himself as the Officer in Charge, gave me his name, shook hands, and asked me which station I had come from. I told him that I had come directly from the training school in Toronto. He gave me a puzzled look and then uttered some words which indicated his total disbelief. That was my welcome to Mould Bay. If I could have, I think I would have gotten back on the airplane.

* * *

At the training school, we had been told that it would be a good idea to take a bottle of liquor with us for the men at the station, and I had done exactly that. I was shown to my room in the barracks. After I unpacked, I walked over to the operations building, where most of the fellows were relaxing and reading mail which had come on the plane. I presented them with the bottle of whiskey. The OIC informed me that I would be on duty with him in four hours and that we would be doing our first radiosonde flight together. Feeling somewhat depressed, a little lonesome, and maybe just a tad homesick, I excused myself and returned to my bedroom where I set my alarm clock, put my head on the pillow, and had a nap.

When I awoke, I put on warm clothes for work. The temperature outside was -30° F. At the operations building, where I had delivered the bottle of whiskey only a few hours before, I was greeted by a fellow from Oklahoma who said, "Mighty tasty whiskey, boy, mighty tasty whiskey!" The two other men there agreed that it was great. My whiskey was a hit. Shortly after the OIC arrived, the two of us walked over to the weather office.

My first upper air observation went well. The OIC was pleased with my effort and apologized for the way he had welcomed me. Following the weather observation, we exchanged stories in the weather office for a short time, and then he gave me a tour of the station. From that day onward, the remainder of the time I worked with him was enjoyable. He turned out to be supportive, helpful, and understanding. A true friend.

* * *

Very little partying was done at the station. A bottle of station liquor was always on a shelf in the operations building, but it was rarely touched. Once in a while on a Saturday night, the fellows would have a shower, get a change of clothes and just maybe, have a drink. I had brought my guitar north, and sometimes we would have a singsong. I never saw anyone get drunk.

The first day of July was different. The four Canadians decided they would celebrate Dominion Day, as it was called then, and show the Americans a good time. The cook cooperated and came up with some special food. Anyone not sleeping joined the party. In a relaxed and friendly atmosphere, we all had a good time with a sing-along, which included few drinks. Then came the Fourth of July. The Americans, not to be outdone, held another party. Again, it was a gala time. The work got done, and the party was great.

A couple of days later, I sensed a strange feeling in the area of my stomach. I thought it might be a result of the Fourth of July celebration, so I said very little about it. After a few days, the pain was still there, but it had moved lower and felt quite pronounced on my right side. It was sort of an off-and-on pain. Sometimes it would go away for a few hours and then it would return. I continued with my station duties without telling anyone.

A week later, the pain returned to stay. I noticed that when I put my right heel down hard as I walked, the sensitive area in my right side would hurt. I walked with a limp. One day, the OIC noticed it and asked if I had hurt my leg. I decided to tell him about my problem. I had a flashback of his words of welcome when I arrived at the station, and I wondered what he was going to say. When I told my story, I kind of felt sorry for him. He had to evacuate a man in April during the spring airlift, and now he had another lame duck in the middle of summer. He listened to my story and then cursed. He walked in circles around the weather office, and eventually came over and sat down beside me. He said we had to tell the others, and then plan a course of action.

As for health services at the station, some of the fellows had taken a first-aid course, and the station had a well-equipped medicine cabinet and a book entitled *Gray's Anatomy*. After a lot of head-scratching, and hours of reading and discussion, the general consensus was that I had appendicitis. Resolute Bay had to be informed. A scheduled radio contact was set up with Resolute, and I was to speak to the RCAF medic. He was in the Registered Officers Training Programme from Dalhousie University and was studying under a Canadian Forces plan. He listened to my story, gave appendicitis as the likely prognosis, and said he would recommend an evacuation order to his commanding officer.

For me, this was good news; but there were problems. The snow had melted. The airstrip was muddy with a few frost boils which oozed out water in the centre, as the permafrost melted. The nearest aircraft were World War II Lancaster Bombers, stationed at Resolute Bay, and used for ice reconnaissance over the Arctic Ocean. We wondered if the aircraft could land successfully at our station, and if it would be possible to obtain enough speed to take off from our muddy airstrip. Some of the fellows figured the only way to find out was to try it. I wasn't so sure, since I was going to be on the plane. But I had few options. The discussion turned to the concept of sacrificing the seven lives of an aircrew for the life of one person. This debate was interesting, but depressing. The crew that was dispatched to evaluate the condition of the airstrip returned with no good news. While waiting for a final decision, I spent more time in bed and each day, I found it more difficult to extend my right leg.

One of the crew at the station was from Pennsylvania. I was never certain what he really looked like, because he had a large bushy beard which masked his face. He was friendly and I liked him. One day he knocked on my bedroom door, entered, and said something like the following, "I have been reading the *Gray's Anatomy* book, and there is a good description of how to remove an appendix. I want you to know there is no way that I'll watch you die without trying to save you. If worse comes to worst, and you want me to operate, I'll give it my best shot." Now that was an offer! He said they had had ham radio contacts with people in the South about my condition, and had even discussed an operation with a doctor. The doctor had told them a major concern was infection, and the cook had agreed to "boil the piss" out of the tools they would use. I don't recall if this was comforting or not.

I finally accepted the fact that it might be impossible to evacuate me and that I might die at Mould Bay. When the station was built in the early 1950s, a family of Eskimos (as they were called then) was flown in from Resolute Bay to assist with the construction. One family member (a little girl) died during the summer. Several times, I had walked up to where her remains had been placed in a cairn on a mountain side overlooking the station. The thought entered my mind that a second cairn might be erected on that mountain – *mine*.

* * *

On July 15, Resolute Bay called to tell us that a Lancaster Aircraft had been dispatched to pick me up. In a letter to my parents sent from Thule Airbase dated July 18, 1956, I wrote the following:

The weather at Resolute was a low overcast condition when the plane left. The weather at Mould Bay could best be described as horrible. We had a low ceiling of 500 feet and it was snowing. Resolute Bay advised the pilot to turn back, but he kept coming and finally landed after three tries.

It was a great relief to look down at the airstrip from my bedroom window and see the plane in the parking lot. For a time, I had forgotten about my condition and was just relieved when the aircrew safely exited the aircraft. In a vehicle with tracks (known as a weasel), they were ferried up to the operations building where the cook had fresh coffee ready. The staff at Mould Bay had packed up some of my belongings, so I was ready and anxious to go, but at the same time I was somewhat apprehensive about leaving. I recalled all the discussions about getting safely airborne from the muddy airstrip. The crew talked about this, and the pilot had an in-depth conversation with the OIC and the chief airstrip mechanic about landing conditions.

When it was time to say goodbye, I couldn't thank the Mould Bay staff enough for all their help and encouragement. I even got a hug from two of them. We were driven to the aircraft, where I was made comfortable and strapped in. The engines were started and warmed up, and we began rolling down the airstrip. From my seat, I could look out a tiny window which I remember being directly behind the left wing. As we increased speed, a lot of mud was flung into the air. About three-quarters of the way down the airstrip, there was a marker which I had hiked past on many occasions. When we passed it, we were still on the ground and labouring to get more speed. I have no idea if this was preplanned or not, but I do know that when we finally left the ground, there was very little runway left. We barely lifted over the end markers and then quickly turned left, away from a hill at the end of the runway. Under normal conditions, this low mountain would not have been a problem. But when an airplane has extra weight from a fair amount of mud on its wings, there is cause for concern.

The flight to Resolute Bay (a distance of 380 miles) took under two hours. We were met by the Commanding Officer and other officials who discussed my condition and where I should be taken. It was generally agreed that the weather going south to Churchill, Manitoba, was unfavourable, and that the best option was to take me to Thule, Greenland, which was about 400 miles from Resolute. The flight lasted about two hours and was without incident. My most vivid memories were of looking out the window at the dark blue ocean with its many icebergs.

* * *

In 1956, Thule was a large American Airbase that was a major part of the defense of North America during the Cold War. About 7000 U.S. armed forces personnel (mostly men) were stationed there. Compared to Mould Bay, it looked like a big city. A great many aircraft were on the airstrip, almost all newer and much larger than the World War II Lancaster in which I was flying. As we taxied into the parking lot, our plane caused quite a stir, and we were well-photographed.

The medical personnel at Thule had been put on notice that we were arriving, and an ambulance stood ready for me in the parking lot. It was raining, and the crew instructed me to sit and stay comfortable until the ambulance came over to pick me up. We waited and waited, until finally one of the crew offered to find out what the problem was. He returned with the news that the ambulance had been there for quite some time and had run out of gas. Eventually, another ambulance arrived, and I was taken directly to the hospital.

It was 5 p.m. when I reached the hospital. The two doctors who examined me decided to operate immediately. My clothes were removed. I was draped in a johnny shirt and wheeled into the operating room. I was probably thinking about many things, but one thought stands out in my mind: I hadn't had a bath for days. This was embarrassing. It was possible to get a bath at Mould Bay, but plumbing and hot water were scarce. I was given a spinal, the operation went well, and afterwards I was taken to a room in one of the hospital wards. I was either given a sedative, or I simply went to sleep.

About midnight, I was awakened by a voice saying, "Wake up. We're going for a walk." I couldn't believe what I heard, for two reasons. First, because I believed there was no way I could walk – as it hurt like the devil just to move. Second, because the voice sounded like that of a woman. I focussed on the face. Sure enough, it was a very pretty blonde nurse who was making the request. She was persuasive and gentle in assisting me, and before I had much time to think about it, she had her arm around me, and we were walking down the corridor. After we took a few steps, she said, "There is no way a 'stupid little appendix' can be allowed to do you in!" She was unbelievable.

There were three female nurses at the hospital. I saw the others, but the one who attended me the most was the blonde nurse who took me on the midnight walk. It is embarrassing to write that I can't think of her name. However, I do recall a few things about her. She was very professional, friendly, and helpful. She cared about others, and she always had a smile.

* * *

Another part of this story should be told. My parents saved all the messages (both official and ham radio) and all of the letters which I wrote from the Arctic. When I returned home for a brief visit after my two-year tour of duty in the Arctic, my mother told me how shocked and confused they were when they were informed of my evacuation from Mould Bay. Only after reading the messages did I fully understand.

I had been reluctant to tell my parents that I was ill. On July 12 (three days before I was evacuated out of Mould), I was working the ham radio. I was in contact with VE6NX, Chuck Gawhichi, in Edmonton, Alberta, who offered to forward the following message to my parents:

Dear Folks,

We have had snow here today, the first time I ever saw snow in July. Have been doing some work around the buildings, making shelves etc. (This was a lie.) The rest of the boys are working on the airstrip. Quite a few flowers here now. Am in good health.

Love, Lowell

On the bottom of this message, my parents had written that they had received it on July 16. Then, on July 17, the following telegraph arrived. (Telegraphs were delivered on Canadian National letterhead and looked very official.)

L.A. DEMOND
SOUTH BROOKFIELD N S

THIS WILL ADVISE THAT YOUR SON L DEMOND WAS EVACUATED BY RCAF FROM MOULD BAY JULY FIFTEEN PM FOR FURTHER EXAMINATION AND PROBABLY OPERATION FOR APPENDICITIS STOP HIS PRESENT ADDRESS IS SIX SIX ZERO SEVENTH USAF HOSPITAL APO TWO THREE CMA NEW YORK STOP WE EXPECT TO RECEIVE ADVICE CONCERNING HIS PROGRESS AND WILL ADVISE YOU BY LETTER

A. THOMPSON 250PM

It is easy to understand how these two messages would create confusion for parents, especially for farm folk who were not used to receiving telegrams.

* * *

In August, 1956, I was flown by the USAF from Thule to the Eureka weather station on Ellesmere Island, 580 miles from the North Pole, where I remained until April, 1958. In the summer of 1957, the USAF sent a C-54 transport plane from Greenland to Eureka. Among the passengers were two nurses from the Thule Air Force Base hospital.

Lack of female companionship and isolation caused several changes in behaviour in the staff at Eureka. Language habits changed: more four-letter words, and vulgar and abusive language were used to describe routine daily happenings. Table manners declined. Please and thank you were often omitted. It was not uncommon to hear someone at the dinner table say, "Pass the damn salt" or "Throw up the pepper." Personal appearance and body cleanliness deteriorated. Clothes were often dirty. (This was partly due to the fact that ice from icebergs had to be cut and hauled in a sleigh in -40° temperatures, and then melted in a tank over a stove to get water.) Baths were delayed, and haircuts reflected the skill of the sculptor.

When the radio operator announced that there were females on board this aircraft (two nurses from Thule) our behavior changed immediately. Almost all of the staff found something clean to wear. When the introductions were made, language habits quickly changed, manners returned, and there was enthusiasm and competition to tell the best stories about station adventures. Cameras flashed, and there was much joy. It was as if the queen was back in the beehive, even if it only lasted for two hours. Freud would have loved it.

One of the two nurses was very special to me. She was the person who had taken me on the midnight walk at the Thule hospital.

Lowell DeMond MEd completed the Radiosonde Technician program with the Federal Department of Transportation at the old Malton Airport in Ontario and the radiosonde school on Toronto Island, in 1956. He was employed as a Met Tech in the Canadian Arctic and served time at Mould Bay and Eureka, NWT. Later he attended Acadia University in Nova Scotia, and received his MEd from the University of New Brunswick. He worked in public schools in New Brunswick and Nova Scotia, and he retired in 1994 as Principal of Bridgewater High School. His hobbies include tree farming and fishing. In an effort to help preserve the Atlantic salmon, he has worked for years with salmon associations. He has published a book of fishing stories entitled *Hooked* and admits he is addicted to fishing – his wife, Marion, agrees. Lowell has two sons, Andrew and Bruce. He lives in Bridgewater, NS.

MEMORIES OF THE CHARLOTTES

Christopher Lemphers

Medevacs over Hecate Strait

The Queen Charlotte Islands are located 90 miles off the coast of Prince Rupert, British Columbia, across a shallow body of water called the Hecate Strait. During the unsettled winter months from late October to early March, medical evacuations from The Charlottes, as they are called by the locals, can become very challenging.

One such medevac that I recall occurred when my wife and I were relatively new to our assignments as nurse practitioners in the Haida community of Masset, on the northern shores of The Charlottes. An elderly Haida woman with advanced pneumonia needed to be medevac'd to Prince Rupert General Hospital. It was late November and dense fog had descended, blanketing the entire north island around Masset. A pilot and a Beaver De Havilland float plane were on standby, waiting for the first opportunity to fly and escape the fog. By noon, the fog had lifted and we departed from Masset, following the finger of land known as Rose Spit that extended into Hecate Strait. Since my patient was in a stretcher and hooked up to intravenous, all the seats, except the pilot's, were removed. The patient's stretcher occupied the area from the co-pilot's space to the tail. I squatted on the floor between the stretcher and the aircraft door.

We lifted off gingerly and followed the contour of Rose Spit, until the pilot realized that the cloud ceiling was lowering to 200 feet. He decided to turn back and wait a bit longer, hoping that by 2 p.m. the fog would have lifted a bit higher, thus allowing us a safer flight. If we postponed the departure until late afternoon, we would lose our opportunity, since the fog would again have descended for another night. By 2 o'clock, although the fog showed no signs of deterioration, we scrambled into our float plane again, and lumbered into the grey, afternoon skies.

The three of us retraced our flight path along the Rose Spit and out over Hecate Strait. The wind had turned from the gentle breezes of a summer morning to a brisk 60 km per hour. The shallow strait was whipped into a frenzy, and whitecaps, with tops being sheared off, were visible from our plane. We passed the point of returning and aborting the medevac. The cloud ceiling had degraded to 150 feet, and the ocean swells below us were at least 30 feet high and rolling. At this point, I regretted having had lunch. The adage: "Have nothing, lose nothing" certainly applied to my stomach. In my case, I had something. The patient was stable, but with all the turbulence, the intravenous had gone interstitial. While I barely maintained my composure and my effectiveness as a nurse, the pilot was expending a great deal of energy controlling the plane. As we banged and rattled across Hecate Strait, we lost sight of the land we had left, and the uniform greyness did not reveal the distant coastlines. The flight seemed much longer than most. Upon our arrival in Prince Rupert, emergency road ambulances were awaiting our landing: one for my patient, and one for me. The pilot slowly walked away.

In retrospect, those early days of nursing practice were full of adventure. Adventures such as this one are still part of nursing in the North today.

Octopus and Spruce Pitch

The Haida Indians of the Queen Charlotte Islands say zero tides are the best times to catch an octopus. It is at such low tides that the den of the octopus can be located in the rocky tidal outcroppings that ring the shores of Masset Inlet. I had been watching the tides until the day of a zero tide finally came.

In preparation, I lashed a large halibut hook onto a pole. I took it and headed to the rocky beaches of the inlet. I zigzagged the shore looking for telltale signs of an octopus den. A shell midden, a quarter of a mile down the beach, was the food source sign that ended my search. Using the blunt end of the pole, I probed the den for the soft body contact of an octopus. I immediately turned the pole around and thrust the hooked end into the den, pulled out the octopus, and quickly dispatched its ink sack before it sprayed.

The next step was to skin the octopus. I sat there with an octopus in one hand and a razor blade in the other. Those who know octopuses will know that their skin is slippery and tends to shift about their bodies. With difficulty and with focussed attention, I chased the skin with my razor blade. Between nicking myself with the blade, and dealing with the movement of the slimy skin, it was not easy to measure my success. In fact I, too, was bleeding from my self-inflicted wounds.

Little did I know that I was being observed. I was obviously entertaining some local Haida boys. After watching me suffer a bit, they asked me if I would like to learn an easier way to skin an octopus. Having lost some of my own blood, I was interested in their offer. One of the boys picked up a handful of beach sand, grasped the skin of the octopus and, with a little traction, removed it.

* * *

On another occasion during my tenure as an outpost nurse, I made a home visit to a Haida woman with a leg ulcer. After taking her initial history, I did a physical assessment and realized the ulcer was infected. We discussed starting antibiotic therapy to treat the infection and to prevent complications. The woman accepted the western medicine of antibiotics, but insisted on wrapping the ulcer with spruce pitch. I followed up on a number of occasions and monitored her health. She made remarkably rapid progress. To this day, I am convinced that the antiseptic and healing qualities of spruce pitch, when used along with oral antibiotics, produced an ideal therapy that was acceptable to both cultures.

These are only two of the many lessons I respectfully learned by living and working with the Haida people.

Harvest after the Storm

A short distance from the Haida village of Old Masset are the northern beaches of the Queen Charlotte Islands. North Beach is particularly interesting because of the adjacent shallow waters of the Dixon Entrance. The waves roll in off the north Pacific and bring an abundance of sea life. Offshore, thirty miles to the north, the islands of the southern Alaska Archipelagos are visible on clear days. During the time I worked at the Masset Nursing Station in the mid 1970s, my wife (who was the other nurse) and I often found solitude on these pristine shores. It was relaxing to stroll the beaches as the waves lapped the shore, while plovers (small shorebirds), raced back and forth, feeding on tiny crustaceans left by each wave. At times like these, the stress of nursing in an isolated location was relieved, and we refocussed on the unique opportunity we had to practise nursing on the Queen Charlotte Islands.

However, the ocean and the wind had another side. On one occasion, a north wind blew at 70 mph for three days. Whitecaps dotted the seascape and crowned the swells like countless sailboats. The wind would gust horizontally and chop the whitecaps, while clouds of white foam sailed across the waves. The beach was definitely not the place to be, for the driving rain and sand stung any exposed flesh. The turbulence above the water was matched below the surf. As the storm waned, the beaches revealed mounds of bull kelp which had been torn from their anchors and tossed ashore.

Two days later, I noticed that an unusual quiet had descended upon the village. On an island, people do not just leave without notice. After making some inquiries, I learned that many of the Haida people had gone to North Beach to harvest shellfish after the recent storm. I was curious about the remarkable natural event that had drawn many people from the village, so I made my way over to North Beach. Cockles as big as softballs, and in mounds two feet high, littered the beach. Dotting these mounds were scallops – larger than any I have ever seen in restaurants. The Haida, who knew the pattern of these occurrences, filled huge sacks full of fresh shellfish. One woman encouraged me to help myself before all the harvest was swept away with the next tide. The same sea that had delivered this bounty would now reclaim it.

The harvest after the storm revealed to me the interrelatedness of health and unique cultural activities. Health and well-being took on a new perspective, unique to the Haida people of the Queen Charlotte Islands. I continued to learn from the First Nations people, as I counted my many blessings of cross-cultural nursing experiences.

Christopher Lemphers RN, BN, MEd graduated in 1972 from Vancouver City College in Vancouver, British Columbia. He completed his BN in 1979 at Dalhousie University in Halifax, Nova Scotia and his MEd at the University of British Columbia in Vancouver in 1984. Chris has worked with the Medical Services Branch in various nursing stations in the Queen Charlotte Islands, off the north coast of BC. He also worked in public health in Campbell River, BC. He is currently with the First Nations and Inuit Health Branch (formerly MSB) in Edmonton, Alberta, where he has worked as a nurse educator and zone nurse manager. He is now a health service delivery analyst in Telehealth.

I ONLY MEANT TO STAY A YEAR

Pearl Herbert

Before I arrived in Canada from Britain in 1962, I had completed my nursing and midwifery training. After working in Ontario and British Columbia, I moved to the Northwest Territories. I had intended to travel around the world for only five years and then return to England. But here I am – still in Canada.

While I was in Kelowna, British Columbia, where I worked from 1963 to 1964, a group of us decided to travel together across Asia and Europe. However, I first wanted to see what the North was like, and I planned to take a cruise to Anchorage. At Easter, just as I was starting to organize my trip, the great Alaska earthquake occurred, and that was the end of my plans. To travel to the Northwest Territories as a tourist was too expensive, so I decided instead to work there – for one year. Having seen an advertisement in *The Canadian Nurse* for nurses to work in the North, I applied to National Health and Welfare, and quickly received a reply from the regional office, which was then located in Ottawa.

In July, 1964, I left Kelowna by train and travelled to Edmonton for an orientation at the Charles Camsell Hospital. There were sessions on pulling teeth, on taking x-rays of chests and limbs, and on how to complete countless forms. (It took me a few months into my first posting before I got everything completely correct.). We were provided with a file binder of guidelines for treating various ailments, but I soon found that the *Textbook for Midwives* by Margaret Myles was one of my main standbys. I was also introduced to a number of people

Although I had originally been told that I would be going to Cambridge Bay, I found out in Edmonton that it would be Coppermine (Kugluktuk). Coppermine is at the mouth of the river of the same name, where it enters Coronation Gulf. One nurse had already left there and the second would be leaving two weeks after I arrived. I would then be on my own for two or three months, until a nurse arrived from Scotland. In preparation, I was given booster shots and I began the typhoid immunizations (TAB) recommended for that area. These made me quite nauseated.

Some orientation information I was given in Edmonton really worried me. A doctor, the zone nursing officer, or others would visit Coppermine every six weeks – depending on the weather. Once a year, the chest x-ray team would be there. These people would stay at the nursing station or at the transient centre (a long building which consisted of about four bedrooms), and I would have to feed them. After that particular day's session, I rushed downtown and bought a couple of basic cookery books (which I still have).

About ten days later, I started on my way north. At the Edmonton airport, I caught a DC7 for Yellowknife. This was my first experience of flying. Looking out the airplane window as we flew north, I saw more lakes and fewer trees. I had been handed a schedule and given the departure time of the plane to Coppermine. However, in Yellowknife, I quickly learned that in the North planes did not fly according to schedule. I took a taxi to the lake where I was to catch the float plane, only to discover upon arrival that the plane would not be leaving that day.

I did not know what to do, but I hoped to get some instructions at the local hospital. At that time, the hospital was an old wooden building with living quarters for the staff upstairs. I met Cora Scott, who informed me that the hospital was a municipal hospital, which did not belong to the federal government (for whom I worked). She directed me to the public health centre, which was on a side street. They told me to check into the Yellowknife Hotel. In 1964, Yellowknife was a small town with one main road, which went down to the Flats (now known as Old Town) from where the float planes departed. At the edges of the town, were the two mines. The next day, while waiting for my flight, I had time for a tour of one of these mines and actually saw gold being poured.

Finally, I left Yellowknife in a single engine Otter on the four-hour flight to Coppermine. Flying over the tundra, I found the scenery fascinating. During the next two years, I would start to recognize some of the lakes. When we approached Coppermine, the pilot pointed out the white, red-roofed buildings of the Hudson's Bay Company by the river bank, the two churches at either end of the community, the RCMP buildings that flew the Union Jack flag, and the orange Department of Transport buildings from where the weather balloon was released and the radio messages were transmitted. The square, flat-roofed school was in the centre of the community, and between it and the Anglican Church, was the green nursing station built on rocks (which I later would learn, were slippery in the winter). When we landed, our float plane was pulled to shore and tied to the dock so that the passengers could disembark safely. Many people were there to meet the plane and to shake hands with the new nurse.

* * *

The Coppermine station was one of the first nursing stations built by the federal government. This facility had a boat with an outboard motor which the janitor used to deliver water from up the river in the summer. There was also a skidoo which he used to meet the plane, in order to collect the mail and to transport patients being evacuated south. At freeze-up time, he would cut ice blocks, which he hauled to the shed where they were stored. With some of these blocks, he would build a porch for the back door. The water was stored in two 45-gallon drums attached to a pump to supply water to the kitchen and the bathroom. Water from the sinks and bathtub would run out under the nursing station through holes cut in the floor.

The toilet was a honey bucket – a green plastic bag into which we poured a small quantity of Mistavan disinfectant. The plastic bag was not removed from the bucket inside the station, as it was common for the bags to split. They would then be taken to the garbage dump. The bathroom was shared with patients. It was located in the general corridor, which also served as a waiting room. There was a room for an office which contained an examining table, a larger room for two patients and a crib, and a smaller room for maternity mothers and babies. This room had space for only one mother at a time, so other mothers would be in the larger room. The clinic was another small room with cupboards on each side. There were two staff bedrooms and a tiny living room.

The spacious kitchen, where we ate our meals, separated the staff quarters from the patient rooms. Whenever we knew the nursing supervisor was coming, the top of the oil range in the kitchen would be polished until it shone. But as soon as the kettle boiled, it would become spattered with water. The range was used not only for cooking but also for sterilizing green towels and dressings in cookie tins placed in the oven. In the ceiling of the kitchen was the trap door to the attic, which was kept open at all times to prevent the items stored there from freezing.

There was a hot-water tank in the bathroom, but we could only bathe when we had sufficient water. One day, while I was having a bath, I heard a noise and the bathroom filled with steam. I jumped out of the tub, grabbed a towel, and rushed out of the room. Fortunately, no patients were in the corridor! The tank had burst and boiling water was pouring out over the floor. There was a spare hot-water tank in the community, so the one at the nursing station could be replaced. Since both patients and staff needed this facility, some extra floor tiles were found to replace the damaged ones.

The staff at the nursing station consisted of a janitor, a housekeeper who did the cleaning and laundry and made the bread, an interpreter, and a community health worker. As the Inuit expected this latter person to do manual work, this title was changed to community health representative (CHR). The health worker had been south to learn how to teach health promotion, to collect water samples, and to advise about matters such as boiling drinking water and disposing of garbage. However, this was a community where manual labour was prized, where hunting skills gave status, and where younger people did not tell older people what to do. This put the community health representative at a great disadvantage.

* * *

I need not have worried about feeding visitors, because I soon obtained a northern book, with instructions for cooking Arctic char, caribou, rabbit, and other foods which they always seemed to like. As long as there was enough fish or game for two helpings each, everyone was happy. Later, when a family left Coppermine, I inherited their manual ice cream maker. If visitors wanted ice cream, I would make the custard, and they would chop the ice and turn the handle until the custard froze. The nurse was expected to cook for inpatients, who also liked the ice cream, as well as the local foods. Fresh meat was always a welcome change to the tins of Irish stew which came in on the sea-lift.

It was in Coppermine that I decided to drink tea without milk because fresh milk was unavailable. Klim (whole milk powder) did not mix well and left lumps floating on top of the tea, and evaporated milk was too sweet, as I did not have sugar in my tea. In addition, evaporated milk separates when frozen, and it sours if stored in a hot place during transportation. None of this results in a good cup of tea.

* * *

At the beginning of the year, an order had to be submitted for all the medications, supplies, and foods which would be needed during the coming year. Hopefully, the order would arrive during the annual sea-lift. Sometimes a DC7 would land on the ice in the winter and bring in extra supplies. During freeze-up and breakup, there would be no planes, as the river was the only place for planes to land. The liquid medications came in gallon glass bottles, the ointments in large tins, and pills in big jars. The nurse would prescribe and then dispense these in smaller containers. In those days, the RCMP officer in charge would check the narcotics and controlled drugs.

* * *

Once when I was the only nurse in the community, the newly arrived RCMP officer came to the nursing station. In his most official manner, he asked immediately to check the locked cupboard and narcotic drug book. At that moment, a couple brought in their baby who was having difficulty breathing. I set up the croupette, treated the baby, and took a chest x-ray, which had to be developed and fixed in the little darkroom that was through the kitchen, by the back door. The baby settled, and just as we began again to count the drugs, the door opened and a man was helped inside. He had been in an accident and had hurt his leg. I examined him, took an x-ray, and after the RCMP officer confirmed that he knew his first aid, I left him to bandage the injured leg, with instructions to call me if the baby's condition deteriorated. Then I went to develop and fix the film. Having ascertained that the man's leg was not broken, I let his friends take him home. It was time to start the drug count again – but then a pregnant woman arrived. At this point, the RCMP officer decided that it was too late to check the drugs and asked if he could take the drug book and keys. I explained that I might need to give drugs during the night, and so I could not part with them. His wife later told me that he had described the hectic afternoon to her. He admitted that he had not realized that the nursing station was such a busy place.

* * *

When I arrived in Coppermine, I quickly had one of the local Inuit women make me a parka, caribou boots, and a pair of gloves. I wore this parka on one of my first trips, during my second week in Coppermine. I went to Holman (Uluqsaqtuuq), on Victoria Island, a community of about 200 people. Some officials from the Department of Northern Affairs were heading there. Since there were no scheduled flights to Holman Island in those days, they had chartered a plane. The nurses in Coppermine covered an area as far north as Holman, and it was thought that this would be a good opportunity for me to go along and to introduce myself. While I was there, the officials were going to visit a seal camp, so I went with them. The boat had to be pulled over ice flows, but eventually we arrived at the camp. When we returned to the community, we were given a welcomed meal of fish and french fries at the RC mission. I was offered a beverage and, being rather naïve, did not ask any questions. I drank it because I was thirsty. I was fine, but I later discovered that I had been given Hudson's Bay overproof rum to drink. After that, I learned to always pour my own drinks, even soft drinks.

On another trip to Holman Island, in a single engine Otter, the heat failed shortly after takeoff. It was winter, and although I was wearing a parka and wind pants, I was frozen. So were the other passengers. Because the aisle was packed with cargo, we had to stay in our seats. When we arrived, we had to be helped off the plane because we were so cold that we could not move. The first year I visited Holman Island, there was no government school. Two lay sisters with the RC Mission held kindergarten classes. I stayed either with these lay sisters or at the Anglican Mission, and when the community relocated, I stayed with a schoolteacher. Then I was able to hold clinics in the school.

Because a one-day visit could last a week, we always travelled with clothes and toiletries to last a few days. A sleeping bag was an essential item in case a plane had to land on the tundra. One such occasion occurred in the middle of the summer when there was a sudden snowstorm. The pilot who was flying between Coppermine and Yellowknife was new to the area. He became disoriented and put down on a lake, until he could get his bearings. However, the lake was rather small, and there was barely room for the plane to take off again. While we waited, it was good to have a sleeping bag to sit in.

* * *

During that time, there were many dogs and sleds (*komatiks*) and very few skidoos. The school principal had husky dogs. One day when there was a visitor in the community I was asked to take him for a ride, as I was comfortable being with the dogs. The dogs were hitched in tandem to the *komatik* which was heavy and quite narrow, with no sides. I borrowed a long caribou parka and we set off across the Coppermine River. After a while, we turned around to go back. I got my bearings on the community and drove straight ahead. I ordered the dogs to "go" and, being rather young, they did just that – right over a cliff. One moment I was looking at the community, and the next moment I was looking at the ice on the river. My one thought was to keep on the sled and not fall off into the dogs. Huskies could easily attack somebody rolling on them in a caribou parka – especially if it were untreated hide. Fortunately, there was a snowbank on the river and the *komatik* slid down and did not land on the dogs. Dogs were expensive, and a heavy *komatik* could have badly injured any of them. I quickly put down the anchor, and we sorted ourselves out. The visitor also had enough sense to stay on the sled. I am sure he never forgot that ride. When people heard what had happened, they told stories of others who had gone over the cliff – and had not survived.

* * *

When I first arrived in Coppermine, there were a few small, one-room houses and a lot of tents. The annual sea-lift had just occurred, and many prefabricated houses had been delivered. The men were busy helping to build the houses, each of which had a living area and kitchen combined, and three bedrooms. However, the Inuit had not been used to sleeping in separate rooms. There were bathtubs, but no running water – only a large plastic barrel with a tap, which held about 100 gallons of water. When the community started hauling water by tractor in the summer, these barrels would be filled two or three times a week – not much water for a large family. In the winter, ice blocks would be delivered and stored outside the houses. The ice would sometimes have yellow stains from stray dogs. A program was set up to teach the local people about this new way of living. Nevertheless, it was not unusual to make home visits and see a snowmobile or hunting gear taking over the main room, while the family all lived in a bedroom. Seal meat would be stored in the bathtub. An oil range would heat the house, and for people who were used to living in a cool climate, especially babies, it was suddenly too hot. For nomadic people, living in permanent housing also meant that garbage would accumulate.

In the summer, families would return to their hunting and fishing areas. I used to enjoy rides in the nursing station's open boat to visit these communities. I could see a difference. The insides of the tents were always tidy. The older Inuit women would sweep the wooden floors with raven wings. The men would exit the tent so that I could perform prenatal assessments, check babies, and attend to any other health problems. It was tranquil to sit in a tent, drink tea and listen to the sea lapping on the shore.

* * *

After I had been in Coppermine for several months, there was the annual chest x-ray survey. Everyone came to get x-rayed and then, on the last day, several *komatiks* arrived with visitors. These Inuit had families here, but they had been living inland. They were dressed in skins – the children had been sewn into these clothes. I did not know that I was seeing this type of clothing for the last time and I wish I had taken photographs.

After the annual chest x-ray survey, the nurse would receive a long list of names of people living in the community and areas covered by that nursing station. The list would indicate those who were to be evacuated to the hospital with suspected tuberculosis, those from whom sputum samples were to be collected, and those who had missed being x-rayed. The list was compiled from the disk list. At birth, all Inuit were given a number and a brown disk to wear. Family names were not used, and grandparents usually named babies after a recently deceased person, regardless of whether they were male or female. Babies would be renamed if they became very ill. It was considered that the spirit of the deceased person, after whom they had originally been named, was not happy with them. Often the persons missing from the x-ray list had moved away or had died.

As many patients who came to the clinic were children, I was glad that I had worked on the paediatric floor in Kelowna. I was also thankful that I was a midwife, because I attended births, some of which were not straightforward. The policy was that mothers having first babies, and any mothers who had definite problems, or who had had a previous Cesarean section, could go to the hospital. Some mothers unexpectedly appeared in the community from other locations and went into labour before the next plane arrived. One such mother had a partial placenta praevia and the baby was born with the placenta between his legs. The mother bled from the beginning of her labour until an hour or two postpartum. We had intravenous solutions and ergometrine, but no blood replacement products. Those who were very anemic received intramuscular iron injections. Another mother, who had a large postpartum hemorrhage, said afterwards that she "woke up" because she heard me calling her. While visiting a camp, I observed a traditional birth and watched how the midwives practised. The women from the camps were very strong, physically and mentally. One became reliant on making accurate antenatal assessments, since a woman in labour could not suddenly be sent to a hospital. However, the majority of births went well. It was helpful for me to know the mother and the whole family, and to watch the baby grow during the two years that I lived in this community.

In order to deal with accidents, I found that I had to teach myself how to suture. Older people came to the clinic, but there were very few deaths during my time in Coppermine. Caring for a sick patient when I was on my own could be very tiring – one time I was up for five days and nights (something I could do in my twenties). Fortunately, the wife of the Anglican minister was a nurse, and could sometimes provide relief, so that I could have a sleep.

* * *

Several cases of tuberculosis showed up in the community, and families were often separated for two years while the father or mother, or sometimes a child, went to a hospital in the South. When the children returned, they may have forgotten how to speak Inuktitut and they may have become used to sleeping on their own, in a bed with sheets. Similar problems occurred when the children were rounded up and flown off to school. When they came back to the community, they looked for hair shampoo, bras and underwear, which the Hudson's Bay store did not stock.

They would come to the nursing station to see if the nurse would ask the store manager to sell these items in his store – especially in Holman Island, where they could not order from catalogues as there was no regular plane schedule.

In Coppermine, however, people could order from catalogues, and the Eaton's catalogue used to sell family planning items. When the Hudson's Bay Company store manager found that condoms were being ordered by mail, he started to display them in the store. He used to say that while the shelves emptied quickly, not one got paid for at the checkout. The nurse was the one who had to explain about family planning and other items for sale in the Eaton's, Sears, and Woodward's catalogues. Nurses, schoolteachers, and others from the South would eagerly study these catalogues to see the latest fashions. Similarly, if anybody received a package of old newspapers or magazines, people would visit and sit quietly, reading. This was before the Anik satellite, when there was no television, short wave radio reception was poor, and urgent messages were transmitted by either the Department of Transport or the RCMP radio phones.

* * *

I took part in community activities in Coppermine. Although, in my childhood I had only "passed up" from Brownies and had never become a Girl Guide, I became a Guide leader. I studied tying knots, and I learned campfire songs that would be translated into Inuktitut and other Girl Guide activities. This gave the girls an opportunity to see me as a person, and not just as somebody who gave needles (immunizations).

Between Christmas and New Year's, a square dance (in one large circle) was held every night in one of the empty warehouses of the Department of Northern Affairs. Here you would meet people who had not visited the nursing station. Everybody would wear new clothes for Christmas, and the churches would be full. Men and boys sat on one side of the church, and women and small children on the other. Whenever babies cried, they were quickly breastfed, regardless of where the mother was. Not all babies wore diapers, and so any baby or child who needed to void was rushed outside. Diaper rash was not a problem.

During the long winter evenings, we often got together to play bridge and cribbage, and each week the Community Association rented films for movie night. Sometimes, between the changing of reels, the nurse was asked to explain what was being shown – such as the time we watched *Days of Wine and Roses*. When the Holman Island community had relocated across the bay and had a new school, I would borrow a film to take with me whenever I went to hold clinics. Films were a special event. Nobody seemed to mind watching Elvis dancing and singing too quickly or too slowly, depending on the speed of the electric generator.

* * *

180

My two years in Coppermine passed quickly. I then decided I would travel around the world – mainly by bus. By the time I got to Australia, I knew that I wanted to return to the North. When I reached Bombay, there was a letter waiting for me, requesting that I write when I made it to England. In January of 1967, I returned to the North. I headed first to the eastern Arctic, before I went on to other places in the Northwest Territories. I have many memories of my time spent nursing in the North between 1964 and 1977. And I had only meant to stay a year.

Pearl Herbert RN, SCM, PHNdip, BN, BEd, MSc finished her training as a registered nurse in 1961 and as certified midwife in 1962, in England. That same year, she left for Canada where she first worked in Brockville, Ontario and in Kelowna, British Columbia. In 1964, she joined Medical Services, Health and Welfare Canada and was stationed in Coppermine, Frobisher Bay, Cape Dorset, and Broughton Island. Pearl earned her Public Health Nursing diploma in 1969, her Bachelor of Nursing in 1972, her Bachelor of Education in 1977, and her Master of Science in Health Education in 1978, all at Dalhousie University in Halifax, Nova Scotia. Meanwhile, she worked in Arctic Bay, Eskimo Point, Hay River, and Rae-Edzo. From 1979 to 1996, Pearl taught at the Memorial University of Newfoundland School of Nursing and coordinated the midwifery diploma program. She was coordinator of the Canadian Confederation of Midwives from 1993 to 1997. In 2003, she received the Atlantic Centre of Excellence for Women's Health Leadership Award. Currently, Pearl works as a consultant and does volunteer work.

THE CENTRE OF MY COUNTRY, THE HIGHLIGHT OF MY CAREER

Mary Flowers Wesko

When I studied and practised Northern Nursing 101, north of Sioux Lookout in Ontario, I learned from the best of nurses. We (two to six nurses, including me) were in a community of about 1000 people, and we had several smaller satellite communities to fly into monthly. Doctors visited regularly from Sioux Lookout and from the Hospital for Sick Children in Toronto. After several years, I carefully selected three communities in the far North with similar population numbers, although a different culture, and I prepared to transfer to the Northwest Territories.

In November, 1972, I arrived at Fort Churchill on a large plane with very few instructions for getting out of the airport. I assumed I would be met, so when the crowd dwindled, I called out "Medical Services," and miraculously someone appeared. I was to go to one of the barracks and get myself settled, and the next morning I was to appear at the office in the hospital. Fort Churchill was a foreign place to me, with people coming and going all night long in the barracks. Hallways linked most of the buildings. If you stepped outside, the snow squeaked, and your breath never left the edge of your nostrils.

After I found the dining hall and the office, I was greeted with *the* Procedure Book and given the rest of the day to familiarize myself with it. I was also asked to consider the possibility of "relieving" in Whale Cove for a while. Whale Cove is a neighbouring community to Rankin Inlet, and it was the location of my choice. Many people went back and forth between the two places. "Oh, Whale Cove is smaller and quieter, and the people are very nice," they assured me. It was also a one-nurse station.

When I was about to board the plane the following day, I heard someone say, "Now, if you don't settle into Whale Cove for six months, I'll be disappointed. It'll likely be the second stop, but check with someone." I looked at my ticket: Whale Cove. I consoled myself, remembering that I had my trunk with all of my stuff in it and my snowshoes strapped on top. Warm clothes, hobby supplies, and the right gear – I was ready for anything.

At the second stop, I got out of the plane and was waved into a Bombardier. This was something new to me. It was a large, covered vehicle with skis on the front and tracked wheels at the rear. At first, it seemed smelly; but the further we went, the more I appreciated that it was enclosed. The day was cold. At one point, when we came to a stop, I could see a railroad-crossing sign through the frosted window. This was my first taste of Whale Cove humour. Many bumps later (that sea ice just won't stay flat), we pulled up at a green house trailer with a porch jammed with children. They were chanting, "Welcome to Whale Cove, Flower. Welcome to Whale Cove, Flower." As it turned out, the teacher had heard on the radio that a new nurse was coming and had only caught the name "Flower." The children had prepared a big welcome in the hope that I would stay for a long time. Nursing stations in small communities were not always highest priority when it came to staffing.

* * *

The nursing station in Whale Cove was three house trailers joined together. In one trailer, there was the clinic/office, a bathroom, and two in-patient bedrooms. I kept one room for newborn deliveries, and I used the other one for sick patients who needed to stay longer, usually because they required IV, oxygen, or a croup tent, or because they needed to go to the hospital and were waiting for the plane. The middle trailer was for supply storage, the x-ray machine, and the darkroom. The third trailer was my residence.

Everyone helped me settle in. Paul K., the interpreter and maintenance man, and Rosie, the part-time housekeeper, were great. The Fredlunds, a long time missionary family, and Sue Lightowler, the school principal, were especially helpful. By helpful, I mean "survival" helpful, as in feeding me, keeping me warm, and providing training on equipment, such as the honey bucket and the water tank which converted ice blocks into my water supply. How to do radio communication and how to get supplies in were also big lessons.

This is how a sea-lift order was supposed to work. About February, the nurse sends an annual order for food and medical supplies into the Churchill Zone Office. After this order has passed through several approvals, it goes to Montreal for the sea-lift ship, which usually unloads in Whale Cove mid-August. You can imagine how many things can go wrong with such an arrangement. That particular year, my first in Whale Cove, most things had gone wrong. In the storage trailer of the nursing station, the inventory included many boxes of powdered mashed potatoes, several cans of whole milk powder, a few cans of egg powder, flour, 10 boxes of cake mix, 3 cans of peas, 20 cans of pimentos, and 10 cans of ripe olives in oil. At the bottom of the big freezer in the station, lay half a char. There was a selection of spices representative of the different nationalities of previous nurses. Very salty canned bacon was available at the Co-op store. It was November, and this supply of food was to last me until next August. Medical supplies were in better numbers, but there were some challenging gaps.

As I said, I learned from the best, and I had come from the land of plenty, where the nurses had the tractor-train annual order down to perfection. Our storeroom would have put the grocery store in my hometown to shame. My first radio call from Whale Cove to Churchill started with me listing all the food I needed. Whenever the person on the other end of the radio apparently didn't like what I was saying, he would say, "You are fading. You are fading. Over." I would plead, "Don't hang up. Send food. Send food, please! Over."

Several days after that call, three maintenance men came in to fix the leaks in my roof. In November, you cannot fix a leaky roof; but you can feed the men canned bacon and powdered potatoes, with olives on the side – for breakfast, lunch, and dinner, and you can communicate a grocery requisition effectively. Our housekeeper, Rosie, made delicious bread, and many people dropped off fish and caribou chunks, and invitations. Soon my larder was healthy.

* * *

Throughout the winter, I met everyone, and I soon became familiar with the village. It was a fairly compact place, with a school, a church, a community hall, the Co-op store/post office, and about 40 houses. There was a freshwater lake where, most of the year, ice blocks were harvested and delivered to the homes. Over the hill, there was a dump area. We even had a lake suitable for swimming, which was fairly shallow with a sandy bottom. There was also a tourist attraction called the Whale's Tail. It was a Centennial project, a "genuine government fluke"– government-funded and built on a hill.

Another interesting government project that became a great conversation topic was the recent "Operation Surname." At birth registration, Inuit had been given an E-number if they were registered in the eastern Arctic (that is, east of Gjoa Haven), or a W-number if they were born in the West. Many soapstone carvings are signed only with this number. When I arrived in the community, the nursing station files were sorted by people's E-numbers, not by their names. Over the years, to satisfy the church, they also took a Christian name at baptism. And culturally, they had a complex tradition of giving a baby an Inuit name as well.

The federal government wanted to stop the registration-by-number system and introduced the idea of a surname, preferably the father's Inuit name. What a funny (and usually unacceptable) idea that was to the Inuit. Many people simply could not call themselves by their father's surname and used either their Christian name and/or their Inuit name as their surname. In the nursing station, the filing system was a major study of family groupings, with the extra complication of custom adoptions, which were very common then. Custom adoptions took place when a child was given to another family, most often within the village. For instance, a couple with several children might offer a newborn to a childless couple. We converted the filing system from the "no mistake numeral" to fluid household groupings. And the spelling was debatable.

When groups of children would visit me on the weekend, a common topic of conversation would be who their real father or mother was and who liked them best. The children were fascinated with the idea that my dad's name was Mr. Flowers, and that his dad's name was Mr. Flowers, and that they were both farmers. They would go through my photo album over and over again.

Several facts about Whale Cove surprised me. It is in the geographic centre of Canada, and yet I felt as if I lived away up north. Although there is snow, it becomes packed down and hard enough to drive a vehicle over it. You never need snowshoes here. The summer sun brings warmth the whole twenty hours it shines, making Whale Cove the hot spot in Canada, with temperatures up into the 90s for several days in June. It matters little that the winter days are dark, because the windows are so thick with frost that you can't see out anyway. And finally, permafrost must be maintained, which is why houses are built up off the ground, allowing free flow of air underneath. If the ground were to melt, the whole area would turn into a swamp.

* * *

When the snow was gone, the sun dried the ground in Whale Cove. As the days lengthened, I noticed that the children played outside longer and later. One of their favourite pastimes was throwing stones. In front of each house was a high wooden stand, where you set the honey bags for the truck to pick up and take over the hill to the dump. These honey bags became favourite targets for stones. It sort of tested the weather as well: if the hole squirted, it was a melt day; if it didn't, it was a freeze day. I was concerned about the raw sewage that seeped into the sand and rock, but I couldn't think of an effective way to stop it. One day, a few kids banged on my door and escorted in a child who was bleeding from the scalp. As I listened, I could see that his head required several stitches, and I came up with a plan. I said I needed to have the kid who threw the stone to come and help me. Naturally, the child didn't want to come in; but as I waited, and the rest became more anxious and persuasive, the stone thrower appeared. I sent the other children out, and I had him sit and comfort his friend by holding his hand, while I cleaned and stitched the wound. After that, this scenario was repeated very few times that summer.

Tuesday was mail day in Whale Cove, with the planes stopping early on their way north and later on their way south. In May, they changed the schedule to north on Monday and Wednesday, and south on Monday and Thursday. Occasionally, I received important mail in the morning and could send a reply in the afternoon. More often, the plane would get delayed somewhere and skip the southbound stop in Whale Cove. The ice landing strip was close to the nursing station. This gave us the advantage of seeing whether or not the plane had landed; however, it could not be used from early June through the summer. While I was there, a land strip was completed. Breakup and freeze-up were no longer the worrisome isolation periods they had been, but the trail to the land strip was an adventure. After bundling sick patients onto a stretcher for the journey out to the plane, I was always thankful that I enjoyed good health.

* * *

One sunny summer day, one of the kids came to ask for my help. Ollie had a beluga tangled in his fishnet, and he needed help to remove the dead whale from the net. Most of the men were working on the airstrip. I was eager to assist, but could not imagine how you would move a

185

smooth, fifteen-foot dead whale in the water. We went out in the motorboat, around the point. As we got beside the whale, Ollie slit its top lip and tied a tow rope through it. Then we towed the whale into shore, where we climbed out of the boat and up on the rocks. There we made tea and took our time enjoying it, while the tide went out and left the whale on shore. Ollie butchered the upper side of the whale, and we cached the meat. We waited for the tide to float the whale again, so that we were able to turn it over and repeat the procedure. I knew I was there to be impressed – and to take pictures. Now, I truly felt welcome in Whale Cove.

* * *

I settled into this small community for more than the suggested six months. In the autumn, I attended university and then moved on to my original destination, Rankin Inlet. It was always exciting for me when people visited from Whale Cove. Occasionally, I would go back for several days, and once, I was weathered in for nearly a glorious week.

Mary Flowers Wesko RN, SCM, DPHN, BScN, CCOH grew up on a farm in southern Ontario. She graduated from the Mack Training School for Nurses in St. Catharines, Ontario, and then studied midwifery in England, in preparation for outpost nursing. Her first nursing station was in Sandy Lake, north of Sioux Lookout, Ontario. In 1972, she was a student of the first federal program for nurse practitioners in Toronto. Mary worked in the Keewatin Zone throughout the 1970s. She nursed in Whale Cove and Rankin Inlet, and was Zone Nursing Officer. After she completed her BScN in Edmonton, she worked for Edmonton Public Health for more than a year and with CUSO for over a year. In 1983, she returned to Rankin Inlet where she stayed until 1985. Since 1988, Mary has worked in southern Ontario as an occupational health nurse for Health Canada.

THE PORT HARRISON FLU EPIDEMIC, 1962

Kathleen Mary (Jo) Lutley

It was the spring of 1962. There were ninety-one Eskimo residents in Port Harrison and two hundred and forty-nine out at the six camps within a fifty mile radius of the settlement. Influenza hit the settlement hard. During the month of April, every man, woman and child, including two babies (born prematurely out at camp to mothers already sick) had influenza. By the end of the month, eight had died, including the two small infants, from complications of this infection. In addition, there were two patients in the nursing station who looked emaciated – like people from the Belsen P.O.W. camp. The man had lost over forty pounds, and the woman of fifty weighed only sixty-nine pounds.

* * *

In Great Whale River, we had almost finished with our share of the epidemic, which had been at its height in March, when Dr. Harvey asked me if I would go to Port Harrison to help Miss Yvonne Newton who had newly arrived there. I was to act as holiday relief while John and Rita McGirl went out on vacation. Miss Newton and the epidemic arrived simultaneously, although the infection probably arrived from Great Whale on an earlier aircraft. When Dr. Harvey and I arrived on the eighth of April, it appeared to be a deserted village. We heard that in the settlement only two or three Eskimo were still on their feet and that the sickness was spreading to the camps.

In the settlement, all of the government agencies and the Hudson's Bay Company helped out. The Department of Transport (DOT) radio and radiosonde operators carried water around to the Eskimo houses. The school principal and his wife, Mr. and Mrs. John McArthur, helped Yvonne Newton to nurse the sick in the two hostels and in the school, which had been turned into a miniature hospital, with rows of mattresses on the floor. Mrs. Doris Newark RN, who had been on the Indian and Northern Health Services staff at Frobisher Bay when I was there, had undertaken the home nursing care of the families on her side of the river, adjacent to the radiosonde site. This was of great help, for it left Yvonne free to divide her time between the school and the hostels, and to do the home visits on her side of the river. The Anglican minister, Rev. W. Graham, a friend from Frobisher days when he was at Pangnirtung, made us a most ingenious oxygen tent out of heavy copper wire and plastic sheeting to fit over a bassinet. (He

---

Port Harrison, now known as Inukjuak, is located on Hudson Bay, in northern Quebec. This is Jo Lutley's April month-end report. It is printed here, with minor changes, with her permission.

later made a second one which we were able to loan to Povungnituk.) His wife, Barbara, also an RN, had offered to help out in the nursing station during the afternoons. Mrs. Carol Fraser, wife of one of the DOT operators, did night duty at the school.

In the nursing station, John and Rita McGirl were hard at work for a week of constant day and night duty. They, and their two children, were already sick with the flu, and we were doubtful whether Rita would be fit to travel. They helped us all they could before they left on the last aircraft before breakup.

Dr. Harvey returned to Moose Factory on April 12. Before he left, he talked to some of the Eskimo on the nature of the infection, the treatment we would give, and what they should do. He also warned the community that we would not be able to save everyone and that they must expect deaths from complications. Up to that time, there had been none. (This was a great help, for they remembered and commented on it when the toll of deaths seemed to be rising alarmingly.) The aircraft that took him south brought in two cylinders of oxygen, more medicines, and an infant resuscitube, which we were required to use over and over again.

* * *

It was not practical for us to make medical trips to the camps; but as the teams came in from the camps, we sent back medicines and advice. We warned them of the most serious complication – severe respiratory embarrassment – and told them that any cases with this symptom should be brought to the nursing station. This obstructed breathing, similar to that in cases of diphtheria, was the worst of the complications that followed the initial influenzal attack. It seemed to be a combination of a naso-pharyngeal edema and laryngeal spasm, and allied with the production of vast quantities of mucoid sputum, some of it coughed up and some of it post-nasal. Altogether, they constituted a deadly hazard, not only with young children and babies, but with adults as well, for suddenly (often with no previous warning other than a little gurgling sigh) they would stop breathing and require all the methods of resuscitation available to start them breathing again.

Mr. Evans, the area administrator for Northern Affairs, returned from Ottawa on April 15 and arranged a tour of the southern camps to see how bad conditions were. We gave him medications to take out, and we showed him how to administer penicillin. Later, he made a trip to the north camp with Mr. McArthur. A second tour of the south camps was undertaken by Mr. McArthur the following week. These trips were made under poor conditions for travelling. Apart from the help it was to us to get full reports on everyone, the reports were greatly appreciated by the Eskimo people. Without these trips, the death toll in the camps would have been greater.

By the fifteenth of April, the settlement people were getting back on their feet, and what seemed like a deserted village when I came was now showing signs of life. It meant, too, that there were women who would just walk in, take off their parkas, and voluntarily give me a helping hand with the care of patients. They would often tackle a formidable mountain of laundry or provide a meal for those who were able to eat. On one occasion, when I was busy with new admissions and three sick babies, I had not eaten lunch. I heard a hammering sound in the ward, and there on the floor was frozen caribou meat being divided out with a meat axe. How good it looked – and how hungry I was. *"Tuktu vini tu gooma voonga"* (caribou that was to partake of want I). Their faces shone with pleasure at my request. A quarter of a pound of this incomparable Eskimo delicacy was chopped off for me, and I sat on the floor among them and ate. I had a twinge of conscience at my flagrant disregard of several public health principles; but by the time I had finished gnawing, I felt so much better that even this was forgotten.

* * *

The sick ones from the camps were now arriving daily. Some of the most pitiful sights that I have seen in the North were the arrival of these teams. Even the dogs were subdued and wore a puzzled frown. The men, often sick themselves, carried in their wives or children and then collapsed on the floor from sheer exhaustion. Sometimes they were too ill to be allowed to return to camp, and we found someone else to take the team back. Usually though, after a warming mug-up by the kitchen stove, they were okay. After giving news of how the rest of the family was, they collected more aspirin or cough medicine and they would be off again.

When the sick were brought to the nursing station, they were laid on mattresses or sleeping bags to thaw out. This gave us time to make a decision as to whether they rated a bed or a mattress, if they were to be admitted here. If they were not too sick, they could go up to the school. Usually, we transferred the convalescent patients to make room for new admissions, for we soon found that everyone tended to get worse before they got better.

One morning, a newborn baby was brought in, wrapped in a fox skin. The mother and everyone in the tent was ill, so they asked a neighbour to bring the baby boy in to the nurse, for he would die if left at home. The baby looked about a month premature, weighed four and a quarter pounds, thrived well and seemed resistant to the infections which surrounded him. When he was five and a half pounds, he was discharged to the care of a foster mother. Three days later, he became sick. When I took him out of the back of the *amouti,* or the carrying parka, when they arrived at the nursing station with him, he was dead.

Another two-day-old premature baby, weighing barely four pounds, was admitted with her mother. The mother had a bad case of bronchopneumonia. Her high temperature probably contributed to her premature labour. This baby became worse, and for twelve days, with a resuscitube, mucus trap, oxygen, and stimulants, we battled for her life. We resuscitated her again and again – but in the end, we lost her.

* * *

By the fifteenth of the month, the four-bed nursing station was accommodating eighteen acutely ill patients. The adults were in the ward and the laundry room, the sitting room was a paediatric ward, and the second staff bedroom was a resuscitation unit for five very sick babies. They all had pneumonia. Practically all of the adults were spitting up bloodstained sputum, and one woman had a lung hemorrhage of nearly a pint. A schoolboy with severe dehydration from persistent vomiting required intravenous therapy and continuous gastric suction for two days. Several patients developed acute retention; many others were incontinent (of urine and feces). Mostly everyone, at some time or other, had to be "willed" into living, because their mental and physical prostration was so severe.

To get them to eat was frequently a major achievement. Often the most successful method was for me to mime an improbable story – such as how I had gone out personally, for instance, to cut a hole in the ice to catch fish. Having caught enough for all of us, a polar bear had come and chased me home, and that was why we all had to have fish cakes made from canned salmon and dehydrated potatoes. They would enter into the spirit of the story and laugh until they almost cried. But, bless them, they would then eat my fish cakes.

The greatest help to them in this time of extreme weakness and apathy was, undoubtedly, their minister, the Rev. W. Graham. He spoke their language fluently and he would come in, talk with them, hold an evening service in the ward, and leave them soothed and strengthened. For, although many heads were shaved (a relic of a more primitive culture, when a person became delirious or mentally disturbed), this was a very devout Christian community. They had more faith in a prayer book shoved into a pillow under the head of a restless patient, than in a sedative tablet.

One occasion when I did not know whether to laugh or cry, or be shocked, was the time they decided to improve upon the Prayers for the Sick offered up on behalf of Mathewsie by Mr. Graham. He had read, and they had listened most attentively to the passage in St. James about anointing with oil. This was translated to them as "seal oil." The minister explained that, since he had no oil, he would just lay his hands on Mathewsie and bless him. The man had been desperately ill for days, and he had been brought in by his wife and another young woman who had handled the team. Not long after, I returned to the ward to find his sister and his wife anointing his brow, chest, hands, and feet with seal oil. To my eyes, Mathewsie looked so near death that I left them to it. It comforted them in their grief. I went to sleep, leaving them in charge. Two hours later, his sister, all excited and with eyes shining, called me to come quickly. "Mathewsie better. Mathewsie okay now." Mathewsie *was* better. The change was dramatic – and although it would be a while before he would recover, at least he was going to recover. Maybe it can be explained by coincidence, but I doubt it. To me, it will always be the result of an act of faith.

* * *

During this same month, forty patients were admitted to the nursing station and thirty-eight to the school. There were fourteen sick children in the two hostels, and two of these were later transferred to the nursing station. There were no deaths in the settlement. In the nursing station, we lost two premature infants, a six-week-old infant who developed meningitis while recovering from pneumonia, and a two-year-old child who died two hours after admission, from acute respiratory embarrassment, secondary to pneumonia and meningitis. After his death, the body of this child broke out in a petechial type of rash that is seen with cerebrospinal fever. In the camps, three adults and one child died. Three of these deaths were in the same house at Johnny Innukpuk's camp, forty miles north. I visited this camp, which was fourteen hours by dog team each way, to bring back a man from the next house with probable encephalitis. From the description they gave of how the illness had developed in the three who died, it may well be that they had developed encephalitis too.

By the end of April, the worst of the sickness was over. The last patients were discharged from the school on the twenty-seventh, and Mr. and Mrs. McArthur were able to resume teaching the next week. In the nursing station, we still had four patients who were waiting for the arrival of an aircraft to take them south to Moose Factory. Two of these patients gave us a harrowing time. They were mentally, as well as physically sick – their minds excited, rather than sedated by the drugs available. Eventually guards had to be employed day and night. These four men, picked by the Eskimo as being the best for the job, did much to help these two unfortunates. Always gentle, but always firm, they were able to re-educate our two patients to acceptable social standards of behaviour. When Lucassie, the janitor, was ill they took over all his duties as well. They took their guard duties very seriously, even dressing as befitted the part. The first morning when they started to work, I was hard put to stop from laughing. Seated on one side of the table was a sheriff from a western film with white wide-brimmed hat, thigh-high boots, a long knife, and a red spotted handkerchief tied over his face. As for Willia Policee, even without any actual RCMP clothes, he somehow looked, behaved, and even had the intangible mannerisms of a Mountie. I learned later that he was employed by them, and that he was a faithful copy of a constable he idolized.

* * *

I returned to Great Whale River, happy to have been given the privilege of helping out in a time of need, in such a friendly and colourful community – and where there was an impressive standard of cooperation among all agencies. Long may it remain thus.

Kathleen Mary Jo Lutley CM, BSc, RN served as a radio operator with the Women's Auxiliary Air Force in England before becoming a nurse. She arrived in Canada in 1956, and worked for the Grenfell Mission in isolated one-nurse stations in northern Labrador. After joining the Medical Services Branch of Health Canada in 1960, she worked in various communities in the North. In 1967, she became a Canadian citizen. She obtained her BSc in Public Health Nursing from the University of Ottawa and a certificate in Community Development from St. Paul University. She travelled throughout northern Manitoba as a zone nursing officer and later became a health educator in Thompson, Manitoba. She retired in 1982, and among other things, is active in wildlife rehabilitation. In 1987, she became a Member of the Order of Canada. The citation for this award reads as follows:

> *During her 26-year career in health services in Canada's North, she delivered babies in teepees, nursing stations and aeroplanes, nursed Inuit patients in snow houses and dog-sledded across miles of ice to immunize children in the remote communities of Labrador and the Northwest Territories.*

In 1995, Mary Jo Lutley received the Manitoba Association of Registered Nurses Outstanding Achievement Award.

INDUSTRIAL NURSING IN NORMAN WELLS

Hilda Doran

In mid-March of 1951, I flew from Edmonton to Norman Wells, which is on the Mackenzie River about 160 km south of the Arctic Circle in the Northwest Territories. On the same flight were a doctor, his wife and my fellow nurse, Julie. We were all going to the Wells for the first time to work for Imperial Oil Ltd. (IOL).

Prior to this assignment, I had IOL orientation in Toronto and in Sarnia, Ontario, and I had one month of x-ray instruction in Calgary, Alberta. This was to be industrial nursing, and our mandate included a yearly medical, with a chest x-ray, for each employee. When the refinery was running and the Mackenzie River was open, there were two nurses and a doctor on staff. The rest of the year, there was one nurse on her own.

During the Second World War, with Canadian approval, the American Army set up Camp Canol across the Mackenzie River from Norman Wells. Their intention was to put in a pipeline to take oil from Norman Wells to Alaska, in the event that the Japanese cut off oil tankers supplying fuel to Alaska. They also built a road from Dawson Creek to Fairbanks, Alaska. When the war was over, we inherited a 16-bed hospital, which the Americans sold to Imperial Oil for a dollar and an ambulance that had a slight list. We looked after the sick in the community, as well as the healthy and visitors. We had to be prepared to handle any situation.

During the early fifties when I was there, the population of the Wells was 60, at most. This included people employed by Imperial Oil and their families. To the East, up river from camp, there were about eight members of the Canadian Army Signal Corps and two families, one Department of Transport couple and, at times, three Royal Canadian Air Force men. A Native family lived a few miles further on. A CPA (Canadian Pacific Airlines) pilot and a Norseman plane were based at the Wells, which then had the northernmost airstrip. (Inuvik didn't exist at that time.) It was usual for this airfield to be "out" for two or three weeks in the spring and in the fall. We hoped nothing would happen during that time. Patients from Aklavik and Fort Good Hope who travelled to and from Charles Camsel Hospital in Edmonton stayed with us overnight. Fort Norman (up river) had no doctor, so we occasionally got patients from there. We tried to fly serious cases to Edmonton. Sometimes one of the medical staff accompanied them. In the first year, I had a flight in a Lancaster Bomber, because the Royal Canadian Air Force were photographing the North and happened to be in when we needed to transport a patient.

For us, it was a six-day work week with Sunday the day of rest. If we had an in-patient, Julie and I did twelve-hour shifts. We split the non-nursing jobs. As the senior nurse, I did the x-ray and secretarial work, while Julie did her best at the lab work – with the help of a book. We both shared the cleaning. (Apparently, the doctors who had been at the Wells before us looked after the lab work; but when I was there, they didn't.) We lived in prefabricated buildings, all of which were heated by steam lines under the floors and were *very* warm. Because the water pipes were alongside the steam lines, water for drinking had to be kept in the refrigerator. I had to put ice into the solutions to try and reach proper temperatures for developing x-rays.

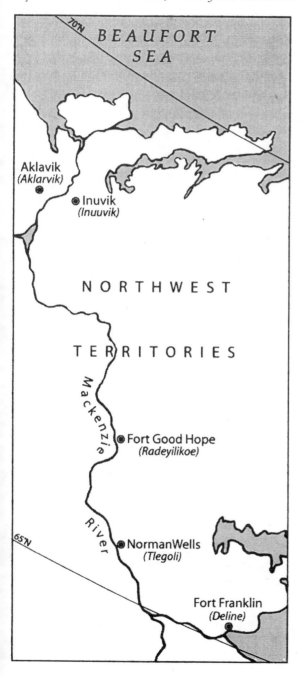

Meals were served in the mess hall. They were hearty and good meals, though fresh vegetables were a rarity, and we had no fresh fruit or salads. Milk was powdered or canned. In the brief summer, we tried our hand at gardening. With the 24-hour sunlight, we were able to grow some vegetables, despite our being on permafrost.

For entertainment, we had a recreation hall where there was a self-serve library and a curling rink with natural ice. Bingo games were held mid-week at the rec hall. We had some Saturday night dances and a movie on Sunday night. I can't remember the dances being well-attended, unless it was a special occasion or a theme night. No liquor was allowed in the hall, and no drinks or popcorn at the movies. In fact, there were no soft drinks or snack foods available at all in camp. Since Norman Wells had no school, the majority of the men were there without their families. Some of them preferred to relax with a drink in their quarters after working six days straight, and they curled a few evenings a week for most of the year. Curling was great fun and it was my favourite form of recreation. There were few women and we were inexperienced curlers, but the men were tolerant.

The couples who were at the Wells frequently entertained at home and sometimes they held card parties. Bridge was a game I played often. Medical personnel were included when the IOL superintendent and his wife invited the administrative staff over when anyone visited from Imperial Oil or from the government, who most likely would have been en route to Aklavik.

Spring breakup on the Mackenzie River was an exciting, and much anticipated, event. Bets were made on when the ice would start to move. Ice piled up as high as 100 feet, and you could not miss breakup, for the noise was tremendous. When the river was open again, freight barges, heavily loaded with supplies, would arrive.

Although we had no telephone service, messages could be relayed by the Signals Corps. Contact with the outside world was by mail – when the planes could land and take off on the dirt airstrip. The arrival of mail was a big event. The first year, I took a small radio, but found that that it could not receive anything. The second year I was there, a bigger radio brought in the Armed Forces station in Los Angeles, which was beamed up to Alaska. We also received a signal from a station in Russia, which sent us good classical music, as well as propaganda in English.

When we left the Wells at the end of October, only a maintenance crew remained. The person in charge of medical care was a nurse, a woman in her sixties who was the wife of an employee. However, before the year was out, she decided that she no longer wanted the responsibility, and I was called back in. I was on my own for two and a half months before a new doctor arrived and Julie returned.

* * *

The most critical experience I had at Norman Wells happened during my second year, when the doctor and I made a mercy flight to Fort Franklin on Great Bear Lake in the CPA Norseman. The population of the village consisted of Native people and five white men: one teacher, two priests and two Hudson's Bay men. The younger of the Bay men had put kerosene on a fire to help it along. He was severely burned and the older man suffered moderate burns. The Hudson's Bay Post burned down and destroyed the only two-way radio in the community, so they could not call for help.

One of the priests had to travel by dog team to Fort Norman to reach us. The two Hudson's Bay men were in pain for twenty-four hours before they received treatment. Although the priests had morphine, they didn't know how to use it. When the doctor and I reached them, we covered their burns with Vaseline gauze (which was the treatment at the time) and gave them something to relieve the pain. We brought them to the Wells on stretchers, with the doctor and me kneeling beside them in the plane as we flipped over the mountains. There was no room to sit and there were no seat belts. A few days later, the RCAF took the men to Edmonton. Both survived.

* * *

When I look back on my years of industrial nursing in Norman Wells, I realize that this was a time I would not have missed.

Hilda Doran RN, DPHN graduated in 1945 from Wellesley Hospital in Toronto, Ontario. She completed her Public Health Diploma at the University of Toronto in 1946. She worked for a year with the Victorian Order of Nurses and then for three years at Sunnybrook Hospital in Toronto, before moving to Norman Wells. Hilda has retired and now lives in Ottawa.

EARLY DAYS IN CAMBRIDGE BAY

Kathleen Dier

In 1957, when Medical Services was known as Indian Health, and the Inuit were called Eskimo, I was sent to Cambridge Bay in the Northwest Territories to open a nursing station. At the time, I was employed at the Charles Camsell Indian Hospital in Edmonton, which was solely for the treatment of Native patients from Alberta, the Northwest Territories, and the Yukon.

Up to this point, there had been no nurse in Cambridge Bay. As in many other small settlements in the North, the RCMP took care of the health and welfare needs of the Native patients. At the Camsell Hospital, I was active in organizing the annual medical orientation course for the RCMP, to help them deal with all emergencies, including deliveries. Sent off with our blessings and a copy of *Canadian Mother and Child*, these men did a truly remarkable job.

However, the influx of labourers working on the construction of the Distant Early Warning (DEW) line meant the RCMP at Cambridge Bay had no time for Native health care, and a nurse was urgently needed. I was happy to be assigned to this new job, and I immediately started packing warm clothes.

In those days, there were no commercial flights into Cambridge Bay, so I went with the RCAF in a B-119 flying boxcar which was used to service their winter survival school. It was a cavernous affair with a great hollow belly and sling-seats around the sides, so your back was against the window. Six hours after takeoff, we descended into the settlement – which looked very small indeed.

Life in Cambridge Bay

Cambridge Bay consisted of the Hudson's Bay Company, the Department of Transport (DOT), the RCMP, and the Anglican and Roman Catholic missions, all spaced about a half-mile apart, with the Inuit dwellings scattered around a three-mile radius. The DEW line site was four miles away (a small bump on the horizon), and fortunately, the community was off-limits to the labourers, so their presence was not disruptive. The population was made up of about 120 Inuit and 12 whites. The wife of the RCMP officer and I were the only white women. The number of Natives fluctuated as the nomadic families came and went. Some had taken employment with

---

This story was first published in *The Canadian Nurse* in January 1984 as "Early Days." It appears here, with minor changes, with permission of the author who was the first nurse in Cambridge Bay.

the DOT or the DEW line, and this had an effect on the traditional migratory nature of Native life.

The shift in lifestyle was reflected in the housing. Those who worked for the government lived in small wooden structures or Quonset hut dwellings. The more nomadic types lived in snow houses, while the majority of the people lived in homes made from old packing cases obtained from the DEW line. These were insulated with snow blocks, but most were simply snowed under. At first, being unaware of this phenomenon, I continually tripped over chimneys protruding from snowbanks. The entrance to each home looked like a giant gopher hole and led into a small passage that you had to negotiate on your hands and knees. The passageway often contained frozen fish and caribou. Occasionally, small puppies huddled there for shelter. A small wooden door opened into the house, which usually consisted of a single room with one or two sleeping platforms covered with blankets or furs, a small oil stove, a few tin dishes, and enamel cups hanging from hooks. There was a container of water, a large pot for making stew, and a frying pan for cooking bannock.

My problem was that Ottawa had sent out a form whereby you had to rate the housing on a scale from one to five. I had no difficulty giving the snow houses top marks because of their excellent biodegradable properties. However, as they aged, they iced over and the roof would drip, so they were no longer warm and comfortable. This motivated the residents to seek more suitable quarters. The packing case houses had no such fail-safe mechanism. They lacked ventilation and became very cluttered and dirty. I, therefore, adjusted the government scale in order to give them a negative rating.

Initially, home visits were confusing. The occupants were never the same as the ones on my previous visit. So I took to numbering the wooden doors in sequence with an old tube of lipstick (starting from what I thought was east and going west). My suspicion was that there was a merry-go-round of tenants: when one family went hunting, another family took over their abode, and anyone coming in from the tundra simply occupied the first available place.

At that time, the Inuit had no family names, only two names – one English, the other Inuit. Thus, Peter Taptit's wife's name was Mary Oguniuk, and their child was Jerry Koogona. This created confusion. So, in trying to enumerate the population, the government came up with the ingenious system of metal discs stamped with a personal number, which most of the people wore on a cord around their neck. This helped to prevent immunizing the same person twice; but it did not eliminate confusion about who belonged to what family, since custom adoption was widely practised among the Inuit. If someone "needed" a son or daughter, the child was given to them. Then the donor parents would often adopt someone else's baby the following year. Everyone knew exactly who their real brothers and sisters were. The only person with a problem was the nurse.

When I arrived, the Anglican minister was attempting to organize a graveyard, which was not easy, considering the rocky terrain and permafrost. An area on a hill was marked out, and wooden caskets were to be buried as deeply as possible, then covered with stones. There were still unmarked graves around the settlement, most of the bodies being enclosed in wooden boxes.

Very few of the Inuit spoke English. A number had completed Grade 1 or 2 at the residential school in Aklavik, before homesickness had drawn them back to Cambridge Bay. And some who had been patients "outside" had picked up a few words of English. I was grateful when Gwen Carter, a Native girl who had been trained as a nursing aid in Camsell, returned to work at the nursing station. She helped to interpret for the people and she explained their customs to me. I was doubly fortunate, for Gwen proved to be good company as well.

The Nursing Station

An old cottage, formerly occupied by the RCMP, had been designated as the new nursing station. Corporal Jones and his wife Liz had recently moved into new quarters, and for the time being, I lived with them. They were reluctant to show me my new quarters because, in the interim since their departure, the cottage had been used for cooking fish for sled dogs. When I entered, I understood: the fish had been removed, but their memory lingered on.

The house had four rooms and an attic, where for some strange reason, the chemical toilet was installed. The room off the kitchen was the obvious choice for the dispensary, as it contained shelves and a cot. It also housed a large box of Army medical supplies left over from some long-forgotten "Operation Musk-ox." A closer examination revealed outdated plasma, old dressings, and even vials of morphine and strychnine, which I promptly disposed of.

The house also contained a kitchen stove, a water barrel, and a set of bunk beds. I immediately sent in a large order for furniture and supplies, and I set about cleaning up the place. I employed a local boy named Pete Atigioyak to help out. He said his name meant "parka," so we affectionately called him Pete the Parka. Pete didn't care much for cleaning, but he threw himself enthusiastically into painting, often getting more paint on himself than the walls.

A generator supplied electricity quite efficiently, as long as no one used too many appliances. The phone system extended only to houses in the settlement; there was no connection to the outside world. DOT operated a radio schedule with neighbouring communities, but it was not very reliable. Telegrams were the major way of communicating. However, they had to go through a number of relays – which resulted in some rather strange messages being exchanged. The clearest radio reception was "Moscow Mollie," who gave somewhat biased news in flawless English and then played records by Guy Lombardo and His Royal Canadians.

Water was a perennial problem. Pete chopped ice blocks out of the river some distance away and these melted slowly in a barrel by the stove. It takes a lot of ice to make a pitcher of water, so you learned to be very frugal. Liz organized a routine for the police compound whereby we had a bath every two weeks (whether we needed one or not). The women went first, then more hot water was added, and the men were each allowed their turn. Even after all these years, I still occasionally pause to appreciate the miracle of water coming out of a tap.

Another serious problem was lack of transportation. Neither the police nor the nurses had a vehicle, which meant we had to walk everywhere – and an Arctic mile seemed longer than the average mile. When it became necessary to transport patients to the plane, the DEW line sent their Bombardier over to pick up the sick. When I went on home visits, I carried medications and supplies in a packsack, and I thawed them before using them. Even when I went out socially, I always had a few supplies like aspirins and cough medicine tucked in my pockets. If I met a client en route, this would save us both the long, cold trek back to the nursing station.

Gradually, the nursing station took on a pleasant homey atmosphere, and the dispensary became orderly and well-stocked. Pete, Gwen and I were pleased with our accomplishments. With every new addition, the Inuit would come to marvel and admire. In fact, they were inveterate visitors who would drop in quietly, sit on the floor and drink tea. They would tell Gwen the latest gossip, smile a lot at me, then bow and leave again as noiselessly as they had come.

Routine Nursing Care

Even before the nursing station had opened, we admitted a patient, Hilda Hipogoak. She was a pleasant older woman who had been left to die, but had been discovered by an RCMP patrol. She was paraplegic due to a TB lesion on her spine. We bathed and fed her, then sent her out to Edmonton where her tattoos, complete from face to waist, caused a sensation. She lived for nearly a year at the Camsell where she enjoyed her celebrity status.

Our days were very busy. Influenza was common, as was measles – a disease that affected both adults and children, and often followed pneumonia. Eye conditions, and skin and ear infections were common, as well as toothaches, since the Bay Store was well-stocked with pop and candy. My first priority, however, was to establish an immunization program, including the new polio vaccination. (Unfortunately, a measles vaccine was yet to be discovered.) I found the best time to immunize was after church, when everyone stopped in at the nursing station to get warm. Gwen and Pete were also excellent at bringing in stragglers who had been hunting and whom they knew "hadn't had their needles yet."

Maternal care caused a dilemma, as it was hard to tell who might be pregnant under the voluminous *atig* (the inner layer of a double-skinned parka with the fur facing the inside), which the women wore. I had to depend on local gossip, as most women considered giving birth a routine happening, and not something that should concern the nurse. There were very few births in the settlement, probably due to the low fertility rate. Also, many women delivered their babies while travelling. Once I saw a premature baby who had been born on the trail, a "little sparrow" kept alive by breastfeeding and his mother's loving care. Today, this baby is a "big man" in the North.

Another mother, Mary, had a Caesarian section in the Camsell and returned when the baby was one month old. Shortly after, in the middle of a 42° below zero night, I got a call. The baby had diarrhea. It was too late. When I arrived, the baby was dead. I thought Mary might have trouble with engorged breasts, so I told her to come and see me the next day. But when she arrived, she had already solved the problem by nursing her four-year-old son. My heart went out to her when she sadly returned the little nightgown and blanket given to her in hospital. It was as if she knew there would not be another baby. And there never was.

My most unusual maternity case also had a sad ending. "Dead Arm Lucy" had been in labour for nearly three days when I was summoned. An informant said her paralyzed arm had been caused by her being dragged by dogs "four babies ago." A number of anxious women had gathered around and the patient was exhausted. After a quick examination, I gave her some Demerol and she drifted off to sleep. Two hours later, she awoke and instantly delivered a bouncing baby girl.

The next morning, Lucy showed up at the nursing station, having walked the three miles with the new baby in her parka, and announced that she was to be named Kathleen Gwen Ekagena. Gwen and I were delighted with our new godchild. Two days later, the baby's father appeared at the door looking rather uncomfortable. He reported that the baby had "stopped breathing." We rushed to see Lucy who resignedly informed us, "Yes, the baby was dead and already buried." Gwen and I tried to place a little marker on the grave of our namesake; but we were unable to locate the burial site in the drifting snow. I reported the death to the police. After questioning the father, Corporal Jones shook his head: "He had too many girls. It was a case of infanticide."

Emergencies

Some emergencies remain particularly vivid. Once I was called to see an older Inuit woman who was obviously having a coronary. Her husband was holding her in a sitting position and gently rocking and crooning to her. Demerol relieved her pain, and the couple beseeched me not to "send her outside." I was moved by their obvious devotion to each other. I could picture this woman lying unhappily between sterile white sheets in an alien environment, far from those she loved. So I relented, on condition that after a period of rest, she would follow a strict regimen. She must not go hunting. She must not walk against the wind, and she must ride on a dog sled if she had to travel any distance. Some months later, when a doctor visited, he agreed that she should continue this routine.

* * *

One evening, a small plane landed directly in front of the nursing station. The pilot delivered a very ill woman from Bathurst Inlet who had apparently been sick all winter. I removed her tattered fur parka and burned it, bathed her, and wrapped her in warm blankets. She was very thin and had a racking, productive cough. I tended her all night, but just before dawn she died. I notified the police, who asked me to sign the death certificate, which I did tentatively, citing the cause of death as pulmonary tuberculosis with superimposed pneumonia. The priest built a coffin, and Pete borrowed his father's dog team. The lonely little procession proceeded through the swirling snow to the new graveyard.

* * *

One Sunday, a rabid dog got loose and terrorized the settlement. Pete joined the posse and after the dog was shot, he reported that it had only bitten one man who, luckily, had a wooden leg. Soon after, a woman who had been bitten and required rabies treatment was sent from another settlement. With great trepidation, I administered the 14 daily injections subcutaneously into her abdomen. All the while, I watched for side effects. One night, she woke up screaming. I was sure she was rabid, and I frantically wondered what one did for humans in a case like this. I knew what happened to dogs! It turned out, however, that a cockroach had stowed away in the borrowed RCAF mattress, and the woman had never seen such a thing before. Gwen promptly stomped on the invader, and we all collapsed into gales of laughter.

X-ray team

The annual x-ray survey from Camsell was conducted at Easter time when the Inuit gathered for their rites of spring which greeted the return of the sun. A team of doctors and technicians crisscrossed the Arctic, x-raying and examining the population for tuberculosis and other health problems. A number of active cases were found in Cambridge Bay. I had the difficult task of telling these people that they would have to leave their homes and families for treatment that would probably take two or three years. One man resisted and only consented to go, after requesting that the police watch his wife. The man's suspicions were well-founded – no sooner had his plane left than a neighbour moved in with his wife. That was the sad thing about TB

202

treatment; it really disrupted families. For example, one child returned home after years in the hospital, unable to remember a word of his own language. His parents were upset because he did not obey them. Eventually he had to be sent away to a residential school, because he could not fit back into the community.

My real difficulty came as the x-ray team moved along the coast and began sending patients back to Cambridge Bay. At one time, we had 14 active TB patients living in the nursing station awaiting transportation to Edmonton. Gwen and I tried to set up a system of separate dishes, and we kept a pot of caribou stew on the stove for them, while Pete made bannock. The patients slept in sleeping bags on the floor. Gwen and I had our double bunk in the bedroom and occasionally shared it with babies who would not stop crying until we took them into the security of our sleeping bags. They were so used to being in their mothers' parkas that the sudden wrench into the outside world was terrifying.

I accompanied the x-ray survey party to Perry River, a small settlement where even the local trader was Inuit. The people were healthy and so prosperous that they owned a large number of commercial fishing boats. These were frozen into the ice so the owners put blocks of snow blocks around the cabins and lived comfortably on board all winter. We tried to reach a camp where part of the population was fishing, but it was impossible to locate white snow houses against the white landscape. The Inuit in the plane were of no help either. They were familiar with the terrain at ground level. However, once they got into the air, they were as confused as the rest of us.

Getting patients sent off to Camsell was an operation of military proportions. Everyone had to be ready to board the RCAF flying boxcar the minute it landed on the ice. Each person had a big yellow tag with name, disc number, and other particulars filled in at the top and bottom. The bottom part was removed at the Yellowknife Hospital where the patients spent the night. The rest of the tag was supposed to remain in place until they reached Camsell, a feat not usually accomplished, as the wind kept blowing them away. This caused great confusion upon arrival at Camsell, confusion compounded by the fact that in fur parkas, it wasn't easy to sort out the men from the women. For the Inuit, the trip south was a bewildering experience. Nevertheless, they coped amazingly well.

Culture Shock

For the Inuit (especially those of Pete and Gwen's generation) the years since I left Cambridge Bay have been tragic. I am glad I had the opportunity of catching a glimpse of the old ways before the full impact of the outside world crashed in upon them.

Today, nurses in the North face social problems unknown in my time. Community expectations have increased in line with the progress of medical technology. The challenge is always to try to improve the quality of life of those who depend on us. Northern nurses are equipped to do this. It is our ability to blend what we know with what the Inuit believe that makes our nursing actions meaningful. The Inuit are a people in transition. They are survivors. They have a long tradition of coping with adversity, and they use this stamina to adapt and master their new environment. Nurses working in the North have a unique opportunity to become a part of this process.

Kathleen Dier RN, BScN, MScN(A) graduated in 1945 from Holy Cross Hospital in Calgary. She obtained her BScN at the University of Alberta in 1960, and her MSc in Nursing Administration at McGill University in Montreal in 1963. She worked for Medical Services for nearly eleven years, during the period from 1947 to 1962. Her postings included: the Charles Camsell Hospital in Edmonton, Yellowknife Red Cross Hospital, Cambridge Bay Nursing Station, and Whitehorse General Hospital. From 1973 to 1976, she was Director of the Northern Nurse Program at the University of Alberta, and served as Associate Dean of Nursing from 1977 to 1980. As a Senior Nurse Educator with the World Health Organization for seven years, she was involved in the development of the first baccalaureate nursing program in Tehran, Iran, and in major projects in Ghana, Malawii, and Thailand. She was also involved in short-term consultations in Pakistan, India, and Thailand. She is now a Professor Emeritus at the University of Alberta, and lives in Edmonton.

ALL WE NEEDED WAS TRIUMPHANT MUSIC

Eleanor Lindsay

In the late 1960s, I was an outpost nurse in Makkovik, a small settlement of about 375 Inuit and white people, on the north Labrador coast, accessible only by plane or boat.

One event that stands out involves the infant of an Inuit woman who had a terrible obstetric history. For her previous deliveries, she was usually sent out to North West River, which is in central Labrador, not far from Goose Bay. However, with this baby, she went into labour unexpectedly early. The weather was dreadful, so I had no choice but to insert an IV and wait nervously. It turned out that she had an uneventful delivery. Afterwards, I wondered how I could have allowed myself to become so scared. As I watched mother and baby set off home by skidoo a few days later, I felt pleased at so satisfactory an outcome.

But the story does not end there. Three weeks later, I got a message that the baby had a cold. I visited her on my morning rounds and found her in good shape, feeding well, and with only a snuffly nose. Her temperature and colour were normal. She was the same the next day. But on the third day, the mother indicated the infant was not feeding well. I started her on a daily dose of procaine penicillin. Because she was in a good home, with a good mother, I left her there with instructions (via a translator) for the mother to let me know if there was any change.

That night I went to bed with a sense of foreboding – and sure enough, around 2 a.m., I woke to a loud hammering on the door. "Come quickly! Come quickly! The baby's blue!" I told the messenger to bring mother and baby to me immediately. In the meantime, I prepared a makeshift oxygen tent – a giant plastic bag between two IV poles, over a bassinet. The family arrived within minutes. When we unwrapped the baby and saw that she was a dreadful grey colour, her mother, who was normally calm, cried out in horror.

Thus began 36 memorable hours. The baby's colour improved with oxygen, and her temperature remained normal. I felt deeply uneasy about her condition, and I lay beside her for the rest of that night. In the morning, the daily RT (radio telephone) rounds with the doctor could not come soon enough. As I waited for my turn, I struggled with how to balance my report of essentially normal vital signs with a gut sense that the infant was in serious trouble. Predictably, the doctor said it sounded as if things were well under control and just suggested to carry on. I squashed my urge to scream, "Send the plane! Take the baby today!" At my insistence, he agreed to call me again in the afternoon, before the RT was shut down for the day.

I sent word to the community that I would not make rounds that day and asked only the really sick to come to the nursing station. The request was fully honoured. The baby's mother came and spent several hours with her daughter, allowing me to lie down, briefly. She tried a number of times (unsuccessfully) to bottle-feed her in the oxygen tent. When the doctor called back in the afternoon, I was again frustrated to report totally normal vital signs. I emphasized my concern that the baby was not feeding and that her colour – even with oxygen – was getting worse. The weather was starting to look ominous, and I asked if a plane could come for her that day. However, the doctor felt things were under control and did not consider transport necessary at this time. He gave me advice about subcutaneous infusions and instructions about adding a second antibiotic – only if her condition deteriorated.

When the baby continued to refuse to feed, I initiated a subcutaneous infusion. Her colour slowly became even greyer, despite increasing the oxygen level. And I now had a new anxiety: my limited supply of oxygen tanks was low. Late that evening, I added the second antibiotic. Again, I spent the night beside the baby. From time to time, I stretched out on one of the ward beds near her.

* * *

The next morning, the baby's colour was very poor, but still the vital signs remained normal. The doctor called me first on his regular schedule. Because the weather was clearly deteriorating, he agreed to call me every hour until mid-morning, so that a decision could be made about a transfer before weather conditions made a flight impossible. The baby's mother arrived, and once more she sat with her daughter, giving me a welcome break. When the doctor called at 11 a.m., I was in the middle of saying, "There is still no change, but my oxygen is running low," when there was a scream from the mother, who came running for me with a stricken face. I yelled "Standby! Standby!" to the doctor and ran to the baby. She appeared to be in full cardiac arrest. I started CPR and, in between breaths, called to the aide to go to the radio telephone and tell the doctor what happened. She did this bravely, having never used the RT before. To this day, I can still hear the doctor's voice calling, "All stations off the air! All stations off the air! North West River standing by for Makkovik."

While I continued to do CPR, the doctor asked the aide if I could hear him. Between puffs, I shouted "Yes!" He gave me instructions about emergency medications for the baby. How was I to do this – while still continuing CPR? There was only one choice. The mother, who spoke no English and who had probably never heard of CPR before, had to take over. I signed to her – positioning her fingers and guiding the strength of compressions. I watched her do mouth-to-mouth resuscitation, and I showed her how to make a proper seal so that the baby's chest rose. Once she seemed to have the hang of it, I ran to the surgery and, with shaking hands, drew up the medications. With no hope of intravenous administration, I gave them IM (intramuscularly) and took over the CPR again.

After about 15 minutes of no response, I remember feeling a sense of unutterable weariness and defeat. I stopped. Resting my hand on the baby's chest, I looked up at the mother and shook my head. At that moment – miracle of miracles – I felt the baby shudder under my hand. She took a breath and in front of our eyes, began to turn pink. The IM medications had begun to work! The sense of wonder exchanged between the baby's mother and me at that moment is unforgettable.

I ran to the RT with the news. The doctor told me that he had a plane on standby to pick up the baby – it was about an hour-and-a-half's flight. He would tell the pilot to take off immediately. A few minutes later, the Beaver pilot called to say that he was leaving, but he cautioned us that he did not like the look of the weather. He would keep me posted. About 30 minutes after that, he radioed very apologetically that he had to turn back. I was seized with despair. I suddenly remembered that a helicopter pilot with a rather daredevil reputation, but considered to be an excellent pilot, was grounded in Makkovik due to the weather. I sent urgently for him. He listened to my story; he thought for a while and then spoke with Goose Bay. Finally, he turned to me and said, "Let's do it – but bring extra food and clothing. Be prepared in the event that we go down for the night somewhere."

A frenzy of activity followed: food and clothing were prepared, the last of the oxygen cylinders were gathered up, and syringes were loaded with adrenalin and solucortef. In no time, I heard the sound of the helicopter landing on the station grounds. I remember the little knot of people struggling out to the helicopter in the wind and blowing snow – me carrying the baby with the IV running, the aide carrying the food and clothing, and the station caretaker carrying the remaining oxygen cylinders, while muttering fiercely that I had no right to risk two peoples' lives for a baby. I had put too much into this to give up now.

* * *

The flight seemed endless. The chopper pitched and wallowed in the wind. The visibility was so poor that the pilot had to fly just above the treetops in order to maintain his bearings. At one point during the flight, I realized that while I had food for myself and the pilot, I had none for the baby – not that she could have eaten any in her present condition – but it just seemed that as a matter of principle, I ought to have had some.

Towards the end of the flight, despite a further increase in oxygen, the baby's colour began deteriorating again. I had the syringes at the ready, but we managed to reach our destination without serious trouble. As we neared North West River, the storm began to ease enough for me to recognize where we were. When we approached the hospital, the wind and snow stopped and the sky was tinged with sunset pinks. All we needed was triumphant music. We had made it and the baby was still alive.

As the helicopter descended in front of the building, I could see a small group of people clustered around a rectangular object (which turned out to be an incubator). When we landed, the door of the helicopter was pulled open, hands reached in for the baby, and suddenly everyone was gone. I was utterly alone and unspeakably exhausted. I put my head down and cried my eyes out.

The rest of the evening is a blur. Somebody finally came and got me. The doctor and his wife gave me a good meal and a comfortable bed at their home. I had a blissful, uninterrupted night's sleep. When I wakened the next morning, the baby was still alive and on her way to the intensive care unit at St. Anthony. After a big breakfast, I was flown back to Makkovik.

Six weeks later, the baby was finally returned to Makkovik. Her mother and I were waiting as the plane arrived. The mother stepped forward to receive her baby, but the pilot came and put her in my arms, saying, "No, this is *your* baby." I held her with my heart full of emotions.

* * *

Several years later, after I had left the North, I revisited Makkovik. One of the most special moments was when the baby's mother presented her now five-year-old daughter to me. I was thankful to see that she appeared in lusty good health, with no obvious side effects from her memorable brush with death.

Eleanor Lindsay RN, SCM, BA received her nursing training in Scotland at the Edinburgh Royal Infirmary from 1961 to 1966. She did her midwifery training at the Elsie Inglis Memorial Maternity Hospital in Edinburgh from 1966 to 1967. From 1968 to 1970, she worked with the International Grenfell Association in Newfoundland and Labrador in St. Anthony, Flowers Cove, and Makkovik. In 1971, she worked at the Montreal General Hospital in Montreal, Quebec. From 1972 until her retirement in 1997, she was at the Izaak Walton Killam Children's Hospital in Halifax, Nova Scotia.

DIARY EXCERPTS FROM SPENCE AND PELLY

Chin Jong Reed

Chin Jong Reed wanted to experience the Arctic, so she took a year's leave of absence in 1991 to work as the community float nurse in the Kitikmeot Region. These are excerpts from the diary she kept during that year. Since 1994, CJ has returned for short term assignments in both the Kitikmeot and Baffin Regions, which are now part of Nunavut.

SPENCE BAY: September, 1991

We are in a big rush to do visual testing in the school in Spence Bay, before the eye technicians arrive for their yearly visit. Visual and hearing screening tests should have been done before school was out for summer vacation. For some reason, it wasn't done in this community.

The local school has classes from kindergarten to grade six, with about 150 students ranging in age from five to eighteen years old. There are three or four Inuit teachers and five white teachers. One morning while I was in the school doing the testing, the teacher warned me there would be a fire drill. When the alarm went off, everyone filed out to the schoolyard in an orderly fashion, all of us in shirtsleeves, some kids without shoes. The temperature was 5°C, and with a wind chill of –10, my teeth were chattering. When two teenage girls were piggybacked into the yard by their boyfriends (they were in grade six and about sixteen or seventeen years old), everyone clapped and some whistled. It was funny, and the incident lightened the ordeal.

* * *

When I arrived at the school this morning, the place was quiet. I noticed there were no coats on the hooks and no shoes in sight, and the classrooms were all empty. I went to the office where the Inuit secretary was hard at work. She hadn't even realized there was no one else in the school, not even the teachers. We looked outside and noticed a lot of activity at the bay. I went to investigate.

The whole town was down by the water. The women were pointing and shouting at fourteen boats that were chasing a pod of narwhal which had come into the bay. Three boats were stationed at the mouth of the bay to prevent them from escaping, while the others circled around looking for the trapped whales. The Inuit have sharp eyesight. The women could see shadows in the water and called to tell the men where the whales were. The narwhal were frantic and confused; they didn't spout, but just swam underwater. When the boats located a whale, they would follow it, and one of the men would throw a spear tied to a buoy. Once the spear hit the whale (it was usually a bull's eye), the boat followed the buoy, and the men fired their guns. The big whales took four or five shots before they died.

That morning, they caught three full-grown narwhal and two babies. The adults were about 18 to 20 feet in length, and gray and white. The babies were five to six feet long, and gray coloured. They have little eyes, a blowhole, no teeth, lateral fins, and skin thick like rubber. Male narwhal have a tusk which can be nine feet long. The boats dragged the bodies to shore in a sea of blood. My heart ached when I saw them. The whole pod had been wiped out – three females and their babies.

The men cut up the whales by the water. After first removing the lateral fins and tail, which are the real delicacies, they made a longitudinal cut from head to tail. The skin and surface blubber, called *muktuk,* is about 1.5 cm thick, and is like gray and white rubber. Then there are 2 mm of connective tissue over the blubber, which is about one foot thick. The knives are so sharp that cutting up the whale looked like cutting into butter. The Inuit used to squeeze oil out of the blubber for light, cooking, and heating; nowadays, they feed it to the dogs. Some people eat the very dark lean meat. Usually the *muktuk* and the meat are boiled and then dipped in salt, ketchup, or soy sauce. Women do not partake in the hunt – but in some communities, they get to cut up the whales. Here the men did it all.

The whole town, including the dogs, had a feast that day. Whoever wanted a piece of *muktuk* or meat was given some. Everyone was smiling. Many people had never seen whales before, and this whale hunt was the first for some of the young men. Apparently, whales stray into the bay only once every four to six years. I was lucky to have seen them, although it was a very sad experience for me and for many *kabloona* (white people).

I took small pieces of *muktuk* and meat home. Only the skin and connective layer is eaten. I ate a tiny piece raw. It tasted salty and was crunchy – not at all fishy as I had expected, but more like soft cartilage. I boiled the rest until a fork could pierce through. It smelled and tasted like a hard-boiled egg. However, I kept seeing the dead little eyes of the whales and found that I couldn't swallow more than just a taste. I fed the rest to my favourite brown husky puppy I named "Fluffy" who just gobbled up the whole lot. I'll cook the meat some other day, when the memory of the lovely creatures is not as fresh. I could have wept.

The excitement of this day will last me a lifetime. I think most *kabloona* were a bit upset. But for the Inuit, it is a source of food, and nothing goes to waste. They had to kill the babies too, because they would never have survived on their own. That morning, the children learned more about their traditions than they would have in a whole school year.

* * *

Last weekend, I took off at 10:30 in the morning and walked towards Pangniktok Lake, northeast of Spence Bay. There were lots of hills and valleys – after every hill I climbed, there was another, even higher. The valleys were wet and in some places, I sank about six inches into the mud. (I wondered if there was quicksand in the Arctic.) Because of the strong winds, I had to fight to maintain a foothold on the high cliffs. Two and a half hours into my hike, it was time for a tea break. A brownish-black, furry animal scurried past – an Arctic fox, about two feet long. When he was 500 or so feet away, he turned around and looked at me as if to ask, "Where did you come from?" He then disappeared into the rocks. Thankfully, it wasn't a wolf for wolves usually travel in packs, and if they were hungry, I wouldn't have stood a chance.

Just then, I noticed something moving on the horizon. Eureka! At last, caribou – fourteen of them. Through my binoculars, I watched them grazing tranquilly on the tundra. The males were much larger in size than the females and they had huge antlers. The young ones were with their mothers, obedient, and quiet. As I watched, I thought that these animals seemed more skilled at raising their young than we humans sometimes are.

After I walked for four hours, I could see Pangniktok Lake in the distance. When a few snow flurries progressed to a whiteout, I felt hopelessly lost. Cape Isabella wasn't visible any more, so I turned back. By the time I had zigzagged the lakes and the lowlands, I knew I was way off course. Everywhere looked so different from the way in, and I had visions of being stranded there for the night. Eventually, the sun peeped through the heavy, dark clouds.

As I continued my trek home, I came upon more caribou grazing. I tried to creep closer, but at about 500 feet one of them stopped eating, looked up, and stared at me. I kept utterly still. More caribou stopped grazing too, until soon all of them were facing me. After what seemed like five minutes, they pretended to resume eating, but immediately looked up again. To play it safe, I assume, one of them turned tail and ran. The others followed. Once they were at a safe distance, they began grazing again. I made it home by 6 o'clock, my face beet red from windburn, and my feet mighty sore.

* * *

It has snowed every night for a week now. Yesterday the snow stayed, and the distant hills are now snowcapped. The husky puppy, Fluffy, which I have sort of adopted, is growing. His fur is getting longer, preparing him to spend the winter outdoors. When he sees me, he jumps up and down with excitement, anticipating the food I always bring. I save every leftover scrap of food for him, and watch it disappear in one gulp. Even through all his fur, I can feel his ribs. It is illegal to feed dogs caribou meat, and seal meat is hard to come by. I wish dog food was cheaper here, not 60 dollars for a 10 kg bag.

November 21

It is hard to believe that I have been back in the Arctic for a month. In the meantime, we have had three blizzards, which have essentially shut down air transport in and out of the community. Except for television, telephone, and fax, we are isolated. It is dry and cold (-30° C) and the snow is fine, like sand, and the wind swirls it everywhere. Once the snow settles, it develops a crunchy crust. There are thin layers in some places, and deep drifts in others.

During the week, I work from 8:30 a.m. to 5 p.m. As the sun rises at 8:30 a.m. and sets by 1 p.m., as a rule I do not go out, except on the weekend. On a clear day, sunrise is glorious red and orange. The sun is a red ball just above the horizon, it moves a short distance from southeast to southwest, and then it disappears. On the weekend, I try to leave for my outings as soon as the sun is up and return before sunset – which means I don't get much exercise. However, for the two and a half hours I am out (on skis, no less), I sweat buckets. Due to exertion and multiple falls, my heart rate is up to 160 beats per minute at times. It takes about an hour for it to return to 80. I guess I don't have an athletic heart. Despite my perseverance, I don't think my cross-country skiing has improved appreciably – I fall on gentle slopes and flat ground alike. I am grateful for the cushioning effect of down-filled clothing. Somehow, I once badly twisted my left arm. Skiing on the frozen lake, where the ice is at least four feet thick, I find all sorts of cracks and trapped air bubbles. Occasionally, there is the reverberation of a hollow, cracking sound. It's fascinating.

One day, I tried to negotiate a 1:3 slope in town. After picking myself up for the third time, I was really discouraged. When the Anglican priest's wife called out from her doorway to see if I would like to stop for a cup of tea, I was more than grateful to take the skis off. They are an English couple who have been in the Arctic for a long time and love the North. The priest speaks Inuktitut to some extent, and his wife teaches English to an adult Inuit student. One drawback for them is that the Inuit, who are not used to making appointments, turn up at their door at any time of the day or night, and consequently, they have no time to call their own. With the isolation and the harsh climate, most clerics just find it too hard and go back south. Our priest is the only *kabloona* clergy left in the whole Central Arctic. He, too, is exhausted from the demands of the job, and he really doesn't know how much longer he will last.

* * *

Mei is the resident dental therapist in Spence Bay. Last weekend, despite the blizzard, Mei and I went out for a walk. Like me, she is 95 pounds, soaking wet. We were pushed and pulled by the 50 mile per hour wind. At times, we literally had to bend forward as we laboured against it. I tripped all over because my glasses were frosted from my breath. The occasional Inuit who passed would stop to offer us a ride back on his vehicle. We thanked them, but declined the offers – we were determined to walk. We were out for one and half hours, sharing a lot of laughs. People must have been thinking, "There go the two crazy Chinese again!" Mei's eyelashes became frosted, and I ended up with second-degree frostbite on my cheeks. There went my beautiful face! Most people here ride; we are the only two who walk.

* * *

In an attempt to get better attendance at the public health sessions, the new nurse in charge decided to change the sick clinics to mornings and the public health programs to the afternoons. The Inuit usually sleep in, so the sick clinic has been slow. They come to the health centre in the afternoons, wanting to be checked out. However, during those hours, we only look after emergencies, sick kids, and elders; the rest have to wait until the next morning. Quite often, they are better by then.

I bought some caribou meat and a couple of big arctic char (cut into steaks) for $2.50 a pound. This will be my protein for the next month or so.

I saw some animal carcasses in the garbage. How wasteful, I thought. When I asked at the house if I could have them to feed to the hungry dogs, I was told they were a wolf and a fox, and the Inuit just harvest the skin. The meat is not fed to the dogs, in case the wild animals were rabid.

November 27

Christmas tea for elders, those 65 and over, took place rather early because the new Spence Bay nurse in charge wanted it held before she left for her two-month vacation. For the event, we all chipped in, decorated the room, put up a Christmas tree, baked, and made sandwiches. There are fourteen elders in Spence Bay, widows outnumbering widowers. They sat in a circle, as we served them "goodies" and afterwards, they all had "doggie bags" to take home.

Next week, I will pack up and go to Pelly Bay. It is with some sadness that I leave Spence Bay, as the last six months have been full of wonder and exhilarating experiences. Just a few days ago after work, Mei and I went for a long walk on the sea ice. The North Star stared down on us, and with a full moon against a clear blue sky, it was as bright as daytime. It was minus 25, with a brisk wind – but lovely. When the days are clear, the sun rises (that is, a thin lip of sun) over the horizon at 10 a.m. and sets at 12:15 p.m. A red and orange hue lights up the southeastern sky for half an hour before and after the blackout. Evenings seem exceptionally long and unproductive, and the long nights are tiring and depressing. Although I sleep eight hours a night, in the morning I still feel tired. Weekends are a race against time – to fit in three hours of outings before darkness falls.

* * *

One night, Annie Buchan (clerk/interpreter for the nursing station) and her Scottish husband showed us their collection of slides of Spence Bay dating from 1956 to the 1970s. In the early

213

days, Spence Bay had only five buildings: a brand-new nursing station, a Hudson's Bay store, an RCMP station, one other building, and of course, a church. On the tundra, people lived in caribou skin tents and igloos. In the 1970s, when the town was more built up, the community still had to haul water from the lake in the summer and chop ice blocks to melt for water in the cold months. Running water has been available since the 1980s, but even today, five old houses have "honey buckets." Due to financial constraints, new houses are not built quickly enough to keep up with the demand. It is not uncommon for a three-bedroom house to be home for 10 to 15 people of three to four generations.

PELLY BAY: December 7

The morning of December 3, I flew into Pelly Bay which is just a half-hour flight southeast of Spence Bay on the Simpson Peninsula. During the descent, I saw many caribou on the tundra. What a lovely sight! There was nothing but ice and snow everywhere, and the temperature was −35° C. Mei had insisted that I bring along her spare cross-country skis and boots, and on the weekend I went out exploring. A lot of local people, who remembered me from my visit last May, greeted me. It was good to see that many of the children I had treated for bronchiolitis had grown a lot since then.

The ear, nose and throat specialist, his wife, and an audiology technician chartered a flight to three communities in this region, including Pelly Bay. Talk about a whirlwind visit! They arrived at 9:30 in the morning and immediately started seeing patients. By 6:40 in the evening, the ENT doctor and the technician had examined people and had had lunch. In the meantime, the doctor's wife and the two pilots walked around town and watched TV in my apartment. They bought 140 pounds of Arctic char at $1.80 per pound, which is cheap, especially when you consider that Pelly Bay has the tastiest char in the Arctic. They also commissioned local women to make them *kamiks* (skin boots). I threw together a fast supper for us all, before they took off for Gjoa Haven at 8:00 the same night. After that, two supervisors from the regional health board came for three days of inspection visits. We two nurses cooked supper for them, and on the third night they cooked for us. With all that lovely food in the last three nights, I am sure I put on five pounds.

* * *

This afternoon, I fed the hungry dogs leftovers and scraps of food. The ones who have to endure the hardest life here are the dogs. Besides being exposed to the natural elements, they are tied up, and frequently left hungry. If one is sick or injured, it is shot and the body thrown into the garbage. Pelly Bay has more dog teams than the other communities. Usually, they are fed only once every three days – if they are lucky. Apparently, on one occasion, an owner did not feed his dogs, and a bitch partially ate her pups. A *kabloona* reported him to the authorities, but nothing was done.

Due to monetary constraints, the RCMP officer and the social worker have been moved out, and the nurses have to pick up the slack. Talk about having to be a Jack-of-all-trades!

December 21

Gale force winds have been blowing for three days, and visibility has been so decreased that the last two scheduled flights did not get here. (The plane usually comes in Tuesdays, Thursdays, and Saturdays.) Consequently, fresh fruit and vegetables have not arrived, and people who are leaving for Christmas are still stranded in the town. The last shipment of fresh tangerines was frozen solid. The plane stops at each community for thirty minutes or so, and while on the ground, the engine is shut off and the door is left wide open for loading and unloading. As the outside temperature is between –50 and –60, with the wind chill, it is no wonder everything inside the plane freezes.

Two weeks ago, the school had its pre-Christmas concert before classes ended for the holidays. It was well-attended. The kids, all in their best Sunday outfits – one eight-year old even wore a black tux – sang Christmas carols in English and in Inuktitut.

One afternoon, thirteen of us: the nurses, the *kabloona* Co-op store manager and his wife, and a few Inuit went house-to-house, singing Christmas carols to the elders. Each elder was given a nicely decorated container of homemade cookies. It was truly the power of persuasion on the part of Marianna (the nurse in charge in Pelly Bay), because heathens like me were not ordinarily game to go out singing carols with the Roman Catholics. As you might have gathered, almost everyone here is RC. Although it was really cold that day, we had fun and the elders appreciated our effort. The sewer exhaust pipe from one of the houses must have been blocked because as we walked inside, we noticed that the stench was absolutely foul. It reminded me of the nurses' residence in Coppermine, which at times stank so badly I felt I was living in an outhouse filled to the brim.

Considering that the Pelly Bay nursing station is fairly new, the construction is very much third-rate. Last May when I was here, the liner of the sewage tank collapsed. It was weeks before the tank could be used to full capacity again. Also, because the front wall of the building was not properly insulated, every time the wind came from the northwest, Marianna's kitchen sink would be blocked for weeks. I guess that is part of living at the "top of the world." One just has to go with the flow, so to speak.

The party for the preschool-aged children, organized by Marianna, had to be cancelled because there were a few cases of measles in the other communities. Spence Bay had carried out the full immunization program, to the tune of over $2,200 worth of measles, mumps and rubella vaccine, and immunoglobulin. Pelly Bay had four possible cases of measles. It takes a week for the serology results to come back. Infection control in Yellowknife told us to get the critical group list ready, so that when they gave the "go," we could start mass immunization.

Unfortunately, the serum of those in question was still sitting in Pelly Bay – there were no flights out because of the weather. In the meantime, the "sickies" were all getting better. I was not sorry about the cancellation of the party, because Marianna said we had to dress up with Christmas hats. I am really not that enthusiastic about Christmas and, less so, about dressing up.

* * *

For weeks now, we haven't seen the sun, even with the bright days. Because the hill to the southeast blocks off even the red rim of the sun, daylight consists of two hours of dusk. I now know what cabin fever is, and I realize that the North is for people who are content within themselves. If they are not happy, the long winter nights can only exacerbate any mental instability they might have. I read a lot. There is an endless supply of books everywhere, for people come and go, and leave their reading material behind. As there is only CBC North radio, as well as CTV and BCTV for entertainment, much of the time I just read, often finishing a book in two or three days.

Last week, there were many sightings of wolves (six different ones to be exact) and foxes. They must be hungry, because as a rule they do not come near town. I was warned to be very careful when I go out. It is rather difficult to be careful, because with my hood up, I am half-deaf and have limited tunnel vision, and because 90% of the time, my glasses are frosted with my expiratory moisture. I am lucky if I can find my way home, never mind watching out for well-camouflaged animals. As a result, my outdoor activities have been very much curtailed. However, one evening when the wind was calm, I persuaded Marianna to go out for a walk on the river ice with me. She was reluctant because of the wolves, but I assured her that they were not likely to attack a group of people; besides, we would carry ski poles. It was a beautiful walk under a clear sky with a three-quarter moon. I was petrified of walking on the slippery ice and was hot and sweating profusely. On the way back, we had to walk into the wind, which had since picked up, and my face became so numb I couldn't talk until I thawed out.

It is four days before Christmas, and I am thinking of my two "orphaned" sons in Oakville in southern Ontario and how this will be the first time we have spent Christmas away from each other. I miss them and I feel homesick. I am thankful that the Rileys will be including them on Christmas Day. As I remember all my good friends in the South, I wish I were home.

December 25

Today is Christmas Day in Pelly Bay. Dorothy phoned from Oakville to wish me a Merry Christmas. It was a delight to hear from friends at home.

The plan to have an early closing of the health centre and to hold a pre-Christmas staff coffee break with Christmas goodies was dashed, when three more people in the community came down with a rash which looked suspiciously like measles. Infectious disease control in Yellowknife gave the go-ahead for mass immunization. Christmas Eve was a hectic time to get all the contacts and the high-risk groups (infants under one year, pregnant women, and the chronically ill) immunized. The nurse in charge had to go on the radio to announce the epidemic, explain the plan of action, and answer phone questions. In the meantime, the rush to get the vaccine and immunoglobulin into the community – and not to forget extra pregnancy testing kits – continued. It was an incredibly busy time for the two nurses. After Boxing Day, we would have to immunize the other group – those born between 1957 and 1980 (about 80 people). Considering the timing of the whole fiasco, we did very well indeed. The stricken families were all quarantined – no visiting and no visitors. An elder told us that during the last measles outbreak, which was in the 1950s, many people became very sick and quite a few died.

Last night, Marianna dragged me to the Christmas Eve midnight service. It was held in the community hall, as nearly everybody attends and the RC church was too small. Everyone dressed in their finery (even a couple of girls in mini-skirts and high heels). Kids ran up and down the aisles. One three-year-old Down's syndrome boy propelled himself like a snake on the floor. When his uncle picked him up, he was most indignant, and started kicking and making angry noises. For someone like me, who understands neither the Roman Catholic service nor Inuktitut, it was very entertaining. With two laymen conducting the service, the congregation sang *Silent Night* and *O Come All Ye Faithful* in Inuktitut. After Communion, everyone shook hands and wished each other Merry Christmas. Knowing they were all RC converts, I wondered what they really thought of the virgin birth and of Christianity as a whole, compared to the shaman and spirits.

The Inuit exchange gifts – mainly homemade garments, mitts or *kamiks*, but Christmas is not nearly as commercialized as in the South. A few houses have Christmas trees up and some have lights. As people in these remote communities travel more and the *kabloona* bring more "stuff" into the community, I am sure commercialism will catch up.

For Christmas Day dinner, Marianna and I shared a Cornish hen, scalloped potatoes, broccoli, and carrots. She even had a Christmas tablecloth, napkins, candles, and red china for the special occasion. During the day, we went for a walk up to the cross on the hill across the river. The hill is a steep 300 feet, so we took the back way, which is gentler. It was still tough-going because the rocks were ice-covered, and the wind was like knives on our faces. We saw caribou tracks and found where they had dug up lichen beneath the snow. At the top of the hill, the cross was 30 feet high, propped up with barrels, and lit with Christmas lights powered by a small generator. Coming back, we slid on our bums down the steep bank. That was fun.

December 26

Today is Boxing Day. I headed out to the cemetery which is two miles from town, past the garbage dump where lots of ravens feast. A few caribou, grazing on the tundra, blended so well into the surroundings that I had a hard time picking them out with my binoculars. An Inuit man, wearing a caribou-skin outfit, came along by dog team on his way to tend his other dogs in the area. By drawing a cross on the snow, I asked him the way to the cemetery. He quickly knew what I was looking for and hand-signaled the up-and-down dips. I thought I was following his directions, but I still went the wrong way. He must have been watching, for soon he came running after me and pointed straight ahead. I would never have noticed the white crosses against the white background. I counted about forty graves: the old ones just had the year of death, while the new ones had the dates of birth and death. Many buried there were only in their twenties to their fifties. From the site of the cemetery, one looked over the open sea – a beautiful place to be laid to rest.

December 27, 1991 to January 1, 1992

Throughout the week from Christmas to New Years, activities were held in the community hall with people gathering there every night from 6 p.m. to 6 a.m. Amid lots of laughter and friendliness, people played games such as untying knots on a piece of string, unravelling yarn, crawling blindfolded on all fours in search of your own parka, high kicking to a wooden bird dangling from a string (which gets higher and higher), and walking on knuckles. All games were competitive, yet done in fun, rather than in earnest. There were large cash prizes, TVs, and skidoos to be won. Besides the games, there was square dancing and disco dancing till morning. I went to only one dance and stayed till 3 a.m. – long past my 9 o'clock bedtime. It was fine for the locals who did not have to be at work at 8:30 in the morning. In hindsight, maybe the authorities should have cancelled these activities in the community hall. I am sure they helped to spread the measles virus. However, it would have been very disappointing for the Inuit if the games had been called off, because they were the highlight of their Christmas celebrations.

I watched a couple of skidoo and dogsled races, which were big money games. Each skidoo racer had to carry an empty five-gallon gas tank on his or her back and drive like hell. With nothing to secure the gas tank, it was a balancing act. If the tank fell off, the competitor had to stop and retrieve it before continuing. The prizes were $300, $200 and $100. Prizes for the dog team races went into the thousands. It is both an art and a skill to command the dogs in a certain direction with a long, thin whip. Everyone laughed when five teams of dogs decided to take a detour and got themselves thoroughly tangled up.

Maybe I am imagining it, but the days are slowly getting longer and brighter. I was told Pelly Bay will not see the sun until it comes higher than the hill in the southeast.

January 18

Since Christmas, work has been hectic in Pelly Bay. So far, there have been almost 30 cases of measles. Those in the older age group (18 and up) are the sickest, with chest and liver complications. Often, their fever is so high it does not respond to acetominophen or entrophen and tepid baths, and we have to put them into cold-air tents. Also, many cases have had such bad sore throats, plus vomiting, that they have become dehydrated, and had to be admitted to the health centre for intravenous therapy. Of course, the medimist machine has been in constant use, and all hours of the day and night, there has been the sound of chest clapping. We instructed the relatives, the clerk/interpreter, and the community health representative how to do chest physio, so the two nurses could get on with seeing other patients. The Ventolin inhalations and vigorous chest physio went on four times a day, and after three days, the sick ones have felt better. I am sure some of them thought they were going to die. Actually, the first case was medevac'd out, because she presented with a mild sore throat, then a fever and sandpaper fine rash (scarlet fever?), an enlarged liver and pneumonia. She got sicker and sicker, and began to look septic. Even the doctor who flew in with the medevac plane couldn't make the diagnosis; he just knew that she was a very sick girl. Anyway, now we were experts in treating measles.

It was a gruelling two weeks for the two nurses. Besides having to treat and look after the stricken people, who seemed to drop like flies, we had to complete all the immunizations and manage busy sick clinics. Of course, the phone never stopped ringing with calls from the infectious diseases head office in Yellowknife and the Regional Health Board constantly wanting more information, updates, and more forms to be filled out. After the first week, the nurse in charge asked for another nurse to be sent, so that she could get the paperwork done. A term nurse came from Coppermine to help for two weeks. She was a recent university graduate, with limited experience; nevertheless, an extra pair of hands helped.

An 80 year-old and a girl who was 35 weeks pregnant, both of whom came down with measles, were medevac'd out to Yellowknife Hospital. As a result, all of the Kitikmeot and Mackenzie Regions had to carry out measles immunizations. At the height of the outbreak, a voluntary restriction on travel was advised for the communities. It was very bad timing, since many Inuit were visiting relatives during the Christmas season.

In the meantime, a girl who was 27 weeks pregnant came to the health centre early one morning, because she had started having pains and bleeding. On examination, I found she was fully dilated, but was having weak contractions. It was a stormy night, and no plane could get in or out. The doctor in Yellowknife told us to medevac her when the weather improved. It didn't get any better before she eventually delivered a 1.4 kg baby girl, who was limp and gasping. Marianna did the delivery (a shoulder and arm presentation), and I tended to the baby, because she said I knew more about resuscitation. However, there wasn't too much we could do for the baby who lived for only about half an hour. I pronounced her dead after the RC priest baptized her. It was all very sad. After the mother and father held the baby for a while, the grandmother washed and dressed her. I improvised a little cardboard box for her to lie in. She was taken to the RC church where she would rest, until the burial the following Monday. Marianne and I both agreed that the mother must have had an incompetent cervix, for she had had a previous 24 week neonatal death, under similar circumstances. She would definitely be referred to an obstetrical specialist early in her next pregnancy. It was sad to fill out both birth and death certificates at the same time.

* * *

Once or twice during lunch hour we walked onto the sea ice. One time there were five caribou — just 50 feet from us. What a sight! On January 15, we saw a sliver of the sun over the southeast ridge of hills. Although it lasted only fifteen minutes, the whole community commented on this special event; everyone was happy to see the sun again. The power of such simple pleasures.

I went cross-country skiing down to the sea ice and to the cemetery. When there was a thin layer of snow on the ice, skiing was good; otherwise, it was treacherous. From there, I could actually see the whole globe of the orange ball which was the sun. The wind was so cold I got frostbite on top of frostbite. My face was a mess.

During the next two weeks, we were very busy. We also had some visitors. The regional district health officer came to investigate the scene and to take notes for the measles study; the general practitioner, who also did obstetrics, came to do ultrasounds and the locum GP arrived for his two-day visit. (This locum GP was Dr. Marcus Coxon from Oakville. Talk about a small world!) Anyway, it was work, and cooking, and hospitality. It was exhausting.

* * *

It took more than a week for the RCMP officers to come from Spence Bay to investigate the problem of the vandalized houses of the local teachers. The teachers were understandably upset to find such a disaster on returning from their Christmas break in the South. Apparently, it was the third time this had happened. To put pressure on the community to reinstate a law-enforcing RCMP, all the teachers put in requests for transfer out of Pelly Bay at the end of the school year. However, no sooner had the news of their action got out, when there was a swarm of applications from teachers in other communities, wanting to fill their jobs. It just shows that when it comes to self-interest, principles take second place.

* * *

This is my last dispatch from the frozen North. I will be returning to Oakville on February 8, 1992. This has been a most rewarding and eye-opening year for me. I will leave here with many unforgettable memories and experiences. Maybe one day I will return.

Chin Jong (CJ) Reed RN, SCM(UK), CCN(C), CEN(US) was born and raised in Padang, Sumatra (Indonesia). She trained as a nurse in London, England, and completed her midwifery certificate in Bristol and Windsor in 1964. Prior to moving to Canada, she practised as a midwife at Westminster Hospital. She worked at the Toronto General Hospital in the ophthalmology, emergency, and recovery room units. After she and her husband moved to Oakville, Ontario, she worked in emergency for 12 years and was night supervisor for six years. Since 1988, she has worked in the intensive care unit. CJ has two grown sons of whom she is very proud, and she still lives in Oakville.

Editors' note: CJ recently took a one-month holiday in New Zealand where she participated in such activities as blackwater and whitewater rafting, sea kayaking, bungee jumping, sky diving, and hang gliding. (The average age of the others in the group was twenty.)

MEDEVAC FROM KENNEDY LAKE CAMP

Greg Neufeldt

Somewhere around 2100 hours, I received an urgent call from Medical Travel for a medevac. It was for a female patient experiencing chest pain at the Kennedy Lake camp, north of Yellowknife. Because of the nature of the call, two nurses would be required for the medevac; so Deb Dunaway and I prepared to go. As I had not heard of this particular camp before, my curiosity was peaked. Upon reaching the office and calling the camp medic for a report, I learned that this is a mining exploration camp owned by DeBeers. Most often, the flights to these camps are done in a Twin Otter because we land on make-shift runways plowed on frozen lakes. Yet for this trip, one of the dedicated medevac King Air 200s that are owned and operated by Air Tindi was being dispatched.

On arrival at the Air Tindi tarmac, the Captain informed us that the weather was not the greatest, and that we may not get in. The temperature was a typical -20°, and it was windy. We took off at 2200 hours, with two Tindi pilots whom I respected, and in whom I had the utmost trust. The flight was roughly 45 minutes. While descending, my partner and I assumed that there was no way we were going to be able to land. The weather was terrible. Flying over the ice strip, we could see the runway lights embedded in the snow and two front-end loaders clearing the runway. The Captain looked back at Deb and me, and told us that he had very good vertical visibility and that he would try to land – but only once. The pilots banked the plane around and shot the approach. To our surprise, we landed. As soon as we touched down on the ice, we came to a lurching halt. The visibility was so poor that the pilots lost sight of the runway lights in the blowing snow, but we managed to come to a stop, dead centre of the runway.

Normally, we are met at the airport by some sort of van, pickup truck, or Suburban-type vehicle. On this night, however, the two front-end loaders that we had just seen clearing the strip moments before pulled up alongside the plane. I looked at Deb and remarked, jokingly, "There is no way!" As we opened the door of the plane, one of the operators jumped down from his cab. He walked up to us, and said, "Put your equipment in the bucket." Pointing at Deb, he said, "You climb up and get in the cab with me." He then pointed at me and said, "You get in the cab with the other guy." So we took our places in the cabs of the front-end loaders and off we went. The cab was so small inside that I was nearly sitting on the lap of the operator. On the way into the camp, I thought, "I don't remember signing up for anything like this when I came to the North."

As we approached the mining camp, the loaders came to a stop. Just an hour prior to our arrival, they had plowed a path to the ice strip on the lake. In that short time, snow had drifted back in on the cleared area to well over eight feet high. We had to get out of the cabs and remove our gear from the buckets, so that the loaders could clear a path for us to get to the camp. In less than five minutes, we were able to walk up to the medical hut. When we entered, we met the medic with whom I had spoken over the phone prior to leaving Yellowknife, a young fellow from Manitoba. The patient who was experiencing chest pain was the camp cook. The medic had already started an intravenous line and had connected the patient to a three-lead cardiac monitor. We initiated our chest pain protocol, which included administering various ICU medications, along with obtaining and interpreting a 12-lead cardiac rhythm strip.

While we were doing this, one of the loader operators went back to the plane to take one of the pilots from one end of the runway to the other, so that he would have an idea of what he was working with for takeoff. We packaged our patient up, which meant we bundled her in the bright orange Medflight sleeping bag, and placed her on the Number 9 folding cot. Once we were ready to go, the medic enlisted the help of other camp employees, and four of us carried the patient to the plane.

* * *

It was close to a quarter-mile walk back to the plane. The wind and snow were blowing so hard that we could barely see where we were going. We stayed close behind one of the loaders which acted as a windbreak and gave us something to follow. Otherwise, under these conditions, we would never have found the plane. I was on the rear left corner of the cot, while Deb was behind us carrying equipment. She describes the conditions as being so blinding that, even though she was only 10 to 20 feet behind us, she could just make out our silhouettes in front of her.

Once we reached the plane, we secured the patient in the usual fashion, stowed our gear, and prepared to leave. The loaders were positioned at either end of the runway to give the pilots a reference for takeoff. Although the runway lights were rapidly being obscured by drifting snow, the elevated headlights of the loaders made the strip visible. We took off from Kennedy Lake into a 20 knot headwind and were on our way to the Stanton Yellowknife Hospital with our patient. Without the expertise of the Tindi pilots, we would never have been able to complete this medevac safely.

Deb and I often talk about the uniqueness of this call, and how only in the North would a nurse be put through an event such as this.

Greg Neufeldt BScN, EMT attended Cariboo College School of Nursing in Kamloops, British Columbia, from 1988 to 1991. After graduating, he worked in Victoria and Smithers, BC. In January of 1992, he went to the United States, with the intention of doing travel nursing for a year. That one year turned into 12 years. He worked various intensive care unit and emergency positions, along with a stint in a cardiac catheterization and pacemaker lab in New Orleans, Louisiana; Hartford, Connecticut, and Seattle, Washington. It was in Seattle that he became involved in critical-care transport and became certified as an Emergency Medical Technician. In 2002, he returned to Canada, to Vancouver Island. He worked in Comox, BC before heading to Yellowknife in 2003 to work for Medflight, where he is currently employed. When not flying with Medflight, his main hobby is aviation photography. In 2003, some of Greg's pictures appeared in The Air Tindi fifteenth anniversary insert in the Yellowknife newspaper.

A SAFE PLACE TO PUT INTO

Colleen Stewart

We were flying at eight thousand feet down the Inside Passage of the British Columbia coastline and my patient's waters had broken. Her contractions were coming every five minutes. Comox, a military base on Vancouver Island, was at least ten to twelve minutes away. I stared, incredulous, at a two-foot square portion of the rear of the plane's cabin. I seriously tried to figure out how "we" were going to deliver the child that was coming into the world. "We" were the young pilot flying the 12-seater Cessna, three Aboriginal elders who years ago had probably delivered most of the babies in Klemtu, and I, a community health nurse, who had intended to head home to Edmonton, after a tough two-month stint in the village.

It was October 31, 1988. I was flying home out of Klemtu, a village of two hundred Kitasoo, on the Pacific Coast of Canada. As we cleared the harbour on the first leg of my trip, my senses were invigorated by the beautiful clear skies, the deep blue waters, and the intense greens of the Pacific Coast. *Klemtu*, in Kitasoo, means "a safe place to put into, or to seek shelter," and so it was, this beautiful village on our Canadian coastline.

* * *

I reflected on the work I had done for the past two months. In northern nursing stations, nurses carry out many added duties and responsibilities. Having had over ten years' experience in emergency nursing and a crisp piece of parchment testifying to my baccalaureate degree, I felt quite confident that I could deal with most of the health problems and concerns of the village. What I couldn't handle was referred to our bi-weekly doctor's clinic, with the assistance of Bruce, the community health representative, with whom I developed a great rapport and friendship.

One of the physicians who flew in to our clinic in Klemtu was Dr. Berry, a beginning general practitioner who had taken a *locum* in Bella Bella. I usually had a lengthy list of referrals for him: orthopaedic injuries, medication reviews for cardiac patients, gallbladder investigations. There were also eight prenatal women in the village who needed attention, due dates all fairly close together. One day, when the clinic was over, Dr. Berry and I got into our usual discussion. I craved the good conversation and comparison of case-notes. (Oh, the memories we shared of our days as students, the long stories we spun over tea and peanut butter cookies with mouth-watering slices of oranges, at the back of the clinic!) I recall his description of a harrowing time he had as an intern, late one night, when he delivered twins by himself. He said that it was one of the most nerve-wracking experiences in his early career. When the doctor's clinic wrapped up, a plane came from Bella Bella to pick him up, while there was still daylight – and our stories were interrupted until the next clinic day.

* * *

On that October day (when I was heading back home from Klemtu), I got no further than the Bella Bella airport, when the local grapevine quickly spread news to the hospital and to Dr. Berry's office, that I was on the flight out. While I waited in the airport – an area slightly larger than a recreation vehicle parking space – I anxiously looked for the pilot and the plane to my connecting flight. At that moment, a phone call came in, and I was paged.

"Colleen, do I understand you're heading down to Vancouver today?" Dr. Berry asked, in a tone that I sensed was more than just, "Good-bye, *au revoir*, and I enjoyed working with you."

"Yes, that's right, Dr. Berry. It's a great day for a flight, and I can't wait to get home. What's up?" I asked.

"Well, Colleen, I have a 36 year-old female with me who needs a nursing escort to Vancouver...." I sensed that my long-awaited flight was turning into work.

"Would you accompany her to Grace Hospital in Vancouver? She hasn't had any prenatal care. Her last, and only, baby was born almost eighteen years ago, so I'm considering her a high-risk *primip*. She has a referral to an attending physician in Vancouver...." *Primip*, medicalese for the Latin term *primipara*, refers to a woman who is pregnant for the first time, and is considered to be high risk. The term frequently makes doctors and nurses a little nervous. I took down the particulars on her condition and requested an emergency delivery bundle. "We're sending her by ambulance from the hospital to the airport. You should see her in ten to fifteen minutes, and her name is ——."

* * *

In the air, a half-hour later, I scuttled back and forth like a crab in the small cabin, conferring with the pilot over the progress of my patient. Sweat broke out on my forehead. We both realized that we had to make a rapid diversion to the nearest safe place to land, preferably one with a runway and a hospital. Comox was the best and the closest facility, and it was only ten to twelve minutes away.

As we headed down the channel at eight thousand feet, I was vaguely aware that the skies were getting darker, with ominous signs of a storm developing. This backdrop echoed the rapid progress of my labouring patient. I continued to check her contractions with my hands, and the thrill of the forces of the birth process startled me even more. I realized how quickly this baby was coming into the world.

The face of my patient reflected stoic determination. She mumbled and moaned to me only once or twice and occasionally, her hands roamed over her large and moving abdomen. When I was a student, obstetrics and case-room experience was one of my best clinical postings. However, that was several years ago, and I now struggled to recall the voices of my nursing instructors, who might serve as long distance guardian angels in my present predicament.

I recalled my conversation with Dr. Berry. "Is she in labour?" I had asked him. He had replied emphatically, "No. Assuredly, no! Due date doesn't look like another three or four weeks. You'll be fine." I knew I'd be fine, but what about my patient? Doctors sometimes overlook that irony, when they ask nurses to do something for a patient.

The pilot radioed ahead with a change in flight plans, and the excitement of the other passengers charged the air. I was sure they were already picking out names and placing bets on whether it would be a boy or a girl. I was aware that they were closely watching "their nurse" of two months being put into action and wondering how I would handle the situation. I, too, was wondering.

We descended very quickly to the Comox airport. The pilot was initially directed to the military landing, but the paramedics who were waiting for us were at the civilian airport. Another precious five to six minutes were spent navigating in a thunder and lightning storm. Rain poured down so heavily we couldn't see four feet in front of us on the tarmac. By this time, a very anxious pilot and nurse were searching through the pelting rain for airport lights and for the red flashers of the ambulance.

My patient became restless and progressed into full labour. Her groans were drowned out by the surrounding passengers, who clapped and cheered, as she was quickly transferred from our small plane to the paramedics' stretcher. The pilot and I shared a collective sigh of relief, now that we were on terra firma and our patient was on her way to the hospital.

* * *

I later learned that she delivered a healthy baby boy, within a half-hour of being admitted to St. Joseph's Hospital. My trusted friend and CHR, Bruce, had heard all about the events of the "labour flight," as the community grapevine continued to chatter. Because no replacement nurse was yet available, Bruce managed the clinic. We chortled long distance over the plight of the next nurse. It was then that I asked Bruce to pass on to Dr. Berry the following message, "No, she was *not* in labour, and I hope your next delivery is twins!"

THE SPELL OF THE STIKINE

Colleen Stewart

In an isolated settlement called Telegraph Creek in the northern wilderness of British Columbia, there is a nursing station where I worked for one winter. It is on the bank and bend of the Stikine, a beautiful and grand river hardly anyone has heard about. Originating far in the Territories, it fills with glacial melt water, and it swells and grows for four hundred miles. For millions of years, it has carved out deep canyons. The Stikine is known for its dangerous rapids. So life-threatening is this river that in some places only one or two teams of rafters have ever shot the waters and lived.

Pristine, innocent and majestic, it flows past the tiny village of Telegraph Creek which was once a jumping-off point for riverboat men, trail guides, and fevered, gold rush explorers of the late 1800s. The river sweeps on to Wrangell, Alaska, creating a huge saltwater delta and then pours itself into the Pacific.

* * *

The week I arrived, the gentle, sloping mountain ranges along the Stikine and around Telegraph Creek, were crisp and white with spring snowfall. Black fringes of spruce and fir hemmed the hillsides in undulating borders. My senses swam and hummed. The countryside was postcard sharp and the air was fresh. The sunlight was so sparkling clear and bright on the snow and on the water, as it broke through the ice in the river, that my eyes hurt. I found myself breathing deeply, my eyes tearing and my fingers reaching out, as if I might capture the unspoiled air, the sunshine, and the purity of it — to hold, if only for a short while.

* * *

One night, after I had been overly attentive to nursing problems: assessments, medications, charts, records, new patients, and insulin orders, I realized that I needed a break. I left the nurses' trailer and I drove the short half mile or so to the airport strip on the edge of the village. I don't know what called me there.

I killed the engine, jumped out of the truck, and walked over the gravel and snow. The only sound was the crunch of my boots on the tarmac. I looked up at the millions of stars in the black velvet sky. For several minutes, I stood under a shower of aurora borealis and smelled the snow. My eyes made out lines of drifts against the trees; my ears ached in the void. I did not hear a thing. Such incredible, profound, soul-stirring silence. Not a bird, not a bear, not a wolf, not another person, not a rumble of far-off traffic. Not a whisper of movement. Such complete and utter silence. This is the place where the wilds are stilled, I thought, where the night simply is night, where time has stopped, and my heart has been touched.

As a philosopher once wrote, "*When meditation is mastered, the mind is unwavering like the flame of a lamp in a windless place.*"   I had entered the temple of Nature, and if only for a brief moment, I had discovered a windless place. For years to come, this created a thirst and a hunger in my soul.

Such was the night I became mesmerized by the spell of the Stikine.

Colleen Stewart RN, BScN, CPMHN(C) graduated in 1978 from the University of Alberta Hospital RN Diploma program. She worked in emergency nursing for several years in Edmonton, in Bermuda, and on Vancouver Island. Some of her travels took her to nursing stations along the British Columbia coastline, where she started writing about her nursing experiences. In 1988, she completed a BScN at the University of Alberta. In 2001, she received her certification in Psychology and Mental Health. She has worked in home care, on general duty, and as a clinical instructor. As a freelance writer, Colleen has had a variety of feature articles published in newspapers, magazines, and on the Web. Colleen moved to Calgary in 2003, and plans to continue working in psychiatry, writing, and enjoying the scenery of the foothills and the Rocky Mountains.

WE ALL HAVE A STORY TO TELL

Florence MacArthur

My admiration for the "Florence Nightingales of the North" is immense. From 1985 to 1988, I worked as a relocation clerk for Health Canada Medical Services Branch in Yellowknife. Many of the nurses that I assisted came from different parts of the world to work in remote areas of the North, and each had a story to tell.

I remember one nurse who came from England after reading an ad in the newspaper, for nurses to work in the Northwest Territories. Her family was horrified. They warned her against the Indians, the cold, and the igloos, and they told her she would get lost in the wilderness. She came anyway, and loved working in the far North, where she went hunting with the Inuit, made moccasins from caribou hide, and heard the stories of the Inuit.

* * *

I came to Yellowknife from Rossland, British Columbia. Only once in my life had I been up in an airplane, and I never dreamt that I would end up in a job which would require that I spend so much time in the sky. In the North, I flew to most remote communities in all sorts of small planes, landing on pontoons on the water, or on pea gravel on runways that you couldn't even see from the sky. When up in the air, looking at the clouds and orange sunsets, I couldn't imagine being anywhere else – and I felt such an overpowering sense of being near to the other world. Looking down on the land and seeing the caribou running and the clear water shining in the sun, I experienced an immense peace. This land is huge and water is everywhere. The land can be unforgiving, yet so unbelievably beautiful, as to make tears fill your eyes.

* * *

We, the workers and nurses of the North, have all these wonderful feelings, which we reflect upon from time to time. They fill our hearts with the knowledge that we are only tiny beings in the large, large world. The North gives us a sense of survival against all odds. Yet there is a beautiful peace when we realize that we are at one with the elements. It's a feeling that only we, the people who have experienced the North, can understand. It is a something special that we save and cherish, for times when we need to be at one with our Creator.

During Florence MacArthur's time as the federal relocation officer for Health Canada in Yellowknife, she knew and made arrangements for every nurse who was either coming to or leaving the North.

Glossary of Some Qualifications and Awards

AOE	Alberta Order of Excellence
BA	Bachelor of Arts
BE or BEd	Bachelor of Education
BN	Bachelor of Nursing
BSc	Bachelor of Science
BScN	Bachelor of Science in Nursing
CCN(C)	Critical Care Nursing (Canada)
CCOHN	Canadian Certified Occupational Health Nurse
CEN(US)	Certified Emergency Nurse (US)
CHN	Community Health Nurse
CHTP	Certified Healing Touch Practitioner
CM	Order of Canada (Member)
CNA	Certified Nursing Assistant
CPMHN(C)	Certification in Mental Health Nursing (Canada)
DPHN or DPM	Diploma in Public Health Nursing
EdD	Doctor of Education
EMT	Emergency Medical Technician
LL.D	Doctor of Laws (honorary degree)
MEd	Master of Education
MPHN	Master of Public Health Nursing
MSc	Master of Science
MScN	Master of Science in Nursing
NP	Nurse Practitioner
OPN	Outpost Nurse
OC	Order of Canada (Officer)
OR Tech.	Operating Room Technician
PHN	Public Health Nurse
PHNdip	Diploma in Public Health Nursing
PHCNP	Primary Health Care Nurse Practitioner
PNC(C)	Prenatal Nursing Certificate (Canada)
RN	Registered Nurse
RNA	Registered Nursing Assistant
RN(EC)	Registered Nurse (Extended Class)
SCM	State Certified Midwife (UK)

Afterword

When the contributions to this second book of northern nursing stories started to arrive – even before we had finished the first one – once again, I couldn't say no to Karen Scott. My admiration for those who deliver health care in remote areas of Canada continues to grow. As Ildiko Luxemburger notes in her story "Dawson City," to work in the North, you must be "tough, tenacious, intelligent, and creative." These health care professionals are indeed special people; they deserve to have their stories heard.

For me, editing a story involves reading it many times. This repetition has not dulled my reactions to the predicaments that these authors bring to life. I feel trapped with Anne Pask Wilkinson as she struggles to keep her patients safe, as their small plane slowly sinks into icy waters. I wait for days with Margaret Hamilton until the weather clears enough for a plane to land so she can medevac her patient. I plead, with Eleanor Lindsay, that the daring helicopter pilot take her and the sick baby to the hospital, when winds and blowing snow have grounded all aircraft. I never tire of revisiting these remarkable adventures.

Although I have had a life-long interest in the North, I have never had the opportunity to visit this part of our country. Yet I feel that through being involved in the publication of these narratives, I have experienced the North with expert guides.

Joan E. Kieser BA

Karen Scott and Joan Kieser